WOOD PELLET SMOKER AND GRILL COOKBOOK

BECOME A PITMASTER OF YOUR WOOD PELLET GRILL WITH 300 DELICIOUS BBQ RECIPES FOR BEGINNER AND ADVANCED GRILLERS TO IMPRESS YOUR FRIENDS AND FAMILY

RALPH PAULEY

TABLE OF CONTENTS

CHAPTER 1. INTRODUCTION

The Wood Pellet Grill and Smoker is the best invention there is. Unlike a charcoal grill, a smoker allows the heat to be adjustable. But how does it work in the first place? The pellet, which burns at a lower temperature than charcoal briquettes, produces a lot of smoke. The smoke is infused into the food as it cooks. This is the key to making the meat flavorful and delicious. You can utilize many of the same techniques that you use with a charcoal grill, like hot and fast, closed-and-vented, indirect smoking, or simple cold smoking. You can use wood pellets to smoke fish, game, vegetables, ribs, and anything else you can think of. The smoke really gives your food a fantastic, rich flavor with a tender and moist meat. Since the food is being smoked and not grilled, the Wood Pellet Grill and Smoker can also be used to cook items like baked potatoes and breakfast eggs. The food is generally very tender and very moist and will taste great. Since the heat is less than it is with a charcoal grill, you will be able to hold on to the food for a longer period of time. This is a very great item for you to have in your home.

The first thing you need to get is a smoker. You can choose from a wide variety of sizes, styles, and types. Remember to check the wood pellet grill and smoker box for a full list of options.

• Wood Pellet Grill and Smoker Kits are the most popular style of pellet grill and they are very affordable.

• Wood Pellet Grills and Smokers come with the following formats: Smokey Mountain Cooker, Camp Chef, Rocket, Granite Gear, MAK, Rec-Tec, and others.

• Wood Pellet Grilling Boxes come in all wood pellet size. Check the wood pellet grill and smoker box for a full list of options.

You can also buy individual wood pellet sizes in bags. You will also find bags of wood pellets in bulk at some suppliers.

The Wood Pellet Grill and Smoker is exactly the same except that it is stationary. While it is stationary, it can easily be parked without taking up too much interior space. It is made of durable materials that are built to last. It has a large cooking surface and can accommodate a lot of food. It is also very easy to use. You can change the cooking temperature to whatever you want it to be and determine how fast the food is cooked.

The Wood Pellet Grill and Smoker is also very safe. The pellet is housed in a metal box that protects the fire. There are no open flames on the Wood Pellet Grill and Smoker, so the food will never catch on fire. The Wood Pellet Grill and Smoker is a smoker that you will truly enjoy, whether you are a weekend cookout enthusiast or a professional chef.

There are three ingredients to better grill: the wood pellet grill, a thermostat controller, and a meat probe thermometer. Together, these three things will create a juicy, tender, delicious meal.

CHAPTER 2. THE CULT OF BARBECUE

Barbeque in the US is a cornerstone in cooking that revolves around the low temperature and prolonged slow cooking of meat, either poultry or meat (and sometimes vegetables) -- the meat is treated with dry heat in a closed environment, a grill. Barbeques are also held in other areas of the world, especially in Canada, Europe, South America, Tunisia, and the Southern Cone of South America. Barbeques are a popular way to prepare food for both social and family functions. The term "Pulled Pork" may sound like a bit of an oxymoron, but it really is the perfect way to describe the smoky flavor that pork gets when you cook it low and slow on a Barbeque.

Every year in America takes place a famous event called Big Apple BBQ where the best barbecue man gathers. This event gathers all the best recipes that you can see that will give newcomers about barbeque that best on what is to be offered. This big barbecue is also for the promoters to make their stuff known to the people who are interested in Barbecue. The barbecue is usually created in the car or home which is fueled by charcoal and wood, they are made of smoke and heat that give the taste of Barbecue by cooking in smoked meats, vegetables.

The best recipes are known by visiting the barbecue festival. This is a barbecue and barbecue cooking skill test with all barbecue specialists from across the nation to answer any query about how they created their barbecue. From your fresh new ingredients and spices to the methods of smoking, taste, additives, basting, marinating, how to offer, and many more other things people need to know.

This comes in the Wood Pellet Grill, revolutionary equipment made exactly for barbecue. It is a gasless outdoor Barbecue that is run by electricity or solar energy. You can barbecue your favorite meats without worrying about the charcoal or wood needed to give the best out of your dish. Cooking will be fast and easy, and it will be less mess to clean up. But it has disadvantages since the wood pellets are not that cheap, and the equipment itself can be costly. But if you want to enjoy a barbecue without the mess, then these grills are the best equipment you can have. The price that you pay is also affordable, you can get this grilled grill for only about $300. If you use it regularly, this can be a great investment and favors your family.

This new equipment flavors the food an authentic experience that cannot be duplicated with any other equipment. Grab your friends and family and celebrate a barbecue extravaganza with the best equipment for your barbecue needs. With this, it will be a whole new experience to know a barbecue without the fear of burning or being messy. Your barbecue will be more convenient with the clean turn, and less hassle of cleaning or disposing of leftover charcoal.

But with this type of grilling just requires a bit of planning, use them with caution and also be sure that the equipment is ready for use.

CHAPTER 3. WHAT IS AND WHY A WOOD PELLET SMOKER-GRILL?

A Wood Pellet barbecue is an ideal product for those who want to give their dishes the taste of wood without excessively getting their hands dirty with coal or firewood. For those who love the taste of dishes cooked over a flame but do not want to manage the drawbacks of temperature regulation or subsequent cleaning. Pellet grills also offer the convenience of combining several cooking options into one unit. Although it is not able to reach the same temperatures as the coal, it still manages to heat the plate or the grill in a few minutes, making the barbecue ready for use in a time much less than that required for the preparation of the barbecue charcoal.

The following reason is why you should buy a pellet grill:

Versatility

There is no denying through the fact that the amount and mammoth variety of food that you can prepare on a wood pellet grill is incredible. Regardless of whether it is beef, pork, chicken, baking dishes or more; you can have all of it in the grill which makes it a very versatile choice.

Time-Saving

The overall design is such that the whole thing is ready in 10 to 15 minutes and when you compare it with other devices to cook food, the speed of cooking is much improved.

Easy

To get the best cooking flavor and taste, the food must be cooked evenly. The wood pellet grills are so designed that the smoke effect can easily be cleared and the smoke spreads evenly thereby giving your food the perfectly evened out cooking taste.

Great Results

Like we have mentioned before, wood pellet grill is known to lend a characteristic flavor of their own. When you use these pellets, you are sure to enjoy the flavor that will give your food a twist you are going to absolutely love.

Temperature Regulation

When you are cooking food, needing to regulate the temperature is an absolute must. There is no denying the fact that we all need to keep a watchful eye on the temperature with this kind of grill. It is a whole lot easier to monitor the heat and the temperature which has generated.

So, these are the umpteen benefits that the wood pellet grill smokers have to offer. No doubt, they enjoy an astounding level of popularity and before you get ahead with some of the most lip-smacking recipes in the book, we want you to find yourself one of the perfect wood pellet grills. Trust us; barbecuing would be so much more fun than you will wish to host a BBQ party every weekend and call your friends over!

Make sure to go through the specifics well, understand the details, and then get yourself a grill you will love to cook on. The smoked effect and the extra infusion of flavor are going to help you earn the title of the most coveted chef. Trust me; you need a wood pellet grill in your backyard right away!

Who makes the best wood pellet grill?

There are many wood pellet grills in the market that claim you can get the very best barbeque in their products. But do they really give you the best barbeque? Do they offer you a perfect taste of the recipe that you like to use? This is a hard, and unfair, question to answer. But the only thing that is certain is that if you really want to get the best barbeque in the market, you have to know about the best wood pellet grills in the market.

I am writing this review in such a concise way because there is so much information that you need to know about these pellet grills.

Traeger Pellet Grills are one of the most premium brands in the industry. They are not just premium but they are also versatile, really convenient to use, and are loaded with the best features. You can do a lot of things in those grills that you will not find in any other grill.

This grill is perfect for anyone looking to do smoking, grilling, searing, and many more. It has got flavor-infused technology. You will be amazed to learn how much this technology can do in your grill.

Pit Boss Pellet Grills are designed to be used with a cooking system designed for it. This is one of the reasons why you may consider buying this model instead of the other ones. One of the systems that are usually designed for pellet grills is a Magellan system.

IF you want to buy the best wood pellet grill in the market, then the Masterbuilt 300 Premium is what you need to get. This is the grill that is packed with features. Everything about the grill is so well thought out that you will become an instant fan of it after you own it.

Camp Chef Pellet Grills has different models in which the company concentrates on the different aspects of grilling. There is a product of them that is designed for searing, smoking, slow cooking, and many other functions. They have been endorsed by famous chefs in the industry.

Z Grills Wood Pellet Grills are the best products that you can use for smoking as well as grilling. This is the product that will bring the excitement that you want whenever you are using it.

It will surely bring a change in your outdoor grilling, and you will not look back at any time. It is designed to make grilling easier than you have ever imagined. It is marketed as the most intelligent grill ever, and this is not an overstatement.

Green Mountain Grills (GMG) It is a three-shelf, pellet grills that are designed to run on all types of pellet fuels. It is a very good burning smoker. This product is very effective, and it has got a lot of features that you will surely love. It has a large shelf that can hold the smoker which will be positioned at the back of the grill. The product is quite easy to assemble. It requires you to work on some screws with a hex wrench.

This is another product of Green Mountain Grills. By owning this product, you have the option to have a professional smoker with the quality that you desire.

As of now, these are some of the very best wood pellet grill brands that you should really take a look at—guaranteed that you will get to experience some of the best barbeque flavors ever.

The most reliable controller?

Types of Temperature Controllers - With the above in mind, you will probably want to learn more about pellet grill temperature controllers. Here are some basics:

- Three-Position Regulators - When you see or hear about a three-position system, it is a system that offers low, medium including high settings. While three settings are better than what you get with charcoal, the control may not be enough for the type of cooking you have in mind.

- Multi-position controllers - With a multi-position controller, you can adjust the temperature up or down at 25-degree intervals. This provides a high degree of control than the three-position controllers, and for some people who use their grill primarily for burgers and sausages, it may be sufficient.
- PID Regulators - A PID (Proportional Integrative Derivative) regulator incorporates digital technology to maintain a more stable temperature in the grill. Rather than having a continuous cranked auger like most other pellet grills, the PID relies on an algorithm that continually monitors internal temperatures and only releases pellets when circumstances demand it.

The best choice on a limited budget

Choose the right pellet

The Wood Pellet Grill requires you to use all-natural wood pellets. The thing is that different kinds of wood pellets can impart different flavors to your food thus improving your gastronomic experience all the time. This section is intended as your in-depth guide on which hardwood pellets to use on your Wood Pellet Grill.

- Alder: Alder wood pellets are versatile, and they add mild flavor and aroma to your food. This wood pellet also gives off a lot of smoke but does not overpower even the most delicate foods. Use it to cook chicken and fish. Surprisingly, alder pellets are also great for baked goods as it imparts a smoky yet sweet aroma to it.
- Apple: Apple pellets are great for cooking pork and poultry. It gives off a light fruity smoke thereby enhancing mild-flavored meats. Similar to alder pellets, it is also great for baked goods. You can make smoke-roasted apple pies with them to elevate the classic American pastry.
- Cherry: Cherry pellets can add hearty flavor and aroma to your dish. It is great for red meats such as beef and pork. It also imparts a cherry fragrance that improves the experience of eating your food.
- Hickory: A favorite wood pellet for savory barbecue, hickory pellets release an extraordinarily strong flavor, yet it complements all kinds of meats. However, if you find hickory pellets a bit strong, you can mix them with milder pellets such as apples and oak. Hickory pellets are great for pork barbecue.
- Maple: Maple pellets give off a mild smoky aroma with a hint of sweetness. They are great for pork and turkey. Maple pellets are great for making holiday meats.
- Mesquite: Mesquite wood pellets are the signature wood used in making Texas BBQ. This type of wood pellet infuses your meats with a hearty and smoky flavor. The strong smoky flavor is great for recipes that call for something extra special. Mesquite is great for game meats as it masks off the gamey flavor of the meat.

- Oak: Oak pellets are great as far as smoke intensity is concerned. It is one of the smoke pellets that give off a light smoky aroma to food. However, it is stronger than both the apple and cherry wood pellets thus making it perfect for all types of meat dishes. But aside from meats, it is also great for smoked and grilled vegetables as well as fish.
- Pecan: Pecan wood pellets impart a nutty as well as a little spicy flavor into your food. It is great with poultry, pork, and beef. You can also use it to make baked goods particularly loaves of bread.

These are the wood pellets that you can use to cook different kinds of foods in your Wood Pellet Grill. It is available on the store's website. You can mix different wood pellets or buy pre-mixed pellets to ensure that you get the right proportion of wood pellets to cook your favorite meals.

The fundamentals of wood pellet grilling and smoking

To proceed with smoking, we will need wood, which in our case we find on the market for this specific use in the following forms:

Wood Chips: they are small wood chips made from untreated trees. They are mainly used in both gas and charcoal kettles (spherical BBQs), and in rectangular gas ones, they generate medium intensity smoke suitable for not excessively large cooking chambers.

Wood Chunks: they are larger pieces of wood (like a punch), they are mainly used in smokers that have a larger cooking chamber, generate a more intense and lasting smoke and give foods a more accentuated smoked flavor, suitable for cooking large pieces of meat such as pork shoulder (pulled pork) and beef brisket (brisket).

Food pellets: small cylinders such as heating pellets. However, they are made from untreated wood and are free of toxic chemicals. They are used exclusively on special BBQs that work with this type of fuel.

Smoke with a charcoal kettle:

We set the BBQ for indirect cooking, make sure that the coal combustion is optimal (you will see a white ash patina on the coal), take the wood chips and place them on the embers. We place the (raw) food on the grill, close the lid of the kettle, and open the vents to the maximum for maximum combustion.

After a short time, you see that the smoke will generate intensely, when the same will fade you can proceed, by adjusting the vents to stabilize the cooking chamber at the desired temperature, and complete the cooking of your dish.

Smoke with a kettle or a gas rectangular:

First, it is also possible to smoke with gas devices and to give our food the aroma of wood smoke. To do this, we will need to have a specific accessory called the smoker box.

The smoker box is a metal box with holes on the top that will be filled with wood chips and placed inside the BBQ near the burner.

The outdoor chef produces both one for the kettle and one for rectangular BBQ and Charcoal Companion.

We proceed by inserting the smoker box with the wood chips inside the BBQ near the burner, reposition the grill, and switch on by setting the BBQ for indirect cooking at the maximum temperature.

Unlike coal, the smoke in the gas device will take longer to generate (about 15-20 min).

Once you see the smoke generated you can insert the food and adjust the BBQ to the desired temperature for cooking.

Smoking with a Bullet Smoker:

These machines are designed to cook food with the Low & Slow cooking technique, their operating temperature ranges from 90 to 130 ° C in a humid cooking chamber.

In these machines a container with water called Water pan is placed between the brazier and the cooking chamber. Moisture has several functions: to make smoking more uniform, to stabilize the temperature, to help convert the collagen into juice.

To smoke with these devices, I recommend using wood chunks (chips are also good but will last less).

For a better quality of the smoke, put the smoking wood on the well-lit embers through the special door.

Place your food on the grill and close the lids, smoke with the ventilation fully open, and then stabilize the smoker at the desired temperature.

Smoke with a pellet barbecue:

Smoking with this device is very simple: once you put our food on the grill with the BBQ turned off we will turn it on in "Smoke" mode and the BBQ will start a smoking cycle, and after 15 ~ 20 minutes of this program we will go to select the desired operating temperature to finish cooking.

CHAPTER 5. FIRST TIME WITH YOUR WOOD PELLET SMOKER-GRILL

Seasoning your grill

Seasoning is an important first step of grill ownership. This will ensure that your grill is in the perfect state for grilling, smoking, roasting or baking. Seasoning helps lock in the non-stick coating meaning you can use less oil when cooking, and it also makes cleaning your grill easier. This is an important step that takes about 1 hour and should not be skipped.

To season your grill, follow these steps the first time you use your Wood Pellet Grill

Step 1: Add wood pellets of your choice to the auger at the side of your grill

Step 2: Plug in the grill and turn the main power switch to "On."

Step 3: Turn the dial to "Select Auger" and choose "Prime Auger." The pellets will now fall into the firepot. Once they have all left the Auger and into the fire pot, select "Done."

Step 4: Turn the dial to 350F and press the dial in to activate

Step 5: Press "Ignite" and close the lid of your grill. Wait and allow the temperature to come up to 350F. Let it run at 350F for 20 minutes.

Step 6: Next, raise the temperature dial to 450F and let it run for an additional 30 minutes.

Step 7: Shut down your grill. This varies by model but will be clear in the user manual for your model.

Once the shutdown of your grill is complete, your grill is fully seasoned and ready to go!

Start-up process

There are two main options for using your Wood Pellet Grill – it is important to know the difference as it will affect the end product and your cooking experience as a whole. If you do not follow these steps, your cooking experience may result in temperature fluctuations, flames and other issues.

The Closed Lid Start-Up Process - This method is super simple! When you've found a recipe you want to cook, simply turn on your grill and select your desired temperature. Let the grill preheat while keeping the lid completely closed for about 15 minutes. This will allow smoke to build in the grill. This time is a great time to get your ingredients ready – this includes patting meat dry, seasoning vegetables or draining marinade from whatever you are cooking.

The Open Lid Start-Up Process - With this method, you will turn on your grill with the lid open. Wait for about 5 minutes and let the fire start before setting the smoke setting. Next, you'll close the lid and set the temperature waiting for 15 minutes or so for it to come up to temperature. Once you add your food to the grill, you will close the grill and allow for smoke to build up inside.

What is the p-setting?

P-settings control the amount of smoke and heat given off by the pellet grill in most pellet grills. It is a critical setting and one of the most important parts of a wood pellet grill. If you want to get the most out of your pellet grill, you must be aware of this setting. The P-setting in a wood pellet grill is critical because it controls the heat in both the convection side and the injection side of a pellet grill and one must be adjusted for the other. If you want to have your wood pellet grill cook quickly, you must increase the P-setting of the convection side. If you want to minimize the heat of the food, you must increase the P-setting of the injection side. Think of the P-setting as the pre-heating setting of a pellet grill. If you have just purchased a pellet grill, it is set at P-5.

If you are a seasoned grillmaster, you will probably want to know how to increase the P-setting so that you can get your food quicker. If you want the food to be done faster, turn the P-setting higher. You might think that the lower the temperature, the better or the healthier the food will be. In fact, food will be healthier if it is at a lower temperature, but don't lower the P-setting too much. It will take longer to cook, and if the P-setting is at P-1, a pellet grill will cook slower than if it were at P-5. You just set your P-setting from P-5 to P-10.

Shut down cycle

This grill will take longer to fully shut down than your average barbeque, because the wood pellets have to burn out and because of the double-lined walls of the grill, it maintains its heat for quite a long time. Each model is equipped with a special timer, so you will know exactly how long it will take for your grill to completely shut down. This is important not only for safety, but also so you know when you can add the recommended cover to your grill (when it's cooled completely.)

CHAPTER 6. MAINTENANCE AND TROUBLESHOOTING FOR THE MOST COMMON PROBLEMS

A barbecue grill can be quite a big investment. They can cost $1000 or more. You need to take some time to learn how to take care of your investment when you spend that much. When it comes to barbecue, taking care of them needs to become a habit. After every use, you should ensure that your grill is thoroughly cleaned. It doesn't matter if you're using an indoor electric grill like the Breville Smart Grill, a barbecue model like a Weber grill, or even a gas grill; most of the maintenance tips that follow will not change.

Phase 1-Using the right equipment

You don't have to go to the hardware store and spend hundreds of dollars to find the right tools to clean your barbecue. All you need are some steel wool sheets, a mild dish cleaner, baking soda, spray cooking oil, a grill brush, aluminum foil, and cloth. Take a few moments to pick and keep these things close to your barbecue, but note that you should store them inside so that the weather does not harm them.

Phase 2 Give A Good Brushing to Your Grill

You should provide your grill with a regular brushing after every single use. One thing you were supposed to get when you gathered materials earlier was a grill brush. They are commonly made of brass wires that can be used to brush the grilling surface to remove all of the unpleasant accumulation so that it won't become permanent. The longer that all of the grease and stuck-on food is left on the grilling board, the more difficult it will be to clean.

Phase 3-The Other Products are used.

Mix a little bit of baking soda with water to make the really nasty bits nice and clean, and put it on your wire brush. By using this baking soda mixture, you can clean every portion of your grill. Next, to make it really clean, crumple up some aluminum foil and wipe down the grill surfaces with a light circular motion. Once your grill is absolutely cold and washed off, spray it down with the cooking oil. This is important because it will avoid the rusting of the grilling surface.

Phase 4-Do not think about the soap.

Get the soap out and wash your shelves. In a bucket, you can combine a bit of soap and water and use a tissue to clean your racks. This may seem like a lot of work, but if you spent a lot of money on your grill, you would certainly want it to be always perfect. It can make them last longer. On top of that, the anti-bacterial properties of the soap will help kill off any bacteria that has been left on your food. The steel wool pads can also be used to remove some of the residual grime.

If you find that you started having habitual problems with your barbecue, consider getting a cover. Some of the worst things that you can expose your grill to, are weather conditions, like rain and snow, so it is best to cover it up. Make this maintenance routine a habit, and your grill will support you for years and years.

You cannot use your grill very much, or maybe you choose to cook in your kitchen because you're not a jockey on the grill, or maybe you just don't have enough time for a barbecue. Well, whatever the reason is, there is no excuse not to take care of it, be it gas or charcoal.

Much like the other appliances you have in your home, you also shelled money on your gas or charcoal grill, so it only fits that you find time to clean and maintain it. How? Here you can find four simple tips on how to take care of your grill. Don't worry; it's so much easier to clean it than to clean the charcoal.

Powder the Grill Grates Before Cooking

Don't put meat and vegetables (also called grids) directly on the grill grates. Instead, before cooking, make it a habit to coat the grill grates with some oil. This prevents excessive food and particles from sticking onto your grates. It may be hard to extract food trapped in the grates. Also, a well-oiled grill grate gives the food better grill marks.

To oil the grill grates, you can use any of these three options: an oiled paper towel or rag, some bacon or beef fat, or cooking spray. If you use the first option, it is best if the grill grates are very hot. Some recommend using bacon or beef fat because it gives the food extra taste. Among the three, the third choice, is the most convenient, however, make sure you apply the spray before you turn the grill on; as the spray appears to catch fire, never try to spray the grates over the flame.

Clean the Whole Grill

The most important part of the grill is the grate since this is where you put your food. That's why they have the priority when it comes to clean the grill. Clean the grill grates only after grilling so that it is easy to remove any food particles that may have stuck on it. To clean the grates, use a wire brush. Long-handled rigid wire brushes are the favorite of serious grillers. Scrub the grates twice; then, you can wash them with soapy water if you are still not pleased.

Next, the whole grill is washed. Wait for the grill to cool down fully. Then, with a wet paper towel or a damp rag, clean off the grease from the surfaces. Grease can cause corrosion if not removed immediately.

You are also advised to schedule a day once a year for thorough cleaning of your grill. Create a combination of half water and half white vinegar. Clean the grill by spraying it inside the grill with the mixture. Leave it for about an hour to 30 minutes. Wipe the whole thing with a wet rag or paper towel afterward.

Drain the drip pan and clear the ash catcher; grilling usually helps to produce a lot of food drippings, such as beef and poultry. Expect that the drip pan (which you ideally set up correctly) is guaranteed to be full of fat and oil after your grilling session. Don't throw the fat instantly, let the drip pan cool off first.

Don't dump the drippings directly into the field once it has cooled down. Use something close to an empty milk carton and pour the fat into it. You may use this fat again, you'll never know. Just ensure that when you decide to use it again, the drippings are absolutely free of ash.

Many charcoal grills, apart from the drip pan, come with an ash catcher. Usually, it is shaped like a saucepan and is placed at the bottom of the grill. As their name suggests, their main purpose is to catch the ashes produced during your grilling session. Remove the ash catcher from the base and toss the ashes after using the grill; however, make sure the ashes are still cold before trying to dump them in the garbage. If you throw them when still hot, it can cause flame among your other flammable garbage. Wait one day, to be sure and secure.

There may be some technical issues with any appliances, primarily since your Wood Pellet Grill and Smoker work with electricity. Here are some of the most frequently asked questions when it comes to general use and troubleshooting.

My grill isn't lighting, what am I doing wrong?

This can happen due to the hotrod not heating up, the induction fan not working, or the auger isn't feeding the fire pot with pellets. Use a process of elimination to find the source of the problem.

The Wood Pellet Grill and Smoker doesn't want to power on.

It's usually due to some or other electrical issues. It can be a bad power outlet, a bad extension cord, a blown fuse on the controller, or the GFCI tripped.

The auger isn't moving.

If you used damp pellets, it might have caused your auger to jam. If that's not the case, the shear pin that holds the motor to the auger may be broken. You can also check if the auger motor is in working order and make sure that it is getting power from the controller.

The induction fan isn't running.

If you haven't used your pellet smoker in a while, the grease on the fan base may have seized—give it a spin to loosen it. In addition, check if there is power from the controller to the orange wires. Lastly, make sure there isn't an obstruction keeping your fan from turning.

My grill is running hot on smoke. Why is this?

The outside weather will play a role in the smoke temperature since it will have to compensate for hotter or colder conditions. It might also be a case of you closing the lid too soon after the grill was started. It is best to leave the top open for at least 10 minutes to give the startup fuel time to burn off.

CHAPTER 7. COMPONENT OF WOOD PELLET GRILLING

We're going to go over all the parts of a wood pellet smoker grill, so you know what you're working with when you get your own. Let's get into it.

The Hopper. You'll be keeping your wood pellets here. When you store your wood pellets, you want to make sure you've got just enough in there to take you through the length of time you'll need for cooking, give you the temperature you need, and meet the capacity recommended for your hopper.

The Auger. The pellets are delivered to the fire pot through the auger.

The Fire Pot. The fire pot is where the pellets go. With the fire pot, you can ignite the wood pellets which will then heat up the grill. You will find there's a big hold in the fire pot. This hole is where you connect the pellet tube. The pellet tube also has the auger in it so that you can feed the pellets directly to the pot. In the fire pot, there is an even bigger hole in the lower, in the middle. This other hole is specifically for connecting the igniter rod. Every other hole in the fire pot is to allow airflow from the fan. You always want to make sure you empty out all the ashes after a few cooking sessions. If you don't do this, then you'll find the igniter won't work as well as it used to over time. You could also vacuum the ashes out as well, if you like.

The Igniter Rod/Element. This is what lights up the wood pellets which are in the fire pot. When you remove the fire pot, you'll be able to see the igniter rod as well as the pellet feed tube which feeds pellets to the fire pot through the auger.

The Fan. This keeps the airflow constant or dynamic, depending on what you're going for. Thanks to the fan, the pellets continue burning, making convection cooking a breeze.

The Thermocouple/Resistive Temperature Detector (RTD). This thermal sensor gives the controller the feedback loop. You must make sure that you always keep the thermocouple clean by wiping it down after a number of cooking sessions. When you do this, you can be assured of more accurate heat measurements.

The Heat Deflector. Just as the name suggests, the heat deflector is what helps absorb heat. It also helps the heat spread out nice and even underneath the drip pan, so that your wood pellet smoker grill functions as convection open. You'll find the head deflector covering the fire pot.

The Drip/Grease Pan. You can use this part of your wood pellet smoker grill for smoking, roasting, baking, and indirect cooking as well. What the pan does is to help move the grease which you'll get naturally from cooking, right to the grease bucket. Now make sure that you always get rid of all residue after each cooking session.

Scrape it off to keep it nice and clean. I cannot stress enough that you should make use of foil. If you do, make sure you change the foil after every few cooking sessions.

The Flame Zone Pan. This is used for grilling directly, at really high temperatures. More often than not, you'll find it being used alongside searing grates, and other griddle accessories.

The Controller. You'll find that there are many forms in which the controller comes. Its function is simple. With the controller, you can adjust the airflow and pellet flow so the temperature you desire remains consistent.

The Grease Bucket. This is what collects all the grease and fat as you cook your yummy meats. Grease definitely will accumulate over time. The amount that does accumulate will depend on the way you handle trimming excess fat and fat caps from poultry and meat. If you would like your clean up sessions to be a breeze, then you definitely should consider lining the bucket with foil. You may then discard all the grease in empty cans, which you can then toss in the trash.

CHAPTER 8. TEMPERATURE CONTROL

One of the best aspects of the Wood Pellet Grill is total control of the temperature. Once you set it, the grill is capable of maintaining consistent heat, even if the weather may not look favorable. The Wood Pellet grills can be set in 5-degree increments, which is a feature not seen in many grills, especially charcoal and gas ones. All you need to do is cook the food using the recipe and not worry about the appliance dropping down the temperature. Additionally, since pellets are essentially electric, you are not tied to your grill like a gas grill. For instance, you do not have to keep checking the grill from time-to-time to ensure that the food has not burned.

CHAPTER 9. SECRET TIPS FOR SUCCESSFUL WOOD PELLET GRILLING

If you are looking for some tips and tricks that can help you better utilize your grill, they are listed for you. If you already have the appliance, you are already on the sweet side of life. Whether you are a grill newbie or a master, there are always things that you can learn to become the ultimate grill and smoker master. Some of the top tricks, tips, and hacks that can make your barbequing, smoking, and grilling experience better include:

1. Always use disposable drip bucket liners

If you get tired of cleaning up that slimy residue every time you decide to grill or smoke some steak or are prone to bumping the bucket off accidentally when putting on the cover, it is recommended that you look for bucket liners - disposable ones of course. With the help of these disposable drip bucket liners, cleaning will become much easier.

2. Grill lights to light the way

If you plan on cooking at night or are always bumping around the grill in the dark, you can look for some grill lights. If you are a serious smoker but are busy dealing with the headlamp or flashlight, these grill lights will come in very handy. No wonder this device is one of the top-sellers on several online shopping sites. The grill lights are fitted with a magnetic base and can clamp and bend according to the shape of the grill.

3. Drip tray liners for easier cleaning

If you want to get serious, then it is time to dump the aluminum foil. Once you have the drip tray liners, you will not have to deal with wadded up, oily, blackened, or small tears in the foil. The overall idea here is to make the cleaning process easier so that you can redirect your focus on the more important things, such as smoking and grilling.

4. Meat temperature and meat smoking magnets to measure the temperature accurately

One of the worst things that can happen while grilling and smoking meat is guessing the cooking temperature. With the help of meat smoking and temperature magnets, you can now leave all the frantic web searches behind. With these devices, you will know the internal temperature that you need to cook meat safely. Then, you will always have perfectly cooked pieces of meat all the time.

5. Wireless thermometer or Tappecue for the perfect temperature

You have already spent hundreds of dollars on a perfect grill. However, you can still end up spending tens and thousands of dollars more each time you decide to cook on it. If you want to protect your important investment from harm, you need to ensure that you do not have to 'peek' while cooking. With the Tappecue, you will get the internal temperature that you are looking for.

6. Swap out pellets with bucket head vacuum

Imagine that you need to move from the apple to the hickory flavor. However, you see that the grill is more than half-full of apple pellets. What can do you in this scenario? Of course, you can choose to wait until the pellets cool down and then remove them. Another solution to this issue is using a bucket head vacuum. Get the appropriate bucket head for a 5-gallon bucket and simply vacuum out the pellets. Once done, you will be left with storage that you can use at any time. Additionally, you do not even need a specialized bucket for this purpose; you can use a simple bucket and storage lid kit that is fitted with a filter.

7. Add extra smoke on any type of cooking with an A-maze-n Smoker Tube

If you love smoking, you should definitely buy a dedicated smoker tube – like the A-maze-n Smoker Tube. Known for its great simplicity, this tube is one of the best tools for a seasoned smoker. All you need to do is to add some pellets and light it at just one end. Then, leave it on the grates. A smoker tube is a great option for cold smoking fish, nuts, and cheese; of course, it can also be used for some extra smoke on meats, like brisket, pulled pork, etc.

CHAPTER 10. COMMON FAQS FOR WOOD PELLET GRILLING

Your Wood Pellet Grill is not only for making smoked meats. In fact, there are so many things that you can make out of this kitchen device. This section will provide you with helpful tips and tricks so that you can optimize your Wood Pellet Grill. Make sure that you are making the most out of your Wood Pellet Grill.

- Use the reverse sear: The reverse sear is a great and exciting way to cook steak. You can smoke your meats at low temperatures (1500F). Cook your meat low and slow (for around 1 hour) then remove the meat from the grill. Adjust the temperature knob to the highest temperature setting to add sear and more flavor to your food. If you are the kind of person who loves some charred parts on their meats, then this is the best setting for you. This will also give you the perfect medium-rare on your meat.

- Put cold meat into the grill at a low setting: This tip is immensely helpful especially if you are cooking large cuts of meat. The secret to cooking large cuts of meat with full flavor is to make sure that it pulls more smoke into the meat. To achieve this, make sure that you put cold meat into the grill and cook it at low temperature (1500F) as it gives a little more time for the smoke to take hold of the meat. Use this tip when cooking Tri-Tip, large brisket, and other large chunks of meats.

- Use the upper racks of the pellet grill for additional space: You can put more food in your grill if you use the upper racks to give you extra space. Using the extra space also decreases radiant heat coming from the grease tray so you will be able to utilize the heat more efficiently.

- Place heat-proof water pan under a rack: Putting a water pan with water under the rack allows long briskets to cook evenly and properly. Putting a water pan inside the grill creates steam that can help cook food. Moreover, it also allows the meat to cook in an ideal environment.

- Use it as you would use an oven: The Wood Pellet Grill is not just a grill. To optimize its use, let your creativity run wild by cooking different kinds of foods on your grill. Think of it as an oven. What you can cook in an oven, you can cook in your pellet grill. To make your food more exciting, use different kinds of pellets to add more flavor to your foods.

- Clean temperature probe regularly: Clean the temperature probe of your grill every after use to ensure that it can effectively read the temperature properly. If you do not clean the temperature probe, the probe will be coated with fat and other drippings that may affect its ability to properly track the temperature inside your grill.

- Preheat the grill before using it: Before you use the grill, make sure that you preheat the grill for at least five minutes at 2000F at the most. Let the grill sit for five

(5) minutes to preheat properly. However, for brand new Wood Pellet Grill units, you can use the Advance Grilling Logic to preheat the grill for 2 minutes. Once the grill finishes preheating, you will hear a roaring noise from the main body. Once you hear the noise, close the lid to build up heat and smoke inside until you are ready to cook.

With these tips and tricks, you will definitely end up making your Wood Pellet Grill the only outdoor kitchen appliance that you will ever need. Happy cooking.

CHAPTER 11. NEW TRENDS AND TECHNIQUES IN BARBECUING

In the last few years, there has been a great resurgence in various forms of "low and slow" cooking. No more do we have to just think of chucking a steak or piece of meat on the barbecue and leaving it to cook for a couple of minutes on each side. No more do we have to fire up a smoker, sometimes almost continuously throughout the day when the meat needs to be turned or checked. No more do we have to stand in front of a grill to rotate steaks or burgers. No more do we have to use "easy" methods such as sticking on your regulator and not worrying about venting away smoke. The latest craze is BBQ that is done well, AND it is done easily.

Not only do we have different methods, but we also have different meat cuts that we can use in our smoking and grilling. More exotic cuts of meat such as ribs, even cheap cuts like brisket, have gained popularity and acceptance that was not there a few years ago. Everyone loves a good pulled pork sandwich or a burger or rib on a plate.

However, the popularity of these different cuts of meat has opened up the field to experimentation. There are different techniques and techniques of cooking that will prepare these cuts and make them succulent and luscious grub for the enjoyment of all.

For instance, there is a method that I have seen that is beautiful to see and to eat. This method is called the "doughing method" and has a home version and an industrial (commercial) version. This is one of the ways in which the industrial version is different from some of the home versions. It guarantees that the meat will be perfectly cooked all the way through. The dough is placed neatly in a pan, and then the meat is layered on top of the dough. This allows the meat to bake until it is done (this can be achieved in a few hours or overnight for up to a day or two. The results are fantastic. The meat is tender to the touch when the dough is opened. However, there is no moisture loss as would happen in other methods such as grilling or roasting. The meat forms a large "crust" that is not dry. The meat still forms small individual patty shapes. When you unwrap the dough (which can be done when the meat is still hot or warm), the aroma that escapes is fantastic.

The dough that I used was fairly soft, though it did not sour. The dough that I used was made of bread-making yeast, flour, and milk, with some salt and butter added in. This dough is perfect for this process.

The bottom line is that there is something just great about being able to pick and choose what you do and how you do it. The smoker has been around for a long time and is here to stay because it just works. Back in the day, you had access to a smoker or not, and you used that method, or you didn't. The amount of smoke being generated by a smoker is often as much a part of the taste of the food as any other ingredient or technique. That said, a smoker is not always easy to use. Since the days of the first Weber kettle BBQ - a smoker underneath the grill - we have come a long way. We now have smokers that do not require constant attention.

CHAPTER 12. THE BEST COMPETITION BBQ SMOKERS

You can't cook good meat if you have an inadequate grill. So you have to obtain a BBQ smoker that's of great quality as well as of a good price. The costliest ones are not necessarily the best smokers. The reason is that the truly good ones don't always leave an enormous opening in your pocket.

There's a brand new distinction in the cooking gear of today. This is the introduction of variation that is brought about by digital or technology types of cooking devices. This is in the form of innovation when compared to the conventional or traditional method of grilling. The contemporary digital technology smokers are best for the optimum in smoking of meat. The ones that are designed to perfection are designed for a specific sort of meat and smoking to compliment it. These best smokers can produce some really good source of meals that a person would be proud to serve.

Louisiana Grills Country Super Hog Series Smoker comes in the particular category of digital burners. However, these digital smokers are only as good as the way it's manufactured, so be sure to have a good dependable place for the processing of your foods. One really good feature of this smoker is the fact that it has a really spacious workspace for your food inside the system. There are special vents that are purposely made so that your meat doesn't lose its juices.

Traeger Pellet Grills TFB30LZB Series Smoker is a bit different from their version of this modern digital technology. However, it has a digital controller for the process. It has both a timer and a temperature gauge, which is constructed so that it will permit the process to work evenly and steadily. For you to be able to eat some really good meat, you should ensure that the control of your smoker will be consistent.

Outdoor Leisure SH36208 -900 26", Smoke Hollow Sideburner is just another device that has a sensible control panel. It has a definite gauge, which lets a person know if your meats are done or not. It is a very nicely designed unit that will permit a specific temperature to be reached. This is very useful for all sorts of meat such as fish, poultry, meats, and vegetables to stop burning when it is done.

Smokin Tex 1400 Pro Series is definitely one of the best smokers in the world. It has a digital remote control and a timer that is perfect for checking meat's temperature. This is the ideal unit for a lot of individuals. It is easy to set up, and also you will not have trouble knowing the temperature of the smoked meat.

In terms of flavor, you can't beat the time tested traditional smokers that did not use technology to digitally develop smoke over the meat. This is really important in developing that special sauce that some individuals just love.

SmokeHouse Red Big Block 1800 - 24" Charcoal Smoker is a good old time favorite that is made by manufacturers that have decades of experience in making smokers. One good feature of this smoker is the fact that it doesn't just have a cooking platform, but it also has built-in side shelves for your food. This severely limits the amount of handling required for the food to be properly placed in the smoker. The days of having to bone out a steak in order to get an evenly cooked meat have all but vanished when the digital technology smokers were designed.

CHAPTER 13. BARBECUE RECIPES

1. Barbecue Pork Chops

Preparation time: 2 minutes

Cooking time: 30 minutes

Servings: 4

Ingredients:

- 4 thick-cut pork chops
- 3 tablespoons sweet dry rub
- 1/2 cup brown sugar
- 1/4 cup molasses
- 2 cloves garlic, minced
- 2 tablespoons honey
- 2 tablespoon Worcestershire sauce
- 1 cup ketchup

Directions:

1. Add the pork chops to a baking pan covered with parchment paper.
2. Season with half of the dry rub.
3. In a bowl, mix the remaining dry rub with the remaining ingredients.
4. Add the sauce to a pan.
5. Set the wood pellet grill to 375 degrees F.
6. Grill the pork chops for 10 minutes per side.
7. Add the pan with sauce on top of the grill.
8. Bring to a boil. Pour the sauce over the chops.
9. Grill for another 3 minutes per side.

Nutrition:

Energy1031 kcal

Calcium, Ca255 mg

Magnesium, Mg168 mg

Phosphorus, P941 mg

Iron, Fe7.32 mg

Potassium, K2166 mg

Sodium, Na1076 mg

Zinc, Zn15.26 mg

2. Barbecue Brisket Sandwich

Preparation time: 20 minutes

Cooking time: 7 hours 40 minutes

Servings: 4

Ingredients:

- 1/2 cup peach preserves
- 2 tablespoons bourbon
- 1/2 cup barbecue sauce
- 1/4 cup beef broth
- 3 lb. beef brisket, fat trimmed
- 4 tablespoons pulled pork rub
- 4 rolls
- Pickles, sliced
- White onions, sliced

Directions:

1. Set your wood pellet grill to smoke.
2. Set it to 225 degrees F.
3. Add the brisket to the wood pellet grill.
4. Smoke the brisket for 5 hours.
5. In a bowl, combine the peach preserves, bourbon and barbecue sauce. Set aside.
6. Transfer the brisket on top of a foil sheet.
7. Pour the broth on top.
8. Sprinkle with the rub.
9. Wrap tightly.
10. Place it back in the smoker.
11. Cook for another 2 hours.
12. Unwrap the foil.
13. Place the brisket back to the grill.
14. Brush with the peach mixture.
15. Smoke for another 30 minutes.
16. Let rest for 10 minutes.
17. Slice and serve with the rolls, onions and pickles.

Nutrition:

Calcium, Ca120 mg

Magnesium, Mg68 mg

Phosphorus, P482 mg

Iron, Fe7.8 mg

Potassium, K1244 mg

Sodium, Na4859 mg

Zinc, Zn10.46 mg

3. Barbecue Pork Shoulder

Preparation time: 30 minutes

Cooking time: 6 hours

Servings: 8

Ingredients:

- 6 lb. pork shoulder
- 2 tablespoons hickory bacon seasoning
- 1 cup apple cider vinegar
- 1 tablespoon sugar

Directions:

1. Turn on your wood pellet grill.
2. Set it to 225 degrees F.
3. Sprinkle all sides of the pork with the seasoning.
4. In a bowl, mix the vinegar and sugar.

5. Mix until the sugar has been dissolved.
6. Inject the vinegar mixture into the pork shoulder.
7. Wrap the pork with foil.
8. Place on top of the grill.
9. Close the lid.
10. Smoke for 6 hours.
11. Uncover the pork slowly.
12. Let rest on a cutting board for 30 minutes.

Nutrition:

Energy 933 kcal

Calcium, Ca91 mg

Magnesium, Mg80 mg

Phosphorus, P711 mg

Iron, Fe6.05 mg

Potassium, K1073 mg

Sodium, Na232 mg

Zinc, Zn16.48 mg

4. Barbecue Pork Butt

Preparation Time: 10 minutes

Cooking Time: 5 hours

Servings: 8

Ingredients:

- 1 pork butt, boneless
- 2 tablespoons sweet dry rub
- 12 oz. dark beer
- 1 tablespoon olive oil
- 1/2 cup brown sugar
- 4 tablespoons honey
- 1 cup ketchup
- 4 tablespoons yellow mustard
- 2 tablespoons granulated garlic
- 2 tablespoons Worcestershire sauce

Directions:

1. Season the pork butt with the dry rub. Place it on a roasting pan. Add half of the beer to the pan.
2. Set the wood pellet grill to high. Add the pan to the grill. Grill for 30 minutes. Remove the pan from the grill.
3. Lessen the heat to 325 degrees F. In a bowl, mix the remaining ingredients. Pour this mixture on top of the roast. Cook for another 5 hours. Shred the pork. Coat with the barbecue sauce.

Nutrition:

Calories: 192

Carbs: 0g

Fat: 14g

Protein: 20g

5. Cajun Barbecue Chicken

Preparation Time: 15 minutes

Cooking Time: 25 minutes

Servings: 4

Ingredients:

- 2 tablespoons sweet spicy dry rub
- 1/4 teaspoon ground thyme
- 1/2 teaspoon oregano
- 1 tablespoon olive oil
- 1 lb. chicken breast fillet
- 2 cloves garlic clove, minced
- 1/2 cup barbecue sauce
- 1 tablespoon butter
- 1/4 cup beer
- 1 tablespoon Worcestershire sauce
- 1 tablespoon lime juice
- 1 teaspoon hot sauce

Directions:

13. Combine the dry rub, thyme and oregano in a bowl.
14. Coat the chicken breasts with olive oil.
15. Season both sides with the dry rub mixture.
16. Set the wood pellet grill to 350 degrees F.
17. Add the chicken breast to the grill.
18. Grill for 7 to 8 minutes.
19. Let rest for 10 minutes.
20. Combine rest of the ingredients in a saucepan. Bring to a boil.
21. Serve the chicken with the sauce.

Nutrition:

Calories: 286

Carbs: 14g

Fat: 5g

Protein: 38g

6. Barbecue Mustard Ribs

Preparation Time: 10 minutes

Cooking Time: 5 hours

Servings: 4

Ingredients:

Sauce

- 1/4 cup dark brown sugar
- 1/4 cup cider vinegar
- 1 cup yellow mustard
- 2 tablespoons ketchup
- 1/4 cup honey
- 1 tablespoon hot sauce

- 1 tablespoon Worcestershire sauce
- 1 tablespoon sweet dry rub

Ribs

- 1 rack ribs
- 1 cup yellow mustard
- 6 tablespoons sweet dry rub
- 2 cups apple juice

Directions:

1. Combine the sauce ingredients in a bowl.
2. Refrigerate while preparing the ribs.
3. Coat the ribs with the remaining mustard.
4. Season both sides with the sweet dry rub.
5. Set the wood pellet grill to 275 degrees F.
6. Grill the ribs for 3 hours.
7. Spray with the apple juice every 30 minutes.
8. Brush with the sauce mixture.
9. Slice and serve.

Nutrition:

Calories: 231

Carbs: 2g

Fat: 15g

Protein: 17g

7. Barbecue Raspberry Pork Ribs

Preparation Time: 5 minutes

Cooking Time: 3 hours

Servings: 6

Ingredients:

- 4 lb. baby back ribs
- 3 tablespoons raspberry chipotle dry rub
- 1 cup barbecue sauce

Directions:

1. Season the ribs with the dry rub.
2. Cover with foil.
3. Refrigerate for 1 hour.
4. Turn on the wood pellet grill.
5. Preheat your grill to 250 degrees F.
6. Add the ribs to the grill.
7. Cook for 2 hours.
8. Brush with the barbecue sauce.
9. Increase temperature to 300 degrees F.
10. Grill for another 1 hour.

Nutrition:

Calories: 114

Carbs: 6g

Fat: 3g

Protein: 14g

8. Barbecue Steak

Preparation Time: 5 minutes

Cooking Time: 45 minutes

Servings: 4

Ingredients:

- 2 bone-in rib eye steaks
- Steak seasoning
- 1 cup barbecue sauce

Directions:

1. Sprinkle both sides of the steak with the rub.
2. Turn on the wood pellet grill.
3. Set it to 400 degrees F.
4. Grill it for 7 to 8 minutes per side.
5. Transfer the steaks to a cutting board.
6. Let sit for 10 minutes before slicing.
7. Using a pan over medium heat, simmer the barbecue sauce for 5 minutes.
8. Serve the grilled steak with the barbecue sauce.

Nutrition:

Calories: 330

Carbs: 47g

Fat: 6g

Protein: 20g

9. Barbecue Kebabs

Preparation Time: 1 hour

Cooking Time: 25 minutes

Servings: 6

Ingredients:

- 1 tablespoon olive oil
- 1/8 cup apple cider vinegar
- 1 tablespoon honey
- 2 tablespoons raspberry chipotle rub
- 1 lb. pork loin, sliced into cubes
- 1 red onion, sliced
- 3 green bell peppers, sliced
- 1/2 cup barbecue sauce

Directions:

1. In a mixing bowl, mix the oil, vinegar, honey and rub.
2. Marinate the pork slices in this mixture.
3. Cover it with a foil and marinate in the refrigerator for 1 hour.
4. Thread the pork cubes into skewers alternating with the red onion and green bell pepper.
5. Set the wood pellet grill to 400 degrees F.
6. Grill the kebabs for 15 to 20 minutes, rotating every 5 minutes.

7. Brush with the barbecue sauce.

Nutrition:

Calories: 165

Carbs: 3g

Fat: 10g

Protein: 10g

10. Cheesy Barbecue Chicken

Preparation Time: 10 minutes

Cooking Time: 2 hours

Servings: 4

Ingredients:

- 4 chicken thigh fillets, skin removed
- 1 teaspoon olive oil
- 1/4 cup barbecue sauce
- 1 tablespoon sweet spicy dry rub
- 4 slices cheese

Directions:

1. Preheat your wood pellet grill to 350 degrees F.
2. Brush the chicken with the mixture of olive oil and barbecue sauce.
3. Sprinkle with the rub.
4. Grill the chicken for 30 minutes.
5. Add some cheese on top of the chicken.
6. Grill until the cheese has melted.

Nutrition:

Calories: 378

Carbs: 7g

Fat: 22g

Protein: 38g

11. Lemon Pepper Barbecue Wings

Preparation Time: 10 minutes

Cooking Time: 30 minutes

Servings: 4

Ingredients:

- 1 tablespoon barbecue sauce
- 2 tablespoons lemon zest
- 1/4 cup ground black pepper
- 2 teaspoons ground coriander
- 2 teaspoons garlic powder
- 3 teaspoons dried thyme
- Salt to taste
- 4 lb. chicken wings

Directions:

1. Set your wood pellet grill to smoke.
2. Set it to 400 degrees F.
3. Using a bowl mix all the ingredients except the chicken wings.
4. Soak the chicken wings in half of the mixture.
5. Place the wings on the grill.
6. Grill for 15 minutes per side.
7. Brush the chicken with the remaining sauce.

Nutrition:

Calories: 211

Carbs: 14g

Fat: 13g

Protein: 9g

12. Barbecue Pulled Pork

Preparation Time: 10 minutes

Cooking Time: 8 hours

Servings: 8

Ingredients:

- 1 teaspoon ground coriander
- 2 teaspoons black pepper
- 1 teaspoon cumin
- Salt to taste
- 7 lb. pork shoulder
- 4 cups chicken broth
- 2 cups barbecue sauce

Directions:

1. Set your wood pellet grill to smoke. Set it to 300 degrees F.
2. Combine the coriander, pepper, cumin and salt in a container. Put the mixture on all sides of the pork shoulder. Pour the broth into a roasting pan. Add the pork shoulder. Add the pan to the grill.
3. Cook for 8 hours. Shred the pork. Toss in the barbecue sauce. Heat through in a grill pan and serve.

Nutrition:

Calories: 207

Carbs: 2g

Fat: 5g

Protein: 34g

CHAPTER 14. BEEF RECIPES

13. Beef Jerky

Preparation Time: 15 minutes

Cooking Time: 5 hours

Servings: 10

Ingredients:

- 3 lb. sirloin steaks
- 2 cups soy sauce
- 1 cup pineapple juice
- 1/2 cup brown sugar
- 2 tbsps. sriracha
- 2 tbsps. hoisin
- 2 tbsps. red pepper flake
- 2 tbsps. rice wine vinegar
- 2 tbsps. onion powder

Directions:

1. Mix the marinade in a zip lock bag and add the beef. Mix until well coated and remove as much air as possible.
2. Place the bag in a fridge and let marinate overnight or for 6 hours. Remove the bag from the fridge an hour prior to cooking
3. Startup the Wood Pellet Grill and set it on the smoking settings or at 1900F.
4. Lay the meat on the grill leaving a half-inch space between the pieces. Let cool for 5 hours and turn after 2 hours.
5. Remove from the grill and let cool. Serve or refrigerate

Nutrition:

Calories 309

Total fat 7g

Saturated fat 3g

Total carbs 20g

Net carbs 19g

Protein 34g

Sugars 15g

Fiber 1g

Sodium 2832mg

14. Smoked Beef Roast

Preparation Time: 10 minutes

Cooking Time: 6 hours

Servings: 6

Ingredients:

- 1-3/4 lb. beef sirloin tip roast
- 1/2 cup BBQ rub
- 2 bottles amber beer
- 1 bottle BBQ sauce

Directions:

1. Turn the Wood Pellet Grill onto the smoke setting.
2. Rub the beef with BBQ rub until well coated then place on the grill. Let smoke for 4 hours while flipping every 1 hour.
3. Transfer the beef to a pan and add the beer. The beef should be 1/2 way covered.
4. Braise the beef until fork tender. It will take 3 hours on the stovetop and 60 minutes on the instant pot.
5. Remove the beef from the ban and reserve 1 cup of the cooking liquid.
6. Use 2 forks to shred the beef into small pieces then return to the pan with the reserved braising liquid.
7. Add BBQ sauce and stir well then keep warm until serving. You can also reheat if it gets cold.

Nutrition:

Calories 829

Total fat 46g

Saturated fat 18g

Total carbs 4g

Net carbs 4g

Protein 86g

Sugars 0g

Fiber 0g

Sodium 181mmg

15. Reverse Seared Flank Steak

Preparation Time: 10 minutes

Cooking Time: 20 minutes

Servings: 2

Ingredients:

- 3 lb. flank steaks
- 1 tbsp. salt
- 1/2 tbsp. onion powder
- 1/4 tbsp. garlic powder
- 1/2 black pepper, coarsely ground

Directions:

1. Preheat the Wood Pellet Grill to 2250F.
2. All the ingredients in a bowl and mix well. Add the steaks and rub them generously with the rub mixture.
3. Place the steak on the grill and close the lid. Let cook until its internal temperature is 100F under your desired temperature. 1150F for rare, 1250F for the medium rear and 1350F for medium.
4. Wrap the steak with foil and raise the grill temperature to high. Place back the steak and grill for 3 minutes on each side.
5. Pat with butter and serve when hot.

Nutrition:

Calories 112

Total fat 5g

Saturated fat 2g

Total carbs 1g

Net carbs 1g

Protein 16g

Sugars 0g

Fiber 0g

Sodium 737mg

16. Beef Tenderloin

Preparation Time: 10 minutes

Cooking Time: 45 minutes

Servings: 6

Ingredients:

- 4 lb. beef tenderloin
- 3 tbsps. steak rub
- 1 tbsp. kosher salt

Directions:

1. Preheat the Wood Pellet Grill to high heat.
2. Meanwhile, trim excess fat from the beef and cut it into 3 pieces.
3. Coat the steak with rub and kosher salt. Place it on the grill.
4. Close the lid and cook for 10 minutes. Open the lid, flip the beef and cook for 10 more minutes.
5. Reduce the temperature of the grill until 2250F and smoke the beef until the internal temperature reaches 1300F.
6. Remove the beef from the grill and let rest for 15 minutes before slicing and serving.

Nutrition:

Calories 999

Total fat 76g

Saturated fat 30g

Total carbs 0g

Net carbs 0g

Protein 74g

Sugars 0g

Fiber 0g

Sodium 1234mmg

17. Beef New York Strip

Preparation Time: 5 minutes

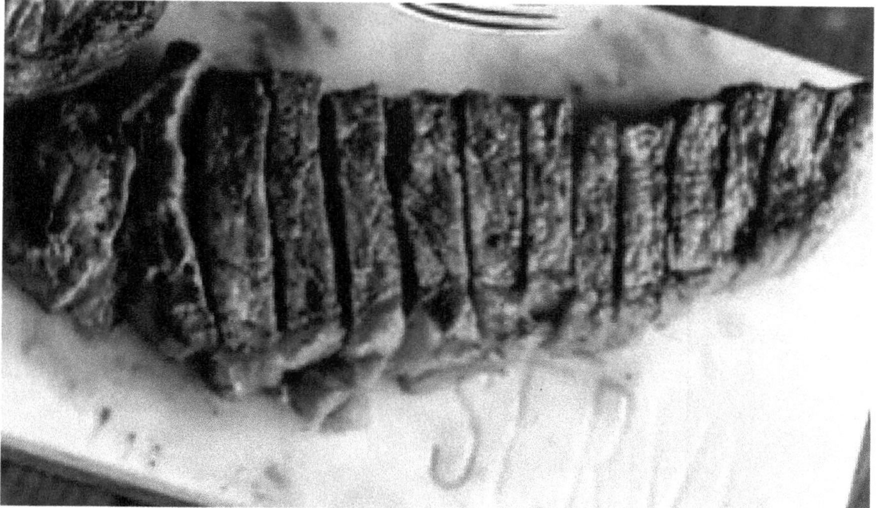

Cooking Time: 15 minutes

Servings: 6

Ingredients:

- 3 New York strips
- Salt and pepper

Directions:

1. If the steak is in the fridge, remove it 30 minutes prior to cooking.
2. Preheat the Wood Pellet Grill to 4500F.
3. Meanwhile, season the steak generously with salt and pepper. Place it on the grill and let it cook for 5 minutes per side or until the internal temperature reaches 1280F.
4. Remove the steak from the grill and let it rest for 10 minutes.

Nutrition:

Calories 198

Total fat 14g

Saturated fat 6g

Total carbs 0g

Net carbs 0

Protein 17g

Sugars 0g

Fiber 0g

Sodium 115mg

18. Stuffed Peppers

Preparation Time: 20 minutes

Cooking Time: 5 minutes

Servings: 6

Ingredients:

- 3 bell peppers, sliced in halves
- 1 lb. ground beef, lean
- 1 onion, chopped
- 1/2 tbsp. red pepper flakes
- 1/2 tbsp. salt
- 1/4 tbsp. pepper
- 1/2 tbsp. garlic powder
- 1/2 tbsp. onion powder
- 1/2 cup white rice
- 15 oz. stewed tomatoes
- 8 oz. tomato sauce
- 6 cups cabbage, shredded
- 1-1/2 cup water
- 2 cups cheddar cheese

Directions:

1. Arrange the pepper halves on a baking tray and set aside.
2. Preheat your grill to 3250F.
3. Brown the meat in a large skillet. Add onions, pepper flakes, salt, pepper garlic, and onion and cook until the meat is well cooked.
4. Add rice, stewed tomatoes, tomato sauce, cabbage, and water. Cover and simmer until the rice is well cooked, the cabbage is tender and there is no water in the rice.
5. Place the cooked beef mixture in the pepper halves and top with cheese.
6. Place in the grill and cook for 30 minutes.
7. Serve immediately and enjoy it.

Nutrition:

Calories 422

Total fat 22g

Saturated fat 11g

Total carbs 24g

Net carbs 19g

Protein 34g

Sugars 11g

Fiber 5g

Sodium 855mg

19. Prime Rib Roast

Preparation Time: 10 minutes

Cooking Time: 2 hours

Servings: 8

Ingredients:

- 5 lb. rib roast, boneless
- 4 tbsps. salt
- 1 tbsp. black pepper
- 1-1/2 tbsp. onion powder
- 1 tbsp. granulated garlic
- 1 tbsp. rosemary
- 1 cup chopped onion
- 1/2 cup carrots, chopped
- 1/2 cup celery, chopped
- 2 cups beef broth

Directions:

1. Remove the beef from the fridge 1 hour prior to cooking.
2. Preheat the Wood Pellet Grill to 2500F.
3. In a small mixing bowl, mix salt, pepper, onion, garlic, and rosemary to create your rub.
4. Generously coat the roast with the rub and set it aside.
5. Combine chopped onions, carrots, and celery in a cake pan then place the bee on top.
6. Place the cake pan in the middle of the Wood Pellet Grill and cook for 1 hour.
7. Pour the beef broth at the bottom of the cake pan and cook until the internal temperature reaches 1200F.
8. Remove the cake pan from the Wood Pellet Grill and let rest for 20 minutes before slicing the meat.
9. Pour the cooking juice through a strainer, then skim off any fat at the top.
10. Serve the roast with the cooking juices.

Nutrition:

Calories 721

Total fat 60g

Saturated fat 18g

Total carbs 3g

Net carbs 2g

Protein 43g

Sugars 1g

Fiber 1g

Sodium 2450mmg

20. Kalbi Beef Short Ribs

Preparation Time: 10 minutes

Cooking Time: 6 hours

Servings: 6

Ingredients:

- 1/2 cup soy sauce
- 1/2 cup brown sugar
- 1/8 cup rice wine
- 2 tbsps. minced garlic
- 1 tbsp. sesame oil
- 1/8 cup onion, finely grated
- 2-1/2 lb. beef short ribs, thinly sliced

Directions:

1. Mix soy sauce, sugar, rice wine, garlic, sesame oil and onion in a medium mixing bowl.

2. Add the beef in the bowl and cover it in the marinade. Cover the bowl with a plastic wrap and refrigerate for 6 hours.
3. Heat your Wood Pellet Grill to high and ensure the grill is well heated.
4. Place the marinated meat on the grill and close the lid ensuring you don't lose any heat.
5. Cook for 4 minutes, flip, and cook for 4 more minutes on the other side.
6. Remove the meat and serve with rice and veggies of choice. Enjoy.

Nutrition:

Calories 355

Total fat 10g

Saturated fat 6g

Total carbs 22g

Net carbs 22

Protein 28g

Sugars 19g

Fiber 0g

Sodium 1213mg

21. Beef Short Rib Lollipop

Preparation Time: 15 minutes

Cooking Time: 3 hours

Servings: 4

Ingredients:

- 4 beef short rib lollipops
- BBQ Rub
- BBQ Sauce

Directions:

1. Preheat your Wood Pellet Grill to 2750F.
2. Season the short ribs with BBQ rub and place them on the grill.
3. Cook for 4 hours while turning occasionally until the meat is tender.
4. Apply the sauce on the meat in the last 30 minutes of cooking.
5. Serve and enjoy.

Nutrition:

Calories 265

Total fat 19g

Saturated fat 9g

Total carbs 1g

Net carbs 0g Protein 22g

Sugars 1g

Fiber 0g

Sodium 60mmg

22. Beef Tri-Tip

Preparation Time: 10 minutes

Cooking Time: 1 hour 30 minutes

Servings: 6

Ingredients:

- 3 lb. tri-tip
- 1-1/2 tbsp. kosher salt
- 1 tbsp. black pepper
- 1 tbsp. paprika
- 1/2 tbsp. cayenne
- 1 tbsp. onion powder
- 1 tbsp. garlic powder

Directions:

1. Preheat the wood pellet grill to 2500F.

2. Mix the seasoning ingredients and generously season the tri-tip.
3. Place it in the grill and cook for 30 minutes. Flip the tri-tip and cook for an additional 30 minutes.
4. Turn up the grill and cook for additional 30 minutes. Pull out the meat at 1250F for medium-rare and 1350F for medium.
5. Let the meat rest for 10 minutes before slicing and serving.

Nutrition:

Calories 484

Total fat 25g

Saturated fat 0g

Total carbs 1g

Net carbs 1g

Protein 59g

Sugars 0g

Fiber 0g

Sodium 650mmg

23. Smoked Ribeye Steaks

Preparation Time: 15 Minutes

Cooking Time: 35 Minutes

Servings: 1

Ingredients:

- ½ pound Ribeye steaks, preferably 2" thick; at room temperature for half an hour
- Steak rub, any of your favorite

Directions:

- Preheat wood-pellet grill over low smoke. Sprinkle the ribeye steaks with the preferred steak rub
- Place the coated Ribeye on wood-pellet grill & permit smoke for 20 to 25 minutes
- Once done; do away with the beef from grill; adjusting the temperature of pellet grill to 400 F
- Place the ribeye over the pellet grill again & sear every side for multiple five minutes.
- Continue to cook dinner the beef till you get your desired doneness (Steak at a hundred 65 F is considered to be nicely done, 145 F is considered to be medium, and 125 F is taken into consideration to be rare). It's important for you to drag off the steak from the grill approximately five degrees before the favored temp. Wrap in aluminum foil & let sit for a couple of minutes then slice into portions. Serve warm and enjoy

Nutrition:

517 Calories

341 Calories from Fat

38g Total Fat

17g Saturated Fat

1.8g Polyunsaturated Fat

18g Monounsaturated Fat

154mg Cholesterol

118mg Sodium

558mg Potassium

0.3g Total Carbohydrates

0g Dietary Fiber

0g Sugars

44g Protein

24. Balsamic Soy Flank Steak Recipe

Preparation Time: 20 Minutes

Cooking Time: 30 Minutes

Servings: 4

Ingredients

- 1 ½ pounds flank steak
- 3 cloves garlic, chopped
- ½ onion, chopped
- 1 tablespoon Dijon mustard
- ½ teaspoon black pepper
- 1 tablespoon dried rosemary
- ¼ cup each of olive oil, balsamic vinegar & soy sauce 1 teaspoon salt

Directions

- For Soy Balsamic Marinade: Whisk the garlic with onion, balsamic vinegar, olive oil, soy sauce, rosemary, Dijon, pepper and salt in a big-sized blending bowl.
- Place the steak in a massive sized zip-lock bag; upload the prepared marinade. Seal the bag & shake the ingredients properly (make certain that the beef pieces are nicely covered with the prepared marinade). Place the bag in a refrigerator for overnight.
- The subsequent day; preheat your wood-pellet grill to 350 F in advance.
- Once done; remove the steak from bag; shake off any extra marinade (booking the excess marinade inside the bag for later use).
- Place the covered steak on the grill & cook dinner until you get your desired doneness, for several minutes on each side. As you're cooking the meat; don 't forgets to comb the pieces with the kept aside marinade. Once done; do away with the steak from grill & allow relaxation for 5 minutes on a reducing board. Thinly cut the grilled steak across the grain. Serve hot and enjoy.

Nutrition:

423 Calories

235 Calories from Fat

26g Total Fat

7g Saturated Fat

0g Trans Fat

2g Polyunsaturated Fat

15g Monounsaturated Fat

111mg Cholesterol

1603mg Sodium

701mg Potassium

7.1g Total Carbohydrates

1.1g Dietary Fiber

3.4g Sugars 38g Protein

25. Beef Tenderloin with Balsamic Glaze

Preparation Time: 20 Minutes

Cooking Time: 1 Hour & 20 Minutes

Servings: 4

Ingredients

- 1 ½ pounds beef tenderloin; trimmed, silver skin removed Beef rub, as required; any of your favorite

For Balsamic Reduction

- 3 cups balsamic vinegar
- 3 tablespoons rosemary, fresh, finely chopped
- 1/3 cup brown sugar
- 3-4 tablespoons softened butter, at room temperature
- 3 garlic cloves; peeled & crushed Pepper & salt, to taste

Directions

1. For flippantly cooking; fold the tail (chain portion) over & secure it with toothpicks or butcher 's twine then, season with your favorite beef rub.
2. Set your wood pellet smoker grill to 250 F in advance. Once done; prepare dinner the tenderloin until the beef reflects an inner temperature of one hundred ten to one hundred fifteen F, for an hour, preferably on the lowest rack.
3. Remove the meat & permit relaxation. In the meantime; set your grill temperature to 500 F.
4. Once done; area the partly cooked tenderloin on the searing rack and prepare dinner until the meat reflects an inner temperature of one hundred thirty F, for a minute on each side.
5. Remove the tenderloin & vicinity it on a clean, large-sized reducing board & relaxation for a couple of minutes earlier than slicing. Slice into favored strips.
6. Serve immediately; drizzled with the organized balsamic reduction on top & enjoy.

For Balsamic Reduction

1. Over moderate heat in a large saucepan; combine the entire ingredients together until mixed well, for a couple of minutes.

Nutrition:

802 Calories

439 Calories from Fat

49g Total Fat

23g Saturated Fat

0.5g Trans Fat

1.9g Polyunsaturated Fat

19g Monounsaturated Fat

150mg Cholesterol

224mg Sodium

778mg Potassium

49g Total Carbohydrates

0.3g Dietary Fiber

44g Sugars

32g Protein

26. BBQ Sweet Pepper Meatloaf

Preparation time: 20 minutes

Cooking time: 3 hours and 15 minutes

Servings: 8

Ingredients:

- 1 cup chopped red sweet peppers
- 5 pounds ground beef
- 1 cup chopped green onion
- 1 tablespoon salt
- 1 tablespoon ground black pepper
- 1 cup panko bread crumbs
- 2 tablespoon BBQ rub and more as needed
- 1 cup ketchup
- 2 eggs

Directions:

1. Switch on the grill, fill the grill hopper with Texas beef blend flavored wood pellets, power the grill on by using the control panel, select 'smoke' on the temperature dial, or set to 225 degrees F and let it preheat for a minimum of 5 minutes.

2. Meanwhile, take a large bowl, place all the ingredients in it except for ketchup and then stir until well combined.
3. Shape the mixture into meatloaf and then sprinkle with some BBQ rub.
4. When the grill has preheated, open the lid, place meatloaf on the grill grate, shut the grill, and smoke for 2 hours and 15 minutes.
5. Then change the smoking temperature to 375 degrees F, insert a food thermometer into the meatloaf and cook for 45 minutes or more until the internal temperature of meatloaf reaches 155 degrees F.
6. Brush the top of meatloaf with ketchup and then continue cooking for 15 minutes until glazed.
7. When done, transfer food to a dish, let it rest for 10 minutes, then cut it into slices and serve.

Nutrition:

Calories: 160.5 Cal

Fat: 2.8 g

Carbs: 13.2 g

Protein: 17.2 g

Fiber: 1 g

27. Blackened Steak

Preparation time: 10 minutes

Cooking time: 60 minutes

Servings: 4

Ingredients:

- 2 steaks, each about 40 ounces
- 4 tablespoons blackened rub
- 4 tablespoons butter, unsalted

Directions:

1. Switch on the grill, fill the grill hopper with hickory flavored wood pellets, power the grill on by using the control panel, select 'smoke' on the temperature dial, or set to 225 degrees F and let it preheat for a minimum of 15 minutes.
2. Meanwhile, prepare the steaks and for this, sprinkle rub on all sides of each steak and let marinate for 10 minutes.
3. When the grill has preheated, open the lid, place steaks on the grill grate, shut the grill and smoke for 40 minutes until internal temperature reaches 119 degrees F.
4. When done, remove steaks from the grill and wrap each in a piece of foil.
5. Change the smoking temperature to 400 degrees F, place a griddle pan on the grill grate, and when hot, add 2 tablespoons butter and when it begins to melts, add steak and sear it for 4 minutes per side until internal temperature reaches 125 degrees F.
6. Transfer steaks to a dish and then repeat with the remaining steak.
7. Let seared steaks rest for 10 minutes, then slice each steak across the grain and serve.

Nutrition:

Calories: 184.4 Cal

Fat: 8.8 g

Carbs: 0 g

Protein: 23.5 g

Fiber: 0 g

28. BBQ Brisket

Preparation time: 12 hours

Cooking time: 10 hours

Servings: 8

Ingredients:

- 1 beef brisket, about 12 pounds
- Beef rub as needed

Directions:

1. Season beef brisket with beef rub until well coated, place it in a large plastic bag, seal it and let it marinate for a minimum of 12 hours in the refrigerator.
2. When ready to cook, switch on the grill, fill the grill hopper with hickory flavored wood pellets, power the grill on by using the control panel, select 'smoke' on the temperature dial, or set the temperature to 225 degrees F and let it preheat for a minimum of 15 minutes.
3. When the grill has preheated, open the lid, place marinated brisket on the grill grate fat-side down, shut the grill, and smoke for 6 hours until the internal temperature reaches 160 degrees F.
4. Then wrap the brisket in foil, return it back to the grill grate and cook for 4 hours until the internal temperature reaches 204 degrees F.
5. When done, transfer brisket to a cutting board, let it rest for 30 minutes, then cut it into slices and serve.

Nutrition:

Calories: 328 Cal

Fat: 21 g

Carbs: 0 g

Protein: 32 g

Fiber: - g

29. Thai Beef Skewers

Preparation time: 15 minutes

Cooking time: 8 minutes

Servings: 6

Ingredients:

- ½ of medium red bell pepper, destemmed, cored, cut into a ¼-inch piece
- ½ of beef sirloin, fat trimmed
- ½ cup salted peanuts, roasted, chopped
- For the Marinade:
- 1 teaspoon minced garlic
- 1 tablespoon grated ginger
- 1 lime, juiced
- 1 teaspoon ground black pepper
- 1 tablespoon sugar
- 1/4 cup soy sauce
- 1/4 cup olive oil

Directions:

1. Place all of its ingredients in a small bowl, whisk thoroughly, then pour it into a large plastic bag.
2. Cut into beef sirloin 1-1/4-inch dice, add to the plastic bag containing marinade, seal the bag, turn it upside down to coat beef pieces with the marinade and let it marinate for a minimum of 2 hours in the refrigerator.
3. When ready to cook, switch on the grill, fill the grill hopper with cherry flavored wood pellets, power the grill on by using the control panel, select 'smoke' on the temperature dial, or set the temperature to 425 degrees F and let it preheat for a minimum of 5 minutes.
4. Meanwhile, remove beef pieces from the marinade and then thread onto skewers.
5. When the grill has preheated, open the lid, place prepared skewers on the grill grate, shut the grill, and smoke for 4 minutes per side until done.
6. When done, transfer skewers to a dish, sprinkle with peanuts and red pepper, and then serve.

Nutrition:

Calories: 124 Cal

Fat: 5.5 g

Carbs: 1.7 g

Protein: 15.6 g

Fiber: 0 g

30. Cowboy Cut Steak

Preparation time: 10 minutes

Cooking time: 1 hour and 15 minutes

Servings: 4

Ingredients:

- 2 cowboy cut steak, each about 2 ½ pounds
- Salt as needed
- Beef rub as needed
- For the Gremolata:
- 2 tablespoons chopped mint
- 1 bunch of parsley, leaves separated
- 1 lemon, juiced
- 1 tablespoon lemon zest
- ½ teaspoon minced garlic
- ¼ teaspoon salt
- 1/8 teaspoon ground black pepper
- 1/4 cup olive oil

Directions:

1. Switch on the grill, fill the grill hopper with mesquite flavored wood pellets, power the grill on by using the control panel, select 'smoke' on the temperature dial, or set to 225 degrees F and let it preheat for a minimum of 5 minutes.
2. Meanwhile, prepare the steaks, and for this, season them with salt and BBQ rub until well coated.
3. When the grill has preheated, open the lid, place steaks on the grill grate, close and smoke it from 45 minutes to 1 hour until thoroughly cooked, and internal temperature reaches 115 degrees F.
4. Meanwhile, prepare gremolata and for this, take a medium bowl, place all of its ingredients in it and then stir well until combined, set aside until combined.
5. When done, transfer steaks to a dish, let rest for 15 minutes, and meanwhile, change the smoking temperature of the grill to 450 degrees F and let it preheat for a minimum of 10 minutes.
6. Then return steaks to the grill grate and cook for 7 minutes per side until the internal temperature reaches 130 degrees F.

Nutrition:

Calories: 361 Cal

Fat: 31 g

Carbs: 1 g

Protein: 19 g

Fiber: 0.2 g

31. Grilled Butter Basted Steak

Preparation time: 10 minutes

Cooking time: 40 minutes

Servings: 2

Ingredients:

- 2 steaks, each about 16 ounces, 1 ½-inch thick
- Rib rub as needed
- 2 teaspoon Dijon mustard
- 2 tablespoons Worcestershire sauce
- 4 tablespoons butter, unsalted, melted

Directions:

1. Switch on the Wood Pellet Grill, fill the grill hopper with hickory wood pellets, power the grill on by using the control panel, select 'smoke' on the temperature dial, or set the temperature to

225F and let it preheat for a minimum of 15 minutes.

2. Meanwhile, take a small bowl, place mustard, Worcestershire sauce, and butter in it and stir until well combined.
3. Brush the mixture on both sides of steaks and then season with rib rub.
4. When the grill has preheated, open the lid, place food on the grill grate, shut the grill, and smoke for 30 minutes.
5. When done, transfer steaks to a dish, let rest for 15 minutes, and meanwhile, change the smoking temperature of the grill to 450 degrees F and let it preheat for a minimum of 10 minutes.
6. Then return steaks to the grill grate and cook for 3 minutes per side until the internal temperature reaches 140 degrees F.
7. Transfer steaks to a dish, let rest for 5 minutes and then serve.

Nutrition:

Calories: 409.8 Cal

Fat: 30.8 g

Carbs: 3.1 g

Protein: 29.7 g

Fiber: 0.4 g

32. Texas Smoked Brisket (Unwrapped)

Preparation Time: 15 minutes

Cooking Time: 16 to 20 hours

Servings: 12-15

Smoke Temperature: 225°F

Preferred Wood Pellet: Mesquite

Ingredients:

- 1 (12-pound) full packer brisket
- 2 tablespoons yellow mustard
- 1 batch Espresso Brisket Rub
- Worcestershire Mop and Spritz, for spritzing

Directions:

1. Supply your smoker with Preferred Wood Pellet pellets and follow the manufacturer's specific start-up procedure. Preheat the grill, with the lid closed, to 225°F.
2. Using a boning knife, carefully remove all but about ½ inch of the deep layer of fat covering one side of your brisket.
3. Coat the brisket all over with mustard and season it with the rub. Using your hands, work the rub into the meat. Pour the mop into a spray bottle.
4. Place the brisket directly on the grill grate and smoke until its internal Smoke Temperature reaches 195°F, spritzing it every hour with the mop.
5. Pull the brisket from the grill and wrap it entirely in aluminum foil or butcher paper. Place the wrapped brisket in a more relaxed, cover the more relaxed, and let it rest for 1 or 2 hours.
6. Remove the brisket from the more relaxed and unwrap it.
7. Separate the brisket point from the flat by cutting along the fat layer and slice the flat. The point can be saved for burnt ends (see Sweet Heat Burnt Ends), or sliced and served as well.

Nutrition:

Energy 523 kcal

Calcium, Ca53 mg

Magnesium, Mg96 mg

Phosphorus, P879 mg

Iron, Fe8.17 mg

Potassium, K1433 mg

Sodium, Na351 mg

Zinc, Zn20.6 mg

33. Mesquite-Smoked Brisket (Wrapped)

Preparation Time: 15 minutes

Cooking Time: 12 to 16 hours

Servings: 8 to 12

Smoke Temperature: 225°F and 350°F

Preferred Wood Pellet: Mesquite

Ingredients:

- 1 (12-pound) full packer brisket
- 2 tablespoons yellow mustard
- Salt
- Freshly ground black pepper

Directions:

1. Supply your smoker with Preferred Wood Pellet pellets and follow the manufacturer's specific start-up procedure. Preheat the grill, with the lid closed, to 225°F.
2. Using a boning knife, carefully remove all but about ½ inch of the deep layer of fat covering one side of your brisket.
3. Coat the brisket all over with mustard and season with salt and pepper.
4. Place the brisket directly on the grill grate and smoke until its internal Smoke Temperature reaches 160°F and the brisket has formed a dark bark.
5. Pull the brisket from the grill and wrap it entirely in aluminum foil or butcher paper.

6. Increase the grill's Smoke Temperature to 350°F and returns the wrapped brisket to it. Continue to cook until its internal Smoke Temperature reaches 190°F.
7. Transfer the wrapped brisket to a calmer, cover the cooler, and let the brisket rest for 1 or 2 hours.
8. Remove the brisket from the more relaxed and unwrap it.
9. Separate the brisket point from the flat by cutting along the fat layer and slice the flat. The point can be saved for burnt ends (see Sweet Heat Burnt Ends), or sliced and served as well

Nutrition:

Energy607 kcal

Calcium, Ca61 mg

Magnesium, Mg111 mg

Phosphorus, P1015 mg

Iron, Fe9.42 mg

Potassium, K1655 mg

Sodium, Na439 mg

Zinc, Zn23.73 mg

34. Sweet Heat Burnt Ends

Preparation Time: 30 minutes

Cooking Time: 6 hours

Servings: 8-10

Smoke Temperature: 225°F and 350°F

Preferred Wood Pellet: Mesquite

Ingredients:

- 1 (6-pound) brisket point
- 2 tablespoons yellow mustard
- 1 batch Sweet Brown Sugar Rub
- 2 tablespoons honey
- 1 cup barbecue sauce
- 2 tablespoons light brown sugar

Directions:

1. Supply your smoker with Preferred Wood Pellet pellets and follow the manufacturer's specific start-up procedure. Preheat the grill, with the lid closed, to 225°F.
2. Using a boning knife, carefully remove all but about ½ inch of the deep layer of fat covering one side of your brisket point.
3. Coat the point all over with mustard and season it with the rub. Using your hands, work the rub into the meat.
4. Place the point directly on the grill grate and smoke until its internal Smoke Temperature reaches 165°F.
5. Pull the brisket from the grill and wrap it entirely in aluminum foil or butcher paper.
6. Increase the grill's Smoke Temperature to 350°F and returns the wrapped brisket to it. Continue to cook until its internal Smoke Temperature reaches 185°F.
7. Remove the point from the grill, unwrap it, and cut the meat into 1-inch cubes. Place the cubes in an aluminum pan and stir in the honey, barbecue sauce, and brown sugar.
8. Place the pan in the grill and smoke the beef cubes for 1 hour more, uncovered. Remove the burnt ends from the grill and serve immediately.

Nutrition:

Energy960 kcal

Calcium, Ca66 mg

Magnesium, Mg58 mg

Phosphorus, P463 mg

Iron, Fe5.18 mg

Potassium, K853 mg

Sodium, Na537 mg

Zinc, Zn11.63 mg

35. Reverse-Seared Tri-Tip

Preparation Time: 10 minutes

Cooking Time: 2 or 3 hours

Servings: 4

Smoke Temperature: 180°F and 450°F

Preferred Wood Pellet: Oak

Ingredients:

- 1½ pounds tri-tip roast
- 1 batch Espresso Brisket Rub

Directions:

1. Supply your smoker with Preferred Wood Pellet pellets and follow the manufacturer's specific start-up procedure. Preheat the grill, with the lid closed, to 180°F.
2. Season the tri-tip roast with the rub. Using your hands, work the rub into the meat.
3. Place the roast directly on the grill grate and smoke until its internal Smoke Temperature reaches 140°F.
4. Increase the grill's Smoke Temperature to 450°F and continues to cook until the roast's internal Smoke Temperature reaches 145°F. This same technique can be done over an open flame or in a cast-iron skillet with some butter.
5. Remove the tri-tip roast from the grill and let it rest 10 to 15 minutes, before slicing and serving.

Nutrition:

Calcium, Ca47 mg

Magnesium, Mg39 mg

Phosphorus, P344 mg

Iron, Fe2.77 mg

Potassium, K575 mg

Sodium, Na98 mg

Zinc, Zn7.04 mg

36. George's Smoked Tri-Tip

Preparation Time: 25 minutes

Cooking Time: 5 hours

Servings: 4

Smoke Temperature: 180°F and 375°F

Preferred Wood Pellet: Hickory

Ingredients:

- 1½ pounds tri-tip roast
- Salt
- Freshly ground black pepper
- 2 teaspoons garlic powder
- 2 teaspoons lemon pepper
- ½ cup apple juice

Directions:

1. Supply your smoker with Preferred Wood Pellet pellets and follow the manufacturer's specific start-up procedure. Preheat the grill, with the lid closed, to 180°F.
2. Season the tri-tip roast with salt, pepper, garlic powder, and lemon pepper. Using your hands, work the seasoning into the meat.
3. Place the roast directly on the grill grate and smoke for 4 hours.
4. Pull the tri-tip from the grill and place it on enough aluminum foil to wrap it completely.
5. Increase the grill's Smoke Temperature to 375°F.
6. Fold in three sides of the foil around the roast and add the apple juice. Fold in the far side, completely enclosing the tri-tip and liquid. Return the wrapped tri-tip to the grill and cook for 45 minutes more.
7. Remove the tri-tip roast from the grill and let it rest for 10 to 15 minutes, before unwrapping, slicing, and serving.

Nutrition:

Calcium, Ca55 mg

Magnesium, Mg47 mg

Phosphorus, P363 mg

Iron, Fe3.11 mg

Potassium, K701 mg

Sodium, Na198 mg

Zinc, Zn7.02 mg

37. Beefy Bolognese

Preparation Time: 25 minutes

Cooking Time: 1 hour 30 minutes

Servings: 4

Smoke Temperature: 180°F and 375°F

Preferred Wood Pellet: Hickory

Ingredients:

- Ground beef (2-lbs, 0.9-kgs)
- Olive oil – 1 tablespoon
- 3 garlic cloves, minced
- 1 yellow onion, peeled and diced
- 3 large tomatoes, chopped
- Tomato sauce – 2 cups
- Dried oregano – 2 teaspoons
- Dried basil – 1 teaspoon
- Paprika – 2 teaspoons
- Salt and black pepper
- Spaghetti (8-ozs, 227-gms)
- Salted butter – 1 tablespoon
- Parmesan cheese, grated

Directions:

1. First, heat the oil in a deep pan. Add the beef, garlic, and onion to the pan. Sauté until the beef browns, and the onion softens.
2. Add the tomatoes followed by the tomato sauce, oregano, basil, paprika, salt, and black pepper. Stir to combine.
3. Bring to a simmer for 5 minutes and stir occasionally.
4. Take the pan off the stove and transfer it to the smoker. Smoke for 1-1½ hours stir occasionally.
5. In the meantime, cook the spaghetti using packet Directions: then drain.
6. Once the meat sauce is ready, take it out of the smoker and stir in the butter until it melts.
7. Spoon the sauce over the cooked pasta.
8. Sprinkle with grated Parmesan and serve.

Nutrition:

Energy911 kcal

Calcium, Ca129 mg

Magnesium, Mg101 mg

Phosphorus, P581 mg

Iron, Fe8.7 mg

Potassium, K1575 mg

Sodium, Na2062 mg

Zinc, Zn15.25 mg

38. Brunch Burger

Preparation Time: 10 minutes

Cooking Time: 20 minutes

Servings: 2

Smoke Temperature: 180°F and 375°F

Preferred Wood Pellet: Hickory

Ingredients:

- Lean ground chuck beef (6-ozs, 170-gms)
- 4 rashers bacon, cooked until crispy
- Salt and black pepper
- Olive oil
- 2 burger buns
- 2 slices American cheese
- 2 medium eggs, fried
- 2 hash browns, cooked and kept warm

Directions:

1. Divide the beef into two portions and form into thin, even patties. Season with salt and black pepper.
2. Brush the grate with oil before placing the patties on top. Grill for 3-4 minutes each side until cooked to your preference.
3. Take the burgers off the grill and place each in a bun. Top each patty with a slice of cheese, bacon, followed by a fried egg and hash brown.
4. Serve straight away.

Nutrition:

Calcium, Ca360 mg

Magnesium, Mg61 mg

Phosphorus, P697 mg

Iron, Fe4.72 mg

Potassium, K640 mg

Sodium, Na1439 mg

Zinc, Zn6.81 mg

39. Classic Pastrami

Preparation Time: 6 Hours

Cooking Time: 29 hours 20 minutes

Servings: 4-6

Smoke Temperature: 180°F and 375°F

Preferred Wood Pellet: Hickory

Ingredients:

- Beef brisket, cut from the point (6-lbs, 2.7 -kgs)
- Kosher salt – 6½ tablespoons
- Brown sugar – 6 tablespoons
- Coriander seeds – ¼ teaspoon
- Curing salt – 1 tablespoon
- Honey – 1 tablespoon
- 3 bay leaves, chopped
- Garlic, peeled and chopped – 1 teaspoon
- Cayenne pepper – ¼ teaspoon
- Warm water – 6 cups
- Whole black peppercorns – ¼ cup
- Brown sugar – 1 tablespoon
- Coriander seeds – ¼ cup
- Garlic powder – 2 teaspoons
- Paprika – 1 tablespoon
- Onion powder – 2 teaspoons

Directions:

1. First, Prepare the brine. Combine the kosher salt, brown sugar, coriander seeds, curing salt, honey, bay leaves, garlic, and cayenne pepper and transfer to a large container. Stir in the warm water to dissolve the sugar and salt. Chill for an hour.
2. Add the meat to the cooled brine and weigh down with a plate.
3. Set the meat aside for one week to brine. Turn the meat in the brine daily.
4. Transfer the brisket to a wire rack and chill for 24 hours, this will dry out the meat.
5. Soak the brisket in a sink full of water for 12 hours; change the water every 3 hours.
6. For the seasoning, in a bowl, combine the black peppercorns, brown sugar, coriander seeds, garlic powder, paprika, and onion powder. Rub the mixture evenly over the outside of the meat.
7. Place the meat on the grill grate and cook for 4 hours.
8. Take the meat off the grill and allow to rest for 60-90 minutes before slicing and serving.

Nutrition:

Calcium, Ca109 mg

Magnesium, Mg85 mg

Phosphorus, P565 mg

Iron, Fe8.81 mg

Potassium, K1463 mg

Sodium, Na13096 mg

Zinc, Zn13.29 mg

40. Fully Loaded Beef Nachos

Preparation Time: 10 minutes

Cooking Time: 25 minutes

Servings: 6

Smoke Temperature: 180°F and 375°F

Preferred Wood Pellet: Hickory

Ingredients:

- Ground beef (1-lbs, 0.45-kgs)
- 1 large bag tortilla chips
- 1 green bell pepper, seeded and diced
- Scallions, sliced – ½ cup
- Red onion, peeled and diced – ½ cup
- Cheddar cheese, shredded – 3 cups
- Sour cream, guacamole, salsa – to serve

Directions:

1. In a cast-iron pan, arrange a double layer of tortilla chips.
2. Scatter over the ground beef, bell pepper, scallions, red onion, and finally the cheddar cheese.
3. Place the cast-iron pan on the grill and cook for approximately 10 minutes until the cheese has melted completely.
4. Take off the grill and serve with sour cream, guacamole, and salsa on the side.

Nutrition:

Energy242 kcal

Calcium, Ca93 mg

Magnesium, Mg23 mg

Phosphorus, P258 mg

Iron, Fe2.37 mg

Potassium, K318 mg

Sodium, Na174 mg

Zinc, Zn5.15 mg

41. Whole Smoked Bologna Roll

Preparation Time: 10 minutes

Cooking Time: 4 hours 20 minutes

Servings: 12

Smoke Temperature: 180°F and 375°F

Preferred Wood Pellet: Hickory

Ingredients:

- Whole beef bologna rolls (3-lbs, 1.4-kgs)
- Black pepper, freshly cracked – 2 tablespoons
- Brown sugar – ¾ cup
- Yellow mustard – ¼ cup

Directions:

1. Combine the black pepper and brown sugar.
2. Score the outside of the bologna with a diamond pattern.
3. Spread mustard over the outside of the bologna and then rub in the black pepper/sugar until thoroughly and evenly coated.
4. Arrange the bologna on the smoker's upper rack and cook for 3-4 hours until the outside caramelizes.
5. Slice the bologna into medium-thick slices and serve.

Nutrition:

Calories: 210kcal

Magnesium, Mg34 mg

Phosphorus, P202 mg

Iron, Fe3.76 mg

Potassium, K434 mg

Sodium, Na1670 mg

Zinc, Zn4.64 mg

42. Hickory Pellets Smoked Beef Roast

Preparation Time: 5 minutes

Cooking Time: 4 – 6 hours

Servings: 6

Ingredients:

4 lbs. of beef roast boneless

1 can (11 oz.) beef stock

1/2 oz. of allspice

Directions:

Combine the beef stock and dry salad dressing mix in a bowl.

Pour this mixture evenly over beef.

Load the wood tray with one small handful of hickory pellet and preheat the smoker to 250° F. Add the tray to the smoker.

Smoke beef for approximately 4 to 6 hours.

Your beef is ready when internal temperature reaches 150 - 160°F.

Remove and let rest for 15 minutes.

Slice and serve warm.

Nutrition:

Calories: 439

Carbs: 1.7g

Fat: 22g

Fiber: 0.5g

Protein: 56g

43. Pellet Smoked "Green" Beef burgers

Preparation Time: 15 minutes

Cooking Time: 1 hour and 30 minutes

Servings: 6

Ingredients:

1 lbs. ground beef

1 lbs. frozen spinach, thawed and drained

1 onion finely diced

1 large egg at room temperature

3 tbsps. of flour all-purposes

1 tsp of fresh basil, chopped

1 tbsps. of fresh parsley chopped

salt and ground pepper

Directions

In a large container, mix all ingredients from the list above.

Knead the mixture until all ingredients combined well.

Form the mixture into equal balls.

Flip the "ON" switch, to preheat, your smoker. Pellets (recommended Hickory or Pecan) from the hopper are automatically delivered to the fire-pot by an auger.

Set to 225°F or to Smoke. It takes 10 minutes.

Place the racks into the smoker, and place burgers onto racks.

Smoke your burgers for 60 to 90 minutes (check burgers on 45 minutes).

Check internal heat must be about 145°F for medium-rare or, if using commercial ground beef, cook to least medium, at 160°F.

Allow burgers to rest for 10 minutes and serve.

Nutrition:

Calories: 238.78

Carbs:

Fat: 17.1g

Fiber: 3g

Protein: 17.5g

44. Pellet Smoked Burgers Simple

Preparation Time: 15 minutes

Cooking Time: 1 hour and 30 minutes

Servings: 6

Ingredients:

1/2 lbs. ground pork

1 1/4 lbs. ground beef

1 onion finely chopped

1 tbsps. fresh parsley finely chopped

1 tbsps. of basil finely, chopped

Pinch of Salt

Ground black pepper

2 tbsps. of olive oil

buns, mayonnaise, mustard or ketchup for serving

Directions

In a bowl, combine all ingredients.

Using your hands, knead the mixture well.

Form the mixture into 6 round patties.

Start the grill on SMOKE, lid open until the fire is good. Set the heat to 225F, lid closed, for 10 to 15 minutes.

Smoke for about 60 to 90 minutes (check burgers on 45 minutes)

Your burgers are ready when the internal temperature is 145F for medium-rare.

Allow burgers to rest for 10 minutes and serve.

Nutrition:

Calories: 397

Carbs: 1.95g

Fat: 32g

Fiber: 0.4g

Protein: 23.3

45. Sheer Spicy Hamburgers on Pellet Grill

Preparation Time: 15 minutes

Cooking Time: 1 hour and 30 minutes

Servings: 6

Ingredients:

3 lbs. of ground beef

1 large egg from free-range chicken

2 tsp of chili flakes

2 tsp of chili powder

2 tbsps. of panko bread crumbs

Sea salt to taste

1 Lemon juice for serving

Directions

In a large bowl, combine and mix we all ingredients.

Form the meat mixture into 6 patties.

Start grill on smoke with the lid open until the fire is established). Set the heat to 380F and preheat, lid closed, for 10 to 15 minutes.

Arrange your patties on a grill and smoke the burgers for 60 to 90 minutes (check burgers on 45 minutes)

Your burgers are ready when the internal temperature is 145F for medium-rare.

In the case that you use commercial ground beef, the internal temperature has to be at least medium, 160F.

Sprinkle with lemon juice and serve immediately.

Nutrition:

Calories: 587

Carbs: 3g

Fat: 48g

Fiber: 0.5g

Protein: 41.6g

46. Smoked Beef Brisket in White Wine Marinade

Preparation Time: 15 minutes

Cooking Time: 5 hours

Servings: 8

Ingredients:

4 lbs. of beef brisket

2/3 cup of soy sauce or tamari sauce

2/3 cup water

1/4 cup of dry white wine

2 tsp fresh lemon juice

1/4 cup of brown sugar

1/2 tsp garlic powder

1/2 tsp of ground ginger

Directions:

In a container, combine together all ingredients for the marinade. Place in the beef and marinate overnight.

Remove from marinade and dry on a kitchen towel.

Start grill on SMOKE with the lid open until the fire is established. Set the heat to 250F then preheat, lid closed, for 10 to 15 minutes.

Smoke from 4 to 5 hours. After the roast has been in the smoker for around 3 hours check the internal temperature. You are looking for a temperature of 150 - 160°F.

Remove from Smoker and let cool for 10 - 15 minutes.

Slice and serve.

Nutrition:

Calories: 486

Carbs: 8.2g

Fat: 33.8g

Fiber: 0.1g

Protein: 33.7g

47. Smoked Beef Fillet with Herb Rubs

Preparation Time: 15 minutes

Cooking Time: 1 hour 30 minutes

Servings: 6

Ingredients:

3 lbs. of beef eye fillet

salt and pepper to taste

1/4 cup of olive oil

2 Tbsps. of basil, fresh and chopped

1/4 cup of parsley, fresh and chopped

2 tbsps. rosemary leaves, fresh and chopped

3 clove garlic finely chopped

Directions

Flavor with salt and pepper and put in a shallow dish.

In a bowl, combine all remaining ingredients well. Rub the meat with the herb mixture from both sides

Start grill on Smoke mode with the lid open until the fire is established. Set the heat to 250F then preheat, close the lid, for 10 to 15 minutes.

Place grill and smoke for 80 to 90 minutes or until they reach an internal temperature of 110F.

When ready, let meat rest for 10 minutes, slice and serve.

Nutrition:

Calories: 570

Carbs: 1.5g

Fat: 41.2g

Fiber: 0.8g

Protein:45.5g

48. Beef Rump Roast

Preparation time: 10 minutes

Cooking time: 6 hours

Servings: 8

Ingredients:

1 teaspoon smoked paprika

1 teaspoon cayenne pepper

1 teaspoon onion powder

1 teaspoon garlic powder

Salt and ground black pepper, as required

3 pounds' beef rump roast

1/4 cup Worcestershire sauce

Directions:

Preheat the Z Grills Wood Pellet Grill & Smoker on smoke setting to 200ºF, using charcoal.

In a bowl, mix together all spices.

Coat the rump roast with Worcestershire sauce evenly and then, rub with spice mixture generously.

Place the rump roast onto the grill and cook for about 5-6 hours.

Remove the beef from the grill and place onto a cutting board for about 10-15 minutes before serving.

With a sharp knife, cut the roast into desired-sized slices and serve.

Nutrition:

Calories: 252

Fat: 9 g

Cholesterol: 113mg

Carbs: 2g

Protein: 37g

49. Spicy Chuck Roast

Preparation time: 10 minutes

Cooking time: 4 hours and 30 minutes

Servings: 8

Ingredients:

2 tablespoons onion powder

2 tablespoons garlic powder

1 tablespoon red chili powder

1 tablespoon cayenne pepper

Salt and ground black pepper, as required

1 (3 pound) beef chuck roast

16 fluid ounces' warm beef broth

Directions:

Preheat the grill setting to 250ºF.

In a bowl, mix together spices, salt and black pepper.

Rub the chuck roast with spice mixture evenly.

Place the rump roast onto the grill and cook for about 1½ hours per side.

Arrange chuck roast in a steaming pan with beef broth.

Cover the pan with a piece of foil and cook for about 2-3 hours.

Remove the chuck roast from grill and place onto a cutting board for about 20 minutes before slicing.

With a sharp knife, cut the chuck roast into desired-sized slices and serve.

Nutrition:

Calories: 645

Fat: 48 g

Cholesterol: 175 mg

Carbs: 4g

Protein: 46g

50. BBQ Spiced Flank Steak

Preparation time: 15 minutes

Cooking time: 30 minutes

Servings: 6

Ingredients:

1 (2-pound) beef flank steak

2 tablespoons olive oil

1/4 cup BBQ rub

3 tablespoons blue cheese, crumbled

2 tablespoons butter, softened

1 teaspoon fresh chive, minced

Directions:

Preheat the grill setting to 225ºF.

Coat the steak with oil evenly and season with BBQ rub.

Put the steak onto the grill and cook for about 10-15 minutes per side.

Remove the steak from grill and place onto a cutting board for about 10 minutes before slicing.

In a bowl, add blue cheese, butter and chives and mix well.

Cut meat into thin strips across the grain.

Top with cheese mixture and serve.

Nutrition:

Calories: 370

Fat: 19g

Cholesterol: 148mg

Carbs: 1g

Protein: 46g

51. Beef Stuffed Bell Peppers

Preparation time: 20 minutes

Cooking time: 1 hour

Servings: 6

Ingredients:

6 large bell peppers

1-pound ground beef

1 small onion, chopped

2 garlic cloves, minced

2 cups cooked rice

1 cup frozen corn, thawed

1 cup cooked black beans

2/3 cup salsa

2 tablespoons Cajun rub

1 ½ cups Monterey Jack cheese, grated

Directions:

Cut the bell pepper in half lengthwise through the stem. Carefully, remove the seeds and ribs.

For stuffing:

Heat a frying pan then cook the beef for about 6-7 minutes or until browned completely.

Add onion and garlic then cook for about 2-3 minutes.

Stir in remaining ingredients except cheese and cook for about 5 minutes.

Take off from the heat and set aside to cool slightly.

Preheat the grill setting to 350°F.

Stuff each bell pepper half with stuffing mixture evenly.

Arrange the peppers onto grill, stuffing side up and cook for about 40 minutes.

Sprinkle each bell pepper half with cheese and cook for about 5 minutes more.

Remove the bell peppers from grill and serve hot.

Nutrition:

Calories: 675

Fat: 14g

Cholesterol: 93 mg

Carbs: 90g

Protein: 43g

52. Brandy Beef Tenderloin

Preparation time: 15 minutes

Cooking time: 2 hours 2 minutes

Servings: 6

Ingredients:

For Brandy Butter:

1/2 cup butter

1-ounce brandy

For Brandy Sauce:

2 ounces' brandy

8 garlic cloves, minced

1/4 cup mixed fresh herbs (parsley, rosemary and thyme), chopped

2 teaspoons honey

2 teaspoons hot English mustard

For Tenderloin:

1 (2-pound) center-cut beef tenderloin

Salt and cracked black peppercorns, as required

Directions:

Preheat the grill setting to 230° F.

For brandy butter:

Melt the butter over medium-low heat.

Stir in brandy and remove from heat. Set aside, covered to keep warm.

For brandy Sauce:

Combine all ingredients and mix until well.

Season the tenderloin with salt and black peppercorns generously.

Coat tenderloin with brandy sauce evenly.

With a baster-injector, inject tenderloin with brandy butter.

Put the tenderloin onto the grill and cook for about ½-2 hours, injecting with brandy butter occasionally.

Remove the tenderloin from grill and place onto a cutting board for about 10-15 minutes before serving.

Cut the tenderloin into desired-sized slices and serve.

Nutrition:

Calories: 496

Fat: 29g	Carbs: 4g
Cholesterol: 180 mg	Protein: 44g

CHAPTER 15. LAMB RECIPES

53. Lamb Shank

Preparation Time: 10 minutes

Cooking Time: 4 hours

Servings: 6

Ingredients:

- 8-ounce red wine
- 2-ounce whiskey
- 2 tablespoons minced fresh rosemary
- 1 tablespoon minced garlic
- Black pepper
- 6 (1¼-pound) lamb shanks

Directions:

1. In a bowl, add all ingredients except lamb shank and mix till well combined.
2. In a large resealable bag, add marinade and lamb shank.
3. Seal the bag then shake to coat completely.
4. Refrigerate for about 24 hours.
5. Preheat the pallet grill to 225 degrees F.
6. Arrange the leg of lamb in pallet grill and cook for about 4 hours.

Nutrition:

Calories: 1507 Cal

Fat: 62 g

Carbohydrates: 68.7 g

Protein:163.3 g

Fiber: 6 g

54. Leg of a Lamb

Preparation Time: 10 minutes

Cooking Time: 2 hours and 30 minutes

Servings: 10

Ingredients:

- 1 (8-ounce) package softened cream cheese
- ¼ cup cooked and crumbled bacon
- 1 seeded and chopped jalapeño pepper
- 1 tablespoon crushed dried rosemary
- 2 teaspoons garlic powder
- 1 teaspoon onion powder
- 1 teaspoon paprika
- 1 teaspoon cayenne pepper
- Salt, to taste
- 1 (4-5-pound) butterflied leg of lamb
- 2-3 tablespoons olive oil

Directions:

1. For filling in a bowl, add all ingredients and mix till well combined.
2. For spice mixture in another small bowl, mix together all ingredients.
3. Place the leg of lamb onto a smooth surface. Sprinkle the inside of leg with some spice mixture.
4. Place filling mixture over the inside surface evenly. Roll the leg of lamb tightly and with a butcher's twine, tie the roll to secure the filling
5. Coat the outer side of roll with olive oil evenly and then sprinkle with spice mixture.
6. Preheat the pallet grill to 225-240 degrees F.
7. Arrange the leg of lamb in pallet grill and cook for about 2-2½ hours. Remove the leg of lamb from pallet grill and transfer onto a cutting board.
8. With a piece of foil, cover leg loosely and transfer onto a cutting board for about 20-25 minutes before slicing.
9. With a sharp knife, cut the leg of lamb in desired sized slices and serve.

Nutrition:

Calories: 715 Cal

Fat: 38.9 g

Carbohydrates: 2.2 g

Protein: 84.6 g

Fiber: 0.1 g

55. Lamb Breast

Preparation Time: 10 minutes

Cooking Time: 2 hours and 40 minutes

Servings: 2

Ingredients:

- 1 (2-pound) trimmed bone-in lamb breast
- ½ cup white vinegar
- ¼ cup yellow mustard
- ½ cup BBQ rub

Directions:

1. Preheat the pallet grill to 225 degrees F.

2. Rinse the lamb breast with vinegar evenly.
3. Coat lamb breast with mustard and the, season with BBQ rub evenly.
4. Arrange lamb breast in pallet grill and cook for about 2-2½ hours.
5. Remove the lamb breast from the pallet grill and transfer onto a cutting board for about 10 minutes before slicing.
6. With a sharp knife, cut the lamb breast in desired sized slices and serve.

Nutrition:

Calories: 877 Cal

Fat: 34.5 g

Carbohydrates: 2.2 g

Protein: 128.7 g

Fiber: 0 g

56. Smoked Lamb Shoulder Chops

Preparation Time: 4 hours

Cooking Time: 25-30 minutes

Servings: 4

Ingredients:

- 4 lamb shoulder chops
- 4 cups buttermilk
- 1 cup cold water
- ¼ cup kosher salt
- 2 tablespoons olive oil
- 1 tablespoon Texas style rub

Directions:

1. In a large bowl, add buttermilk, water and salt and stir till salt is dissolved.
2. Add chops and coat with mixture evenly.
3. Refrigerate for at least 4 hours. Remove the chops from bowl and rinse under cold water.
4. Coat the chops with olive oil and then sprinkle with rub evenly. Preheat the pallet grill to 240 degrees F. Arrange the chops in pallet grill grate and cook for about 25-30 minute or till desired doneness. Meanwhile preheat the broiler of oven. Cook the chops under broiler till browned.

Nutrition:

Calories: 328 Cal

Fat: 18.2 g

Carbohydrates:11.7 g

Protein: 30.1 g

Fiber: 0 g

57. Lamb Skewers

Preparation Time: 5 minutes

Cooking Time: 8-12 minutes

Servings: 6

Ingredients:

- One lemon, juiced
- Two crushed garlic cloves
- Two chopped red onions
- One t. chopped thyme
- Pepper
- Salt
- One t. oregano
- 1/3 c. oil
- ½ t. cumin
- Two pounds cubed lamb leg

Directions:

1. Refrigerate the chunked lamb.
2. The remaining ingredients should be mixed together. Add in the meat. Refrigerate overnight.
3. Pat the meat dry and thread onto some metal or wooden skewers. Wooden skewers should be soaked in water.
4. Add wood pellets to your smoker and follow your cooker's startup procedure. Preheat your smoker, with your lid closed, until it reaches 450.
5. Grill, covered, for 4-6 minutes on each side.

Serve.

Nutrition:

Calories: 201 Cal

Fat: 9 g

Carbohydrates: 3 g

Protein: 24 g

Fiber: 1 g

58. Brown Sugar Lamb Chops

Preparation Time: 2 hours

Cooking Time: 10-15 minutes

Servings: 4

Ingredients:

- Pepper
- One t. garlic powder
- Salt
- Two t. tarragon
- One t. cinnamon

- ¼ c. brown sugar
- 4 lamb chops
- Two t. ginger

Directions:

1. Combine the salt, garlic powder, pepper, cinnamon, tarragon, ginger, and sugar. Coat the lamb chops in the mixture and chill for two hours.
2. Add wood pellets to your smoker and follow your cooker's startup procedure. Preheat your smoker, with your lid closed, until it reaches 450. Put chops on the grill, cover, and smoke for 10-15 minutes per side. Serve.

Nutrition:

Calories: 210 Cal

Fat: 11 g

Carbohydrates: 3 g

Protein: 25 g

Fiber: 1 g

59. Grilled Lamb and Apricot Kabobs

Preparation Time: 15 Minutes

Cooking Time: 8 – 10 minutes

Servings: 4

Ingredients:

- ½ cup olive oil
- ½ cup lemon juice
- 2 tablespoons minced fresh mint
- 1 tablespoon lemon zest
- ½ tablespoon finely chopped cilantro
- ½ tablespoon salt
- 2 teaspoons black pepper
- 1 teaspoon cumin
- 3 pounds (1.4 kg) boneless leg of lamb, cut into 2-inch cubes
- 15 whole dried apricots
- 2 whole red onions, cut into 1/2 - inch thick

Directions:

1. In a bowl, mix the lemon juice, mint, olive oil, lemon zest, cilantro, salt, pepper and cumin. Add the lamb shoulder to the bowl and toss to coat. Set in the refrigerator and marinate overnight.

2. Remove from the marinade and thread lamb, apricots, and red onion alternatively until the skewer is full.

3. When ready to cook, set temperature to 400ºF (204ºC) and preheat, lid closed for 15 minutes.

4. Lay the skewers on the grill grate and cook for 8 to 10 minutes, or until the onions are lightly browned and the lamb is cooked to the desired temperature.

5. Remove the skewers from the grill and serve immediately.

60. Spicy Braised Lamb Shoulder

Preparation Time: 10 Minutes

Cooking Time: 5 hours 2 minutes

Servings: 4

Ingredients:

- 2 ounces (57 g) guajillo peppers, deseeded
- 2 tablespoons plus ½ cup water, divided
- 3 cloves garlic
- 2 tablespoons olive oil
- 1 tablespoon lime juice
- 1 tablespoon smoked paprika
- 1 tablespoon fresh oregano
- 1 tablespoon salt
- ¼ tablespoon ground coriander seeds
- ¼ tablespoon ground cumin seeds
- ¼ tablespoon ground pumpkin seeds
- 3 pounds (1.4 kg) lamb shoulders

Directions:

1. In a microwave-safe bowl, cover the guajillo chilies with water and microwave on high for 2 minutes. Let cool slightly, then transfer the soft chilies and 2 tablespoons of the water to a blender.
2. Mix the remaining ingredients, except for the lamb shoulders, to the blender. Pulse until smooth.
3. Arrange the lamb in a roast pan and rub ½ cup of the sauce all over the meat. Marinate lamb at room temperature for at least 2 hours and up to 12 hours.
4. When ready to cook, set temperature to 325F (163C) and preheat, lid closed for 15 minutes.
5. Add ½ cup of the water to the roast pan and cover the pan loosely with foil. Cook the lamb for 2½ hours, adding water to the pan a few times.
6. Remove the foil and cook for another 2½ hours, or until the lamb is browned and tender, occasionally spooning the juices on top.
7. Take off from the grill and let cool for 20 minutes before shredding. Spoon the remaining liquid in the bottom of the pan over the lamb.
8. Serve immediately.

61. Grilled Lamb Leg

Preparation Time: 10 Minutes

Cooking Time: 30 – 40 Minutes

Servings: 8

Ingredients:

- 5 pounds (2.3 kg) leg of lamb, butterflied and boneless
- 1 whole onion, sliced into rings
- Marinade:
- 1 whole lemon, juiced and rinds reserved
- 4 cloves garlic, minced
- 1 cup olive oil
- ¼ cup red wine vinegar
- 2½ teaspoons minced rosemary
- 1 teaspoon thyme
- 1 teaspoon salt
- 1 teaspoon ground black pepper

Directions:

1. In a mixing bowl, whisk together all the ingredients for the marinade.
2. Remove netting from the lamb and place into a large resealable plastic bag. Pour the marinade inside the bag and add the onion. Massage the bag to evenly mix the marinade. Refrigerate for several hours or overnight.
3. Remove the lamb from the marinade then dry with paper towels. Discard the marinade.
4. When ready to cook, set to High and preheat for 15 minutes, lid closed.
5. Fix the lamb on the grill grate, fat-side down. Grill for 30 to 40 minutes per side, or until the internal temperature reaches 135F (57C) for medium-rare.
6. Let the lamb leg cool for 5 minutes before slicing. Serve warm.

62. Roasted Breaded Rack of Lamb

Preparation Time: 10 Minutes

Cooking Time: 200 Minutes

Servings: 4

Ingredients:

- 1 rack of lamb, frenched (about 1½ pounds / 680 g)
- ½ cup yellow mustard
- 1 tablespoon salt
- 1 teaspoon ground black pepper
- 1 cup panko bread crumbs
- 1 tablespoon minced Italian parsley
- 1 teaspoon minced rosemary
- 1 teaspoon minced sage

Directions:

1. Rub the rack of lamb with the mustard and season with salt and pepper.
2. In a shallow baking dish, combine the remaining ingredients. Dredge the lamb in the bread crumb mixture.
3. When ready to cook, set temperature to 500ºF (260ºC) and preheat, lid closed for 15 minutes.
4. On the grill place the lamb, bone-side down, and cook for 20 minutes, or until the internal temperature reaches 120F (49C).
5. Take off the lamb from the grill and let rest for 5 to 10 minutes before slicing. Serve warm.

63. Garlicky Grilled Rack of Lamb

Preparation Time: 5 Minutes

Cooking Time: 30 Minutes

Servings: 4

Ingredients:

- 8 cloves garlic
- 1 bunch fresh thyme
- 1 tablespoon kosher salt
- 2 teaspoons extra-virgin olive oil
- 1 teaspoon sherry vinegar
- 2 pounds (907 g) rack of lamb

Directions:

1. Blend all the ingredients using a blender except for the rack of lamb. Pulse until smooth. Put the mixture all over the rack of lamb.
2. When ready to cook, set temperature to 450ºF (232ºC) and preheat, lid closed for 15 minutes.
3. Place the lamb fat-side down on the grill and cook for 20 minutes. Turn over so that fat side is up then cook for an additional 10 minutes.
4. Let the meat rest for 10 minutes. Serve warm.

64. Smoked Lamb Chops (Lollipops)

Preparation Time: 10 minutes

Cooking Time: 1 hour

Servings: 4

Ingredients:

- 1 rack of lamb
- 2 tbsp. Fresh rosemary, approx. 3 sprigs
- 2 tbsp. fresh sage
- 1 tbsp. fresh thyme
- 1/2 tsp coarse ground pepper
- 1/4 cup olive oil
- 1 tsp honey
- 2 large cloves garlic, roughly chopped
- 2 tbsp. shallots, chopped (about 1 shallot)
- 1/2 tsp salt

- Fruitwood

Directions:

1. Preheat the Wood Pellet Grill and Smoker at 225°F.
2. Remove the silver skin & excess fat from the rack of lamb.
3. Combine all the ingredients together and make a thick paste.
4. Coat the lamb gently with the paste.
5. Place in the middle rack of the smoker for about 45-60 minutes or until it reaches 120°F internal temperature.

7. When done, remove and then sear the lamb for 2 minutes/ side.
8. Keep it sitting for 5 minutes before serving.

Nutrition:

Calories: Cal 185
Carbs: 4.9g
Fat: 15.6g
Protein: 6.2g
Fiber: 1.4g

65. Pulled, Low and Slow Smoked Lamb Shoulder

Preparation Time: 40 minutes

Cooking Time: 8-9 hours

Servings: 10

Ingredients:

- 1 lb. boneless lamb shoulder
- 1 tbsp. whole mustard seeds
- 2 tbsps. sweet paprika
- 2-1/2 tbsp. sea salt
- 1-1/2 tbsp. freshly ground black pepper
- 4 garlic cloves, crushed
- 4 tablespoons mild American mustard
- 1-1/2 tbsp. brown sugar
- 2 tbsps. freshly chopped rosemary leaves

Directions:

1. Preheat the Wood Pellet Grill and Smoker at 250°F.
2. Trim the excess fat from the lamb.
3. Take a bowl and mix together salt, pepper, paprika, whole mustard seeds, brown sugar, garlic, rosemary leaves.
4. Coat the lamb with mustard sauce and then evenly apply the spice mixture.
5. Add wood chips and a bowl of water in the smoker.
6. Put the lamb on the top rack of the smoker and let it smoke for 8-9 hours at low heat.
7. Keep checking and refilling the wood and bowl every 2 hours.
8. When done, wrap in an aluminum foil and let it rest for 30 minutes.
9. Pull the meat apart using the forks.
10. Serve and enjoy.

Nutrition:

Calories: Cal 173
Carbs: 15.3g
Fat: 5.7g
Protein: 15.2g
Fiber: 1.9g

66. Smoked Boneless Leg of Lamb

Preparation Time: 15 minutes

Cooking Time: 3 hours

Servings: 6

Ingredients:

- 2 to 2 1/2 pounds of boneless leg of lamb
- 1 tbsp. fresh ground black pepper
- 2 tbsps. oregano
- 4 garlic cloves, minced
- 2 tbsp. salt
- 1 tsp thyme
- 2 tbsps. olive oil
- Wood Chips

Directions:

1. Cut down the excess fat and maintain a uniform thickness of the meat.
2. Take a bowl and mix spices, oil, and garlic together. Apply the mixture to the meat.
3. Cover it with a plastic sheet and refrigerate it for 1 hour.
4. Put the meat on the middle rack of the smoker.
5. Set the Wood Pellet Grill and Smoker at a temperature of 250F. Add wood chips in the side tray and half bowl of water.
6. Smoke it for 3-4 hours or until it reaches an internal temperature of 145F.
7. Serve and enjoy.

Nutrition

Calories: Cal 352
Carbs: 3g
Fat: 16g
Protein: 49g

Fiber: 1g

67. Turkish Marinated Smoked Lamb Leg

Preparation Time: 20 minutes

Cooking Time: 2 – 3 hours

Servings: 10

Ingredients:

- 6 lb. deboned lamb leg
- 2 medium-size or one large onion
- 1 tbsp. kosher salt
- 4-6 cloves of garlic
- 1 cup flat-leaf parsley
- 1 teaspoon cumin
- 2-3 tbsps. Hardcore Carnivore Camo seasoning

Directions:

1. Marinade: Whisk together and make a paste of onion, parsley, garlic, and cumin.
2. Cut the strings to open the leg of the lamb if needed.
3. Coat the meat with kosher salt on either side and put it in a container.
4. Generously apply the onion paste over the meat. Cover and refrigerate for 24 hours.
5. Preheat the Wood Pellet Grill and Smoker at 250F.
6. Season the inner side of the meat with 1/3 of the Camo seasoning. Tie the lamb back into a roast.
7. Apply the remaining Camo rub on the outside of the tied lamb leg. Put it into the smoker.
8. Smoke until it reaches an internal temperature of 138°F or 2-3 hours.
9. When done, wrap the meat in one to two layers of butcher paper and put it in a cooler for 45 minutes.
10. Remove, cut twine, and serve by slicing it down.

Nutrition:

Calories: Cal 259
Carbs: 2.3g
Fat: 9.7g
Protein: 40.7g
Fiber: 0.6g

68. Smoked Lamb Shoulder

Preparation Time: 15 minutes

Cooking Time: 2 – 3 hours

Servings: 6-8

Ingredients:

Lamb Shoulder:

- 5 lb. boneless lamb shoulder
- 2 tablespoons kosher salt
- 2 tablespoons freshly ground black pepper
- 1 tablespoon dried rosemary
- Injection:
- 1 cup apple cider vinegar

Spritz:

- 1 cup apple cider vinegar
- 1 cup apple juice

Directions:

1. Preheat the Wood Pellet Grill and Smoker at 225F. Add a bowl of water in the smoker.
2. Remove excess fat and then rinse in water. Pat dry and then inject apple cider vinegar into the lamb.
3. Rub olive oil, rosemary, salt, and pepper and then tie with kitchen twine.
4. Mix together 1 cup apple cider vinegar and 1 cup apple juice and store in a spritz bottle.
5. Place the meat on the middle rack of the smoker without covering. Smoke for one hour and then every 15 minutes, spritz the mixture and let it smoke until it reaches 165F internal temperature.
6. When done, wrap the lamb in aluminum foil and place it back into the smoker until it reaches a temperature of 195F.
7. Remove when done and place in a cooler for at least one hour.
8. Serve and enjoy.

Nutrition

Calories: Cal 528
Carbs: 5.1g
Fat: 20.9g
Protein: 79.8g
Fiber: 0.6g

69. Lamb Shoulder Chops with Smoky Red

Preparation Time: 20 minutes

Cooking Time: 1-2 hours

Servings: 4

Ingredients:

- 2 medium cloves garlic, smashed & peeled
- Kosher salt

- 1 tbsp. chopped fresh oregano
- 1/8 tsp sweet hot pimento (smoked paprika)
- 1 tbsp. extra-virgin olive oil
- 4 (3/4- to 1-inch-thick) lamb shoulder or arm chops (2 lb. total)
- 2 oz. (4 tbsps.) unsalted butter
- 1-1/2 tsp cumin seed coarsely ground
- 1/2 tbsp. finely chopped shallot
- 1/2 tbsp. chopped piquillo pepper
- 1 tbsp. Sherry vinegar

Directions:

1. Make a smooth paste of garlic and one tsp salt. Then add cumin, oregano, and 1/2 -tsp. of the pimento. Stir in the olive oil until it becomes smooth.
2. Rub the paste over the lamb chops uniformly and let them rest for one hour.
3. Take another medium bowl, and mix shallot, butter, vinegar, piquillo pepper, and remaining pimento.
4. Place the lamb chops in a container and add to the middle rack of the smoker.
5. Let it smoke until it reaches 125F internal temperature.
6. When done, check if the chops are rosy in texture. If not, then smoke for another 20 minutes.
7. Add some melted butter over the chops when done and serve.

Nutrition:

Calories: Cal 488
Carbs: 2g
Fat: 40g
Protein: 30g
Fiber: 1g

70. Smoky Lamb's Leg with Bone

Preparation Time: 20 minutes

Cooking Time: 3 hours

Servings: 6

Ingredients:

- 5-7-pound leg of lamb, bone-in
- 4 shallots
- 1/2 cup kosher salt
- 1 cup olive oil
- 1/4 cup Dijon mustard
- 10 garlic cloves
- 12 rosemary sprigs
- 6 tablespoons lemon juice
- 12 thyme sprigs
- 2 tablespoons black pepper
- Cherry or apple wood chunks (one hand)

Directions:

1. Preheat the Wood Pellet Grill and Smoker at 225F. Add wood chips to the side tray and half bowl of water.
2. Blend to make a semi-liquid paste of lemon juice, mustard, garlic, olive oil, rosemary, shallots, thyme, salt, and pepper. Blend until it forms a semi-liquid paste.
3. Rub the mix over the lamb' leg uniformly.
4. Put the leg of lamb into the smoker and smoke for 2-3 hours or until the temperature reaches 145F.
5. Remove from the smoker and cover with aluminum foil loosely packed. Rest it for 30 minutes.
6. Slice and serve.

Nutrition:

Calories: Cal 1025
Carbs: 7.9g
Fat: 62.5g
Protein: 107.7g
Fiber: 2.8g

71. Smoked Pulled Lamb Sliders

Preparation Time: 30 minutes

Cooking Time: 8- 9 hours

Servings: 4 - 6

Ingredients:

Lamb:

- 4-5 lb. boneless lamb shoulder
- 1/4 cup olive oil
- 1/4 cup dry rub
- 10 ounces spritz

Dry Rub:

- 1/3 cup kosher salt
- 1/3 cup coarse ground pepper
- 1/3 cup granulated garlic

Spritz:

- 4 ounces Worcestershire sauce
- 6 ounces' apple cider vinegar

Directions:

1. Preheat the Wood Pellet Grill and Smoker at 250F. Add wood chips to the side tray and one bowl of water.
2. Remove the excess fat and coat with the dry rub and olive oil.
3. Put the lamb in the smoker without covering for one and a half hours.
4. After 90 minutes, start spritzing every 30 minutes for the next 4-6 hours until it reaches an internal temperature of 165F.
5. When done, remove from the smoker and add to a pan.
6. Spritz the remaining liquid and cover tightly in an aluminum foil.
7. Smoke again for two to three hours until it reaches a temperature of 200F.
8. Remove and place it ideal for 30 minutes in a cooler. Then add to the bun.
9. Serve and enjoy.

Nutrition:

Calories: Cal 658

Carbs: 9.5g

Fat: 30.6g

Protein: 86.2g

Fiber: 0.7g

72. Smoked Lamb with Rosemary

Preparation Time: 15 minutes

Cooking Time: 4 hours

Servings: 8

Ingredients:

- 5-7-pound boneless leg of lamb
- 1/4 cup olive oil
- 6 cloves garlic
- 2 tbsps. fresh mint chopped
- 2 tbsps. fresh rosemary chopped
- 1/4 cup white wine
- 2 tbsps. fresh thyme chopped
- Half cup juice and zest of 2 lemons

Directions:

1. In a zipper bag, mix all the ingredients together.
2. Put the lamb in a plastic bag and toss evenly. Refrigerate the bad for 24 hours.
3. Preheat the Wood Pellet Grill and Smoker at 225F. Add pecan wood chips and half bowl of water.
4. Place the lamb on the top rack of the smoker and smoke for 3-4 hours until internal temperature reaches 130F.
5. For crispier edges, raise the temperature to 400F and smoke for 20-30 more minutes.
6. Let it rest for 20 more minutes and then serve.

Nutrition:

Calories: Cal 291

Carbs: 2g

Fat: 15g

Protein: 37g

Fiber: 1g

73. Smoky Dry Lamb's Shoulder

Preparation Time: 20 minutes

Cooking Time: 4 hours

Servings: 6 - 8

Ingredients:

- 1 4-8Lb Lamb shoulder
- 2 tbsps. Olive oil

Rub:

- 2 tbsps. Salt
- 1 tbsp. Dried parsley
- 1 tbsp. dried oregano
- 1 tbsp. Dried basil
- 2 tbsps. Dried crushed sage
- 1 tbsp. ground black pepper
- 1 tbsp. Dried rosemary
- 1 tbsp. dried thyme
- 1 tbsp. Dried crushed bay leaf
- 1 tbsp. Sugar

Directions:

1. Preheat the Wood Pellet Grill at 250°F. Add pecan wood chips and a bowl of water to the side dish.
2. Combine the mix ingredients in a medium bowl.
3. Take olive oil and coat the lamb generously with it.
4. Sprinkle some salt over the lamb.
5. Coat the lamb with the dry rub uniformly.

9. Place it in the smoker with the fat side up.
10. Smoke for 3-4 hours until the temperature reaches 250°–300F.
11. In the last hour of smoking, raise the temperature to 300°–325°F for rendering the fat.
12. Remove it from the smoker once the temperature reaches between 195 – 203F.

13. Wrap in an aluminum foil and keep it ideal for 10-20 minutes.
14. Slice and serve.

Nutrition:
Calories: Cal 197
Carbs: 2.9g
Fat: 9.9g
Protein: 24.1g
Fiber: 0.8g

74. Rosemary-Smoked Lamb Chops

Preparation Time: 15 minutes

Cooking Time: 2 hours and 5 minutes

Servings: 4

Ingredients:

- Wood Pellet Flavor: Mesquite
- 4½ pounds bone-in lamb chops
- 2 tablespoons olive oil
- Salt
- Freshly ground black pepper
- 1 bunch fresh rosemary

Directions:

1. Supply your smoker with wood pellets and follow the manufacturer's specific start-up procedure. Preheat the grill to 180°F.
2. Rub the lamb generously with olive oil and season on both sides with salt and pepper.
3. Spread the rosemary directly on the grill grate, creating a surface area large enough for all the chops to rest on. Place the chops on the rosemary and smoke until they reach an internal temperature of 135°F.
4. Increase the grill's temperature to 450°F, remove the rosemary, and continue to cook the chops until their internal temperature reaches 145°F.
5. Take off the chops from the grill and let them rest for 5 minutes before serving.

Nutrition:

Calcium, Ca57 mg

Magnesium, Mg123 mg

Phosphorus, P1011 mg

Iron, Fe8.43 mg

Potassium, K1789 mg

Sodium, Na424 mg

Zinc, Zn16.14 mg

75. Classic Lamb Chops

Preparation Time: 10 minutes

Cooking Time: 30 minutes

Servings: 4

Ingredients

- Wood Pellet Flavor: Alder
- 4 (8-ounce) bone-in lamb chops
- 2 tablespoons olive oil
- 1 batch Rosemary-Garlic Lamb Seasoning

Directions:

1. Supply your smoker with wood pellets and follow the manufacturer's specific start-up procedure. Preheat the grill to 350°F. Close the lid
2. Rub the lamb generously with olive oil and coat them on both sides with the seasoning.
3. Put the chops directly on the grill grate and grill until their internal temperature reaches 145°F. Remove the lamb from the grill and serve immediately.

Nutrition:

Calcium, Ca48 mg

Magnesium, Mg61 mg

Phosphorus, P454 mg

Iron, Fe4.23 mg

Potassium, K841 mg

Sodium, Na147 mg

Zinc, Zn7.23 mg

76. Seared lamb chops

Preparation Time: 10 minutes

Cooking Time: 20 minutes

Servings: 4

Ingredients:

- Wood Pellet Flavor: Alder
- 4 (8-ounce) bone-in lamb chops
- 2 tablespoons olive oil
- 1 batch Rosemary-Garlic Lamb Seasoning

Directions:

1. Supply your smoker with wood pellets and follow the manufacturer's specific start-up procedure. Preheat the grill to 500F. Close the lid
2. Rub the lamb chops all over with olive oil and coat them on both sides with the seasoning.
3. Put the chops directly on the grill grate and grill until they reach an internal temperature of 120°F for rare, 130°F for medium, and 145F for well-

done. Remove the lamb from the grill then serve immediately.

Nutrition:

Calcium, Ca48 mg

Magnesium, Mg61 mg

Phosphorus, P454 mg

Iron, Fe4.23 mg

Potassium, K841 mg

Sodium, Na147 mg

Zinc, Zn7.23 mg

77. Roasted Leg Of Lamb

Preparation Time: 15 minutes

Cooking Time: 1-2 hours

Servings: 4

Ingredients:

- Wood Pellet Flavor: Hickory
- 1 (6- to 8-pound) boneless leg of lamb
- 2 batches Rosemary-Garlic Lamb Seasoning

Directions:

1. Supply your smoker with wood pellets and follow the manufacturer's specific start-up procedure. Preheat the grill to 350°F. Close the lid
2. Using your hands, rub the lamb leg with the seasoning, rubbing it under and around any netting.
3. Put the lamb directly on the grill grate and smoke until its internal temperature reaches 145°F.
4. Take off the lamb from the grill and let it rest for 20 to 30 minutes, before removing the netting, slicing, and serving.

Nutrition:

Calcium, Ca136 mg

Magnesium, Mg222 mg

Phosphorus, P1778 mg

Iron, Fe16.82 mg

Potassium, K3070 mg

Sodium, Na729 mg

Zinc, Zn31.88 mg

78. Hickory-Smoked Leg Of Lamb

Preparation Time: 15 minutes

Cooking Time: 5-7 hours

Servings: 4

Ingredients:

- WOOD PELLET FLAVOR: Hickory
- 1 (6- to 8-pound) boneless leg of lamb
- 2 batches Rosemary-Garlic Lamb Seasoning

Directions:

1. Supply your smoker with wood pellets and follow the manufacturer's specific start-up procedure. Preheat the grill to 225F. Close the lid
2. Using your hands, rub the lamb leg with the seasoning, rubbing it under and around any netting.
3. Move the lamb directly on the grill grate and smoke until its internal temperature reaches 145F.
4. Take off the lamb from the grill and let it rest for 20 to 30 minutes, before removing the netting, slicing, and serving.

Nutrition:

Calcium, Ca136 mg

Magnesium, Mg222 mg

Phosphorus, P1778 mg

Iron, Fe16.82 mg

Potassium, K3070 mg

Sodium, Na729 mg

Zinc, Zn31.88 mg

79. Smoked Rack Of Lamb

Preparation Time: 25 minutes

Cooking Time: 4-6 hours

Servings: 4

Ingredients:

- Wood Pellet Flavor: Hickory
- 1 (2-pound) rack of lamb
- 1 batch Rosemary-Garlic Lamb Seasoning

Directions:

1. Supply your smoker with wood pellets and follow the manufacturer's specific start-up procedure. Preheat the grill to 225°F.Close the lid
2. Using a boning knife, score the bottom fat portion of the rib meat.
3. Using your hands, rub the rack of lamb all over with the seasoning, making sure it penetrates into the scored fat.

4. Place the rack directly on the grill grate, fat-side up, and smoke until its internal temperature reaches 145°F.
5. Take off the rack from the grill and let it rest for 20 to 30 minutes, before slicing it into individual ribs to serve.

Nutrition:

Calcium, Ca50 mg

Magnesium, Mg56 mg

Phosphorus, P424 mg

Iron, Fe3.72 mg

Potassium, K748 mg

Sodium, Na154 mg

Zinc, Zn6.1 mg

80. Roast Rack Of Lamb

Preparation Time: 10 minutes

Cooking Time: 1 hour

Servings: 6-8

Ingredients:

- Wood Pellet Flavor: Alder
- 1 (2-pound) rack of lamb
- 1 batch Rosemary-Garlic Lamb Seasoning

Directions:

1. Supply your smoker with wood pellets and follow the manufacturer's specific start-up procedure. Preheat the grill to 450°F.
2. Using a boning knife, score the bottom fat portion of the rib meat.
3. Using your hands, rub the rack of lamb with the lamb seasoning, making sure it penetrates into the scored fat.
4. Place the rack directly on the grill grate and smoke until its internal temperature reaches 145F.
5. Take off the rack from the grill and let it rest for 20 to 30 minutes, before slicing into individual ribs to serve.

Nutrition:

Calcium, Ca50 mg

Magnesium, Mg56 mg

Phosphorus, P424 mg

Iron, Fe3.72 mg

Potassium, K748 mg

Sodium, Na154 mg

Zinc, Zn6.1 mg

81. Buttermilk Brined Shoulder Chops

Preparation Time: 15 minutes

Cooking Time: 30 minutes

Servings: 4

Ingredients:

- 4 lamb shoulder chops
- 4 cups buttermilk
- 1 cup cold water
- ¼ cup kosher salt
- 2 tablespoons olive oil
- 1 tablespoon Texas style rubs

Directions:

1. In a large bowl, add buttermilk, water and salt and stir until salt is dissolved.
2. Add chops and coat with mixture evenly.
3. Refrigerate for at least 4 hours.
4. Remove the chops from bowl and rinse under cold running water.
5. Coat the chops with olive oil and then sprinkle with rub evenly.
6. Preheat the Wood Pellet Grill & Smoker on smoke setting to 240 degrees F, using charcoal.
7. Arrange the chops onto grill and cook for about 25-30 minute or until desired doneness.
8. Meanwhile preheat the broiler of oven. Grease a broiler pan.
9. Remove the chops from grill and place onto the prepared broiler pan.
10. Transfer the broiler pan into the oven and broil for about 3-5 minutes or until browned.
11. Remove the chops from oven and serve hot.

Nutrition:

Calories 414

Total Fat 22.7 g

Saturated Fat 6.9 g

Cholesterol 123 mg

Sodium 7000 mg

Total Carbs 11.7 g

Fiber 0 g

Sugar 11.7 g

Protein 41.2 g

82. Herbed Rack of Lamb

Preparation Time: 15 minutes

Cooking Time: 2 hours

Servings: 3

Ingredients:

- 2 tablespoons fresh sage
- 2 tablespoons fresh rosemary
- 2 tablespoons fresh thyme
- 2 garlic cloves, peeled
- 1 tablespoon honey
- Salt and ground black pepper, as required
- ¼ cup olive oil
- 1 (1½-pound) rack of lamb, trimmed

Directions:

1. Mix all ingredients, except for oil and rack of lamb rack, in a food processor and pulse until well combined.
2. While motor is running, slowly add oil and pulse until a smooth paste is formed.
3. Coat the rib rack with paste generously and refrigerate for about 2 hours.
4. Preheat the Wood Pellet Grill & Smoker on grill setting to 225 degrees F.
5. Arrange the rack of lamb onto the grill and cook for about 2 hours.
6. Remove the rack of lamb from grill and place onto a cutting board for about 10-15 minutes before slicing.
7. Using a knife, slice the rack into individual ribs and serve.

Nutrition:

Calories 566

Total Fat 37.5 g

Saturated Fat 9.7 g

Cholesterol 151 mg

Sodium 214 mg

Total Carbs 9.8 g

Fiber 2.2 g

Sugar 5.8g

Protein 46.7 g

83. Cola Flavored Rack of Lamb

Preparation Time: 15 minutes

Cooking Time: 3 hours

Servings: 12

Ingredients:

- 4 (1½-pound) racks of lamb, trimmed
- 1 tablespoon unsweetened cocoa powder
- 1 tablespoon brown sugar
- 1 tablespoon smoked paprika
- Salt and ground black pepper, as required
- 1 cup cherry cola

Directions:

1. Preheat the Wood Pellet Grill & Smoker on grill setting to 225 degrees F.
2. With a sharp knife, make ½x¼-inch cuts in each rack of lamb.
3. In a bowl, place remaining ingredients except for cherry cola and mix until well combined.
4. Rub the racks with sugar mixture generously.
5. Arrange the racks onto the grill and cook for about 2½-3 hours, coating with cherry cola after every 1 hour.
6. Remove the racks from grill and place onto a cutting board for about 10-15 minutes before slicing.
7. With a sharp knife, cut each rack of lamb into individual ribs and serve.

Nutrition:

Calories 437

Total Fat 16.8g

Saturated Fat 6 g

Cholesterol 204 mg

Sodium 186 mg

Total Carbs 3.6 g

Fiber 0.4 g

Sugar 2.7 g

Protein 63.9 g

84. Wine Flavored Leg of Lamb

Preparation Time: 15 minutes

Cooking Time: 5 hours

Servings: 8

Ingredients:

- ½ cup olive oil
- ½ cup red wine vinegar
- ½ cup dry white wine
- 1 tablespoon garlic, minced
- 1 teaspoon dried marjoram, crushed
- 1 teaspoon dried rosemary, crushed
- Salt and ground black pepper, as required
- 1 (5-pound) leg of lamb

Directions:

1. In a bowl, add all ingredients except for leg of lamb and mix until well combined.
2. In a large resealable bag, add marinade and leg of lamb.
3. Seal the bag and shake to coat completely.
4. Refrigerate for about 4-6 hours, flipping occasionally.
5. Preheat the Wood Pellet Grill & Smoker on grill setting to 225 degrees F.
6. Arrange the leg of lamb onto the grill and cook for about 4-5 hours.
7. Remove the leg of lamb from grill and place onto a cutting board for about 20 minutes before slicing.
8. With a sharp knife, cut the leg of lamb into desired-sized slices and serve.

Nutrition:

Calories 653

Total Fat 33.4 g

Saturated Fat 9.2 g

Cholesterol 255 mg

Sodium 237 mg

Total Carbs 1 g

Fiber 0.1 g

Sugar 0.2 g

Protein 79.7 g

85. Stuffed Leg of Lamb

Preparation Time: 20 minutes

Cooking Time: 2½ hours

Servings: 8

Ingredients:

- 1 (8-ounce) package cream cheese, softened
- ¼ cup cooked bacon, crumbled
- 1 jalapeño pepper, seeded and chopped
- 1 tablespoon dried rosemary, crushed
- 2 teaspoons garlic powder
- 1 teaspoon onion powder
- 1 teaspoon paprika
- 1 teaspoon cayenne pepper
- Salt, as required
- 1 (4-5-pound) leg of lamb, butterflied
- 2-3 tablespoons olive oil

Directions:

1. Preheat the Wood Pellet Grill & Smoker on smoke setting to 225-240 degrees F, using charcoal and cherry wood chips.
2. For filling: in a bowl, add all ingredients and mix until well combined.
3. For spice mixture: in another small bowl, mix together all ingredients.
4. Place the leg of lamb onto a smooth surface.
5. Sprinkle the inside of leg with some spice mixture.
6. Place filling mixture over the inside surface evenly.
7. Roll the leg of lamb tightly and with a butcher's twine, tie the roll to secure the filling
8. Coat the outer side of roll with olive oil evenly and then sprinkle with spice mixture.
9. Arrange the leg of lamb onto the grill and cook for about 2-2½ hours.
10. Remove the leg of lamb from grill and place onto a cutting board.
11. With a piece of foil cover the leg of lamb loosely for about 20-25 minutes before serving.
12. With a sharp knife, cut the leg of lamb into desired-sized slices and serve.

Nutrition:

Calories 700

Total Fat 37.2 g

Saturated Fat 15.2 g

Cholesterol 294 mg

Sodium 478 mg

Total Carbs 2.2 g

Fiber 0.5 g

Sugar 0.5 g

Protein 84.6 g

86. Seasoned Lamb Shoulder

Preparation Time: 15 minutes

Cooking Time: 5¾ hours

Servings: 6

Ingredients:

- 1 (5-pound) bone-in lamb shoulder, trimmed
- 3-4 tablespoons Moroccan seasoning
- 2 tablespoons olive oil
- 1 cup water
- ¼ cup apple cider vinegar

Directions:

1. Preheat the Wood Pellet Grill & Smoker on smoke setting to 275 degrees F, using charcoal.
2. Coat the lamb shoulder with oil evenly and then rub with Moroccan seasoning generously.

3. Place the lamb shoulder onto the grill and cook for about 45 minutes.
4. In a food-safe spray bottle, mix together vinegar and water.
5. Spray the lamb shoulder with vinegar mixture evenly.
6. Cook for about 4-5 hours, spraying with vinegar mixture after every 20 minutes.
7. Remove the lamb shoulder from grill and place onto a cutting board for about 20 minutes before slicing.
8. With a sharp knife, cut the lamb shoulder in desired sized slices and serve.

Nutrition:

Calories 563

Total Fat 25.2 g

Saturated Fat 7.5 g

Cholesterol 251 mg

Sodium 1192 mg

Total Carbs 3.1 g

Fiber 0 g

Sugar 1.4 g

Protein 77.4 g

87. Lemony & Spicy Lamb Shoulder

Preparation Time: 15 minutes

Cooking Time: 2½ hours

Servings: 8

Ingredients:

- 1 (5-pound) bone-in lamb shoulder, trimmed
- 2 tablespoons olive oil
- 1 tablespoon fresh lemon juice
- 1 tablespoon fresh ginger, peeled
- 4-6 garlic cloves, peeled
- ½ tablespoon ground cumin
- ½ tablespoon paprika
- ½ tablespoon ground turmeric
- ½ tablespoon ground allspice
- Salt and ground black pepper, as required

Directions:

1. Using a sharp knife, carve the skin of the lamb shoulder into diamond pattern.
2. Combine all the ingredients in a food processor and pulse until smooth.
3. Coat the lamb shoulder with pureed mixture generously.
4. Arrange the lamb shoulder into a large baking dish and refrigerate, covered overnight.
5. Remove the baking dish of shoulder from refrigerator and set aside at room temperature for at least 1 hour before cooking.
6. Preheat the Wood Pellet Grill & Smoker on grill setting to 225 degrees F.
7. Place the lamb shoulder onto the grill and cook for about 2½ hours.
8. Remove the lamb shoulder from grill and place onto a cutting board for about 20 minutes before slicing.
9. With a sharp knife, cut the lamb shoulder into desired-sized slices and serve.

Nutrition:

Calories 41

Total Fat 18.8

Saturated Fat 5.6 g

Cholesterol 188 mg

Sodium 222 mg

Total Carbs 2 g

Fiber 0.5 g

Sugar 0.1 g

Protein 58.1 g

88. Sweet & Tangy Braised Lamb Shank

Preparation Time: 15 minutes

Cooking Time: 10 hours

Servings: 2

Ingredients:

- 2 (1¼-pound) lamb shanks
- 1-2 cups water
- ¼ cup brown sugar
- 1/3 cup rice wine
- 1/3 cup soy sauce
- 1 tablespoon dark sesame oil
- 4 (1½x½-inch) orange zest strips
- 2 (3-inch long) cinnamon sticks
- 1½ teaspoons Chinese five spice powder

Directions:

1. Preheat the Wood Pellet Grill & Smoker on smoke setting to 225-250 degrees F, using charcoal and soaked apple wood chips.
2. With a sharp knife, pierce each lamb shank at many places.
3. In a bowl, add remaining all ingredients and mix until sugar is dissolved.
4. In a large foil pan, place the lamb shanks and top with sugar mixture evenly.
5. Place the foil pan onto the grill and cook for about 8-10 hours, flipping after every 30 minutes. (If required, add enough water to keep the liquid ½-inch over).
6. Remove from the grill and serve hot.

Nutrition:

Calories 1200

Total Fat 48.4 g

Saturated Fat 15.8 g

Cholesterol 510 mg

Sodium 2000 mg

Total Carbs 39.7 g

Fiber 0.3 g

Sugar 29 g

Protein 161.9 g

89. Cheesy Lamb Burgers

Preparation Time: 10 minutes

Cooking Time: 18 minutes

Servings: 4

Ingredients:

- 2 pounds ground lamb
- 1 cup Parmigiano-Reggiano cheese, grated
- Salt and ground black pepper, as required

Directions:

1. Preheat the Wood Pellet Grill & Smoker on grill setting to 425 degrees F.
2. In a bowl, add all ingredients and mix until well combined.
3. Make 4 (¾-inch thick) patties from mixture.
4. With your thumbs, make a shallow but wide depression in each patty.
5. Arrange the patties onto the grill, depression-side down and cook for about 8 minutes.
6. Flip the patties and cook for about 8-10 minutes.
7. Remove the patties from grill and serve immediately.

Nutrition:

Calories 502

Total Fat 22.6 g

Saturated Fat 9.9 g

Cholesterol 220 mg

Sodium 331 mg

Total Carbs 0 g

Fiber 0 g

Sugar 0 g

Protein 71.7 g

90. Roasted Leg of Lamb

Preparation Time: 30 minutes

Cooking Time: 1 hour

Servings: 8

Ingredients:

Pellets: Cherry

- 8lbs bone-in leg of lamb
- 2 teaspoons extra-virgin olive oil
- 4 cloves garlic, half minced and half sliced
- 4 sprigs rosemary
- 2 lemons
- Salt and pepper

Directions:

1. Mix olive oil and minced garlic. Rub mixture into the leg of lamb.
2. Make small holes in the lamb and stuff them with the rosemary sprigs and sliced garlic.
3. Zest the lemons and juice, spreading across the lamb and finishing with salt and pepper.
4. When ready to cook, set your smoker temperature to 500°F and preheat. Put the leg of lamb on the smoker and cook for 30 minutes.
5. Lower grill temperature to 350°F and cook for 90 minutes.
6. Rest the lamb for 15 minutes before carving.

91. Lamb Wraps

Preparation Time: 1 hour

Cooking Time: 2 hours

Servings: 4

Ingredients:

Pellets: Apple

- 1 leg of lamb
- 3 lemons, juiced
- Olive oil
- Big game rub
- 2 cups yogurt
- 2 cucumbers, diced
- 2 cloves garlic, minced
- 4 tablespoons dill, finely diced
- 2 tablespoons mint leaves, finely diced
- Salt and pepper
- 12 pitas
- 3 tomatoes, diced
- 1 red onion, thinly sliced
- 8 oz. feta cheese

Directions:

1. Rub your lamb with the lemon juice, olive oil, and the rub.
2. When ready to cook, set your smoker temperature to 500°F and preheat. Put the leg of lamb on the smoker and cook for 30 minutes.
3. Lower the heat to 350F and keep cooking for another hour.
4. While the lamb is roasting, create the tzatziki sauce by mixing the yogurt, cucumbers, garlic, dill, mint

leaves, in a bowl and mix to combine. Place in the refrigerator to chill.
5. Get the pittas and wrap in foil, then place on the grill to warm.
6. Put the lamb at a cutting board and leave to rest for 15 minutes before slicing.
7. Fill the warm pita with red onion, lamb, diced tomato, tzatziki sauce, and feta.

92. Moroccan Kebabs

Preparation Time: 20 minutes

Cooking Time: 30 minutes

Servings: 2

Ingredients:

Pellets: Cherry

- 1 cup onions, finely diced
- 1 tablespoon fresh mint, finely diced
- 1 teaspoon paprika
- 1 teaspoon salt
- 1/2 teaspoon ground coriander
- 1/4 teaspoon ground cinnamon
- Pita Bread
- 2 cloves garlic, minced
- 3 tablespoons cilantro leaves, finely diced
- 1 tablespoon ground cumin
- 1 1/2 lbs. ground lamb

Directions:

1. In a bowl, mix the ingredients except for the pita bread. Mix into meatballs, and skewer each meatball.
2. Next, wet your hands with water and shape the meat into a sausage shape about as large as your thumb. Cover and refrigerate for 30 minutes.
3. When ready to cook, set your smoker temperature to 350°F and preheat. Put the kebabs on the smoker and cook for 30 minutes.
4. Serve with the pita bread.

93. Braised Lamb Shank

Preparation Time: 15 minutes

Cooking Time: 4 hours

Servings: 4

Ingredients:

Pellets: Mesquite

- 4 lamb shanks
- Prime rib rub
- 1 cup beef broth
- 1 cup red wine
- 4 sprigs rosemary and thyme

Directions:

1. Season the lamb with the prime rib rub.
2. Turn your smoker to 500F and preheat.
3. Place the lamb straight on the grill and smoke for 20 minutes.
4. Transfer the lamb to a pan and pour in the wine, beef broth, and herbs. Cover and put back on the grill, lowering the temperature to 325F.
5. Braise the lamb for 4 hours before serving.

94. Braised Lamb Tacos

Preparation Time: 2 hours

Cooking Time: 5 hours

Servings: 4

Ingredients:

Pellets: Mesquite

- 1/4 tablespoon cumin seeds
- 1/4 tablespoon coriander seeds
- 1/4 tablespoon pumpkin seeds
- 2 oz. guajillo peppers
- 1 tablespoon paprika
- 1 tablespoon lime juice
- 1 tablespoon fresh oregano, diced
- 3 cloves garlic, minced
- 2 tablespoons olive oil
- 1 tablespoon salt
- 3 lbs. lamb shoulders

Directions:

1. Grind all of the seeds together before microwaving the chili with water for two minutes on high.
2. Mix the seeds, lime juice, paprika, garlic cloves, salt, oil, and oregano with the chili.
3. Put the meat in a pan, then rub the seasoning mixture over it. Leave for two hours in the fridge.
4. When ready to cook, turn your smoker to 325F and preheat.
5. Pour 1/2 cup of water to the pan and cover with foil. Cook the lamb for two hours, adding water when needed.
6. Discard the foil and cook for 2 hours more, then leave for 20 minutes before shredding.
7. Serve on corn tortillas.

95. Lamb Kebabs

Preparation Time: 15 minutes

Cooking Time: 10 minutes

Servings: 4

Ingredients:

Pellets: Mesquite

- 1/2 tablespoon salt
- 2 tablespoons fresh mint
- 3 lbs. leg of lamb
- 1/2 cup lemon juice
- 1 tablespoon lemon zest
- 15 apricots, pitted
- 1/2 tablespoon cilantro
- 2 teaspoons black pepper
- 1/2 cup olive oil
- 1 teaspoon cumin
- 2 red onion

Directions:

1. Combine the olive oil, pepper, lemon juice, mint, salt, lemon zest, cumin, and cilantro. Add lamb leg, then place in the refrigerator overnight.
2. Remove the lamb from the marinade, cube them, and then thread onto the skewer with the apricots and onions.
3. When ready to cook, turn your smoker to 400F and preheat.
4. Lay the skewers on the grill and cook for ten minutes.
5. Remove from the grill and serve.

96. Ultimate Lamb Burgers

Preparation Time: 20 minutes

Cooking Time: 30 minutes

Servings: 4

Ingredients:

Pellets: Apple

Burger:

- 2 lbs. ground lamb
- 1 jalapeño
- 6 scallions, diced
- 2 tablespoons mint
- 2 tablespoons dill, minced
- 3 cloves garlic, minced
- Salt and pepper
- 4 brioche buns
- 4 slices manchego cheese

Sauce:

- 1 cup mayonnaise
- 2 teaspoons lemon juice
- 2 cloves garlic
- 1 bell pepper, diced
- salt and pepper

Instructions

1. When ready to cook, turn your smoker to 400F and preheat.
2. Add the mint, scallions, salt, garlic, dill, jalapeño, lamb, and pepper to the mixing bowl.
3. Form the lamb mixture into eight patties.
4. Lay the pepper on the grill and cook for 20 minutes.
5. Take the pepper from the grill and place it in a bag, and seal. After ten minutes, remove pepper from the bag, remove seeds and peel the skin.
6. Add the garlic, lemon juice, mayo, roasted red pepper, salt, and pepper and process until smooth. Serve alongside the burger.
7. Lay the lamb burgers on the grill, and cook for five minutes per side, then place in the buns with a slice of cheese, and serve with the homemade sauce.

97. Lamb Lollipops

Preparation Time: 15 minutes

Cooking Time: 10 minutes

Servings: 4

Ingredients:

Pellets: Apple

- 6 lamb chops
- 2 tablespoons olive oil
- 1/2 tablespoon salt

Chutney:

- 1 mango
- 3 cloves garlic
- 1/2 habanero pepper
- 3 sprigs cilantro
- 1 tablespoon lime juice
- 1 teaspoon salt
- 5 tablespoons pepper
- 2 tablespoons mint

Directions:

1. Start by cutting the fat off your lamb chops.
2. Mix all of the chutney ingredients together in a processor until well blended and smooth.
3. When ready to cook, turn your smoker to 400F and preheat.
4. Drizzle the lamb with olive oil and season with salt and pepper before grilling for five minutes on each side, leave to rest.
5. Serve with chutney and chopped mint.

98. Smoked Lamb Chops

Preparation Time: 15 minutes

Cooking Time: 15 minutes

Servings: 6

Ingredients:

Pellets: Apple

- 1/2 cup extra-virgin olive oil
- 1/4 cup onion, diced
- 2 cloves garlic, minced
- 2 tablespoons soy sauce
- 2 tablespoons balsamic vinegar
- 1 tablespoon rosemary
- 2 teaspoons mustard
- 1 teaspoon Worcestershire sauce
- 8 oz. lamb chops
- Salt and pepper

Directions:

1. In a pan, sauté the onion with garlic and olive oil over medium heat.
2. Take the mixture and place in a blender with vinegar, soy sauce, rosemary, Worcestershire sauce, and mustard.
3. Next, season the mixture with black pepper and set to one side.
4. When ready to cook, set the smoker temperature to 500°F and preheat.
5. Brush the lamb with olive oil then flavor with salt and pepper.
6. Smoke the lamb chops for six minutes per side. Serve alongside your homemade sauce.

99. Greek Style Leg of Lamb

Preparation Time: 25 minutes

Cooking Time: 2 hours

Servings: 8

Ingredients:

Pellets: Oak

- 7 lbs. leg of lamb
- 8 cloves garlic
- 2 sprigs fresh rosemary
- 1 sprig fresh oregano
- 2 lemons, juiced
- 6 tablespoons olive oil
- Salt and pepper

Directions:

1. Slice a series of thin cuts into the leg of lamb.
2. On a chopping board, mince the rosemary, oregano, and garlic and combine. Stuff into the holes in the lamb.
3. Rub the lamb with oil and lemon juice, then cover and refrigerate for eight hours.
4. Take out of the refrigerator and season with salt and pepper before placing it on a roasting pan.
5. When ready to cook, set your smoker to 450F and preheat.
6. Put the pan straight onto the grill and roast for 30 minutes. Then drop the temperature to 350F and keep cooking for another 90 minutes.
7. Rest for 15 minutes before serving.

CHAPTER 16. CHICKEN RECIPES

100. Buffalo Chicken Wings

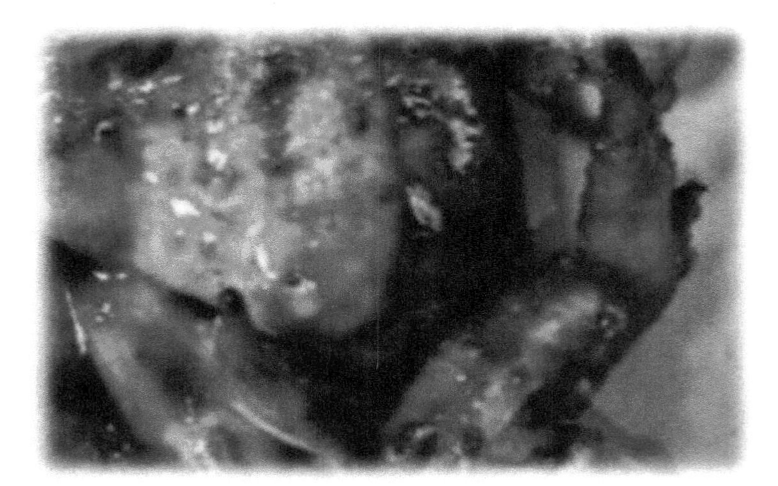

Preparation Time: 15 Minutes

Cooking Time: 25 Minutes

Servings: 6

Ingredients:

- 2 lb. chicken wings
- 1/2 cup sweet spicy dry rub
- 2/3 cup buffalo sauce
- Celery, chopped

Directions:

1. Start your wood pellet grill.
2. Set it to 450 degrees F.
3. Sprinkle the chicken wings with the dry rub.
4. Place on the grill rack.
5. Cook for 10 minutes per side.
6. Brush with the buffalo sauce.
7. Grill for another 5 minutes.
8. Dip each wing in the buffalo sauce.
9. Sprinkle the celery on top.

Nutrition:

Calcium, Ca235 mg

Magnesium, Mg248 mg

Phosphorus, P1483 mg

Iron, Fe9.58 mg

Potassium, K2556 mg

Sodium, Na2784 mg

Zinc, Zn15.3 mg

101. Sweet & Sour Chicken

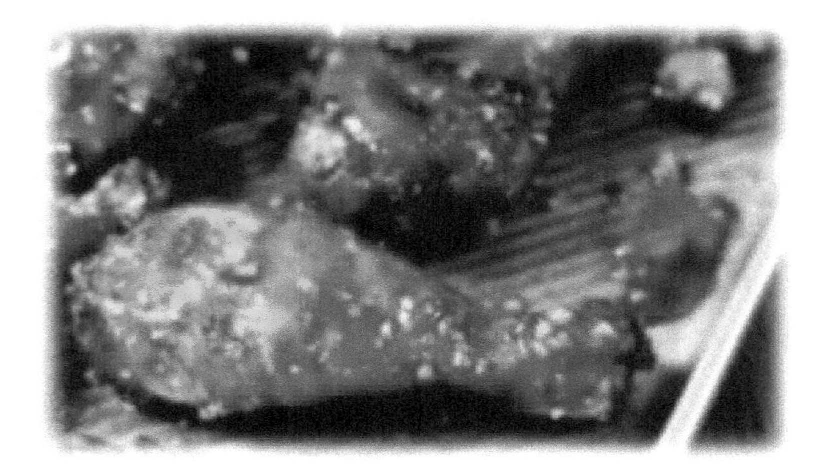

Preparation Time: 4 Minutes

Cooking Time: 3 hours

Servings: 4

Ingredients:

- 8 chicken drumsticks

Sauce

- 1/4 cup soy sauce
- 1 cup ketchup
- 2 tablespoons rice wine vinegar
- 2 tablespoons lemon juice
- 2 tablespoons honey
- 2 tablespoons garlic, minced
- 2 tablespoons ginger, minced
- 1 tablespoon sweet spicy dry rub
- 3 tablespoons brown sugar

Directions:

1. Combine all the sauce ingredients in a bowl.
2. Mix well.
3. Take half of the mixture, transfer to another bowl and refrigerate.
4. Add the chicken to the bowl with the remaining sauce.
5. Toss to coat evenly.
6. Cover and refrigerate for 4 hours.
7. When ready to cook, take the chicken out of the refrigerator.
8. Discard the marinade.
9. Turn on your wood pellet grill.
10. Set it to smoke.
11. Set the temperature to 225 degrees F.
12. Smoke the chicken for 3 hours.
13. Serve the chicken with the reserved sauce.

Nutrition:

Calcium, Ca175 mg

Magnesium, Mg266 mg

Phosphorus, P1873 mg

Iron, Fe9.61 mg

Potassium, K3234 mg

Sodium, Na4252 mg

Zinc, Zn20.68 mg

102. Honey Glazed Whole Chicken

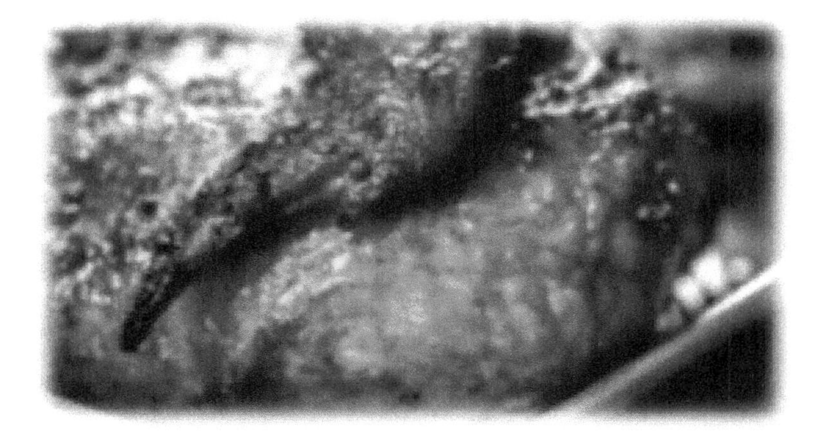

Preparation Time: 10 Minutes

Cooking Time: 3 hours 8 Minutes

Servings: 4

Ingredients:

- 1 tablespoon honey
- 4 tablespoons butter
- 3 tablespoons lemon juice
- 1 whole chicken, giblets trimmed
- 4 tablespoons chicken seasoning

Directions:

1. Set your wood pellet grill to smoke.
2. Set it to 225 degrees F.
3. In a pan over low heat, add the honey and butter. Pour in the lemon juice.
4. Add the seasoning.
5. Cook for 1 minute, stirring.
6. Add the chicken to the grill.
7. Smoke for 8 minutes.
8. Flip the chicken and brush with the honey mixture.
9. Smoke for 3 hours, brushing the sauce every 40 minutes.
10. Let rest for 5 minutes before serving.

Nutrition:

Calcium, Ca495 mg

Magnesium, Mg1101 mg

Phosphorus, P9463 mg

Iron, Fe49.27 mg

Potassium, K11424 mg

Sodium, Na3944 mg

Zinc, Zn56.88 mg

103. Chicken Lollipops

Preparation Time: 15 Minutes

Cooking Time: 2 hours 15 Minutes

Servings: 6

Ingredients:

- 12 chicken lollipops
- Chicken seasoning
- 10 tablespoons butter, sliced into 12 cubes
- 1 cup barbecue sauce
- 1 cup hot sauce

Directions:

1. Turn on your wood pellet grill.
2. Set it to 300 degrees F.
3. Season the chicken with the chicken seasoning.
4. Arrange the chicken in a baking pan.
5. Put the butter cubes on top of each chicken.
6. Cook the chicken lollipops for 2 hours, basting with the melted butter in the baking pan every 20 minutes.
7. Pour in the barbecue sauce and hot sauce over the chicken.
8. Grill for 15 minutes.

Nutrition:

Calcium, Ca241 mg

Magnesium, Mg489 mg

Phosphorus, P4123 mg

Iron, Fe21.77 mg

Potassium, K5159 mg

Sodium, Na2497 mg

Zinc, Zn24.78 mg

104. Asian Wings

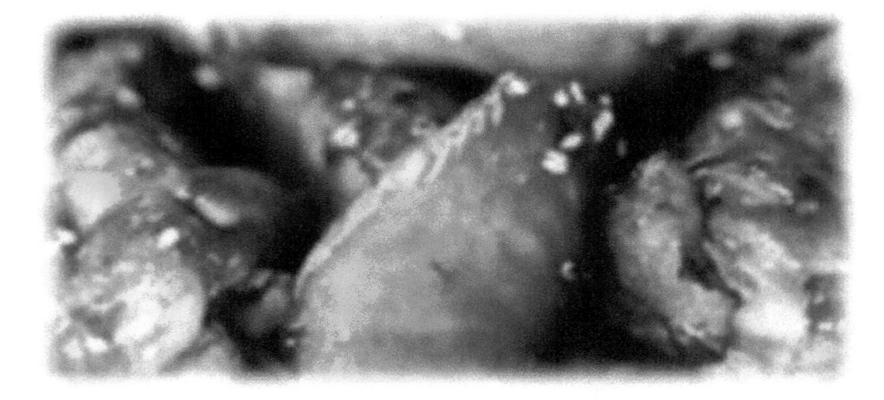

Preparation Time: 2 hours 30 minutes

Cooking Time: 1 hour

Servings: 6

Ingredients:

Sauce

- 1 teaspoon honey
- 1 teaspoon soy sauce
- 2 teaspoon rice vinegar
- 1/2 cup hoisin sauce
- 2 teaspoon sesame oil
- 1 teaspoon ginger, minced
- 1 teaspoon garlic, minced

- 1 teaspoon green onion, chopped
- 1 cup hot water

Wings

- 2 lb. chicken wings

Directions:

1. Combine all the sauce ingredients in a large bowl. Mix well.
2. Transfer 1/3 of the sauce to another bowl and refrigerate.
3. Add the chicken wings to the remaining sauce.
4. Cover and refrigerate for 2 hours.
5. Turn on your wood pellet grill.
6. Set it to 300 degrees F.
7. Add the wings to a grilling basket.
8. Cook for 1 hour.
9. Heat the reserved sauce in a pan.
10. Bring to a boil and then simmer for 10 minutes.
11. Brush the chicken with the remaining sauce.
12. Grill for another 10 minutes.
13. Let rest for 5 minutes before serving.

Nutrition:

Calcium, Ca32 mg

Magnesium, Mg40 mg

Phosphorus, P245 mg

Iron, Fe1.58 mg

Potassium, K327 mg

Sodium, Na481 mg

Zinc, Zn2.55 mg

105. Lemon Chicken in Foil Packet

Preparation Time: 5 Minutes

Cooking Time: 25 Minutes

Servings: 4

Ingredients:

- 4 chicken fillets
- 3 tablespoon melted butter
- 1 garlic, minced
- 1-1/2 teaspoon dried Italian seasoning
- Salt and pepper to taste
- 1 lemon, sliced

Directions:

1. Turn on your wood pellet grill.
2. Keep the lid open while burning for 5 minutes.
3. Preheat it to 450 degrees F.
4. Add the chicken fillet on top of foil sheets.
5. In a bowl, mix the butter, garlic, seasoning, salt and pepper.
6. Brush the chicken with this mixture.
7. Put the lemon slices on top.
8. Wrap the chicken with the foil.
9. Grill for 7 to 10 minutes per side.

Nutrition:

Calcium, Ca101 mg

Magnesium, Mg223 mg

Phosphorus, P1898 mg

Iron, Fe10.01 mg

Potassium, K2329 mg

Sodium, Na823 mg

Zinc, Zn11.4 mg

106. Sweet & Spicy Chicken

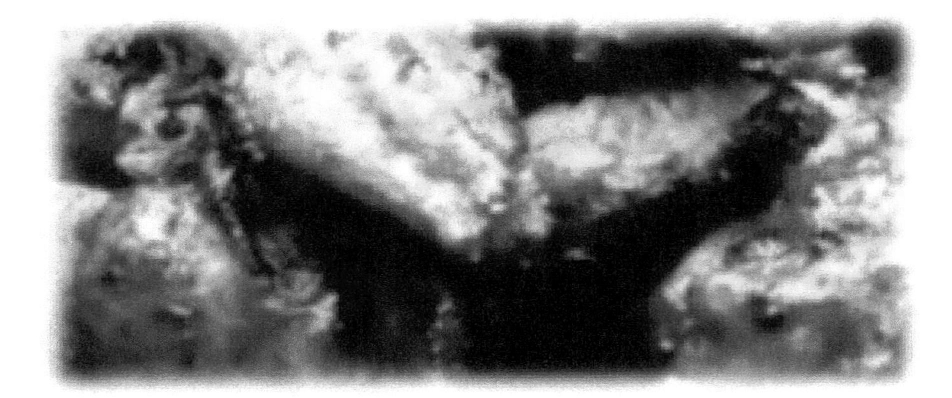

Preparation Time: 1 hour

Cooking Time: 40 Minutes

Servings: 4

Ingredients:

- 16 chicken wings
- 3 tablespoons lime juice
- Sweet spicy rub

Directions:

1. Arrange the chicken wings in a baking pan.
2. Pour the lime juice over the wings.
3. Sprinkle the wings with the seasoning.
4. Set your wood pellet grill to 350 degrees F.
5. Add the chicken wings to the grill.
6. Grill for 20 minutes per side.

Nutrition:

Calcium, Ca22 mg

Magnesium, Mg31 mg

Phosphorus, P187 mg

Iron, Fe1.1 mg

Potassium, K274 mg

Sodium, Na95 mg

Zinc, Zn1.92 mg

107. Tandoori Chicken Wings

Preparation Time: 20 minutes

Cooking Time: 1 hour 20 minutes

Servings: 4-6

Ingredients:

- ¼ Cup Yogurt
- 1 Whole Scallions, minced
- 1 Tablespoon minced cilantro leaves
- 2 Teaspoon ginger, minced
- 1 Teaspoon Masala
- 1 Teaspoon salt
- 1 Teaspoon ground black pepper
- 1 ½ pound chicken wings
- ¼ cup yogurt
- 2 tablespoon mayonnaise
- 2 tablespoon Cucumber
- 2 teaspoon lemon juice
- ½ teaspoon cumin
- ½ teaspoon salt
- 1/8 cayenne pepper

Directions:

1. Combine yogurt, scallion, ginger, garam masala, salt, cilantro, and pepper ingredients in the jar of a blender and process until smooth.
2. Put chicken and massage the bag to cat all the wings
3. Refrigerate for 4 to 8 hours. Remove the excess marinade from the wings; discard the marinade
4. Set the temperature to 350F and preheat, lid closed, for 10 to 15 minutes. Brush and oil the grill grate
5. Arrange the wings on the grill. Cook for 45 to 50 minutes, or until the skin is brown and crisp and meat is no longer pink at the bone. Turn once or twice during cooking to prevent the wings from sticking to the grill.
6. Meanwhile combine all sauce ingredients; set aside and refrigerate until ready to serve.
7. When wings are cooked through, transfer to a plate or platter. Serve with yogurt sauce

Nutrition:

Calories 241kcal

Carbohydrates 11g

Protein 12g

Fat 16g

Saturated Fat 3g

108. Asian BBQ Chicken

Preparation Time: 12 to 24 hours

Cooking Time: 1 hour

Servings: 4-6

Ingredients:

- 1 whole chicken
- To taste Asian BBQ Rub
- 1 whole ginger ale

Direction:

1. Rinse chicken in cold water and pat dry with paper towels.
2. Cover the chicken all over with Asian BBQ rub; make sure to drop some in the inside too. Place in large bag or bowl and cover and refrigerate for 12 to 24 hours.
3. When ready to cook, set the Wood pellet grill to 372F and preheat lid closed for 15 minutes.
4. Open can of ginger ale and take a few big gulps. Set the can of soda on a stable surface. Take the chicken out of the fridge and place the bird over top of the soda can. The base of the can and the two legs of the chicken should form a sort of tripod to hold the chicken upright.
5. Stand the chicken in the center of your hot grate and cook the chicken till the skin is golden brown and the internal temperature is about 165F on an instant-read thermometer, approximately 40 minutes to 1 hour.

Nutrition:

Calories 140kcal

Carbohydrates 18g

Protein 4g

Fat 4g

Sodium 806 mg

Potassium 682 mg

Fiber 5g

Sugar 8g

109. Smoke Roasted Chicken

Cooking Time: 1 hour 20 minutes

Servings: 4-6

Ingredients:

- 8 tablespoon butter, room temperature
- 1 clove garlic, minced
- 1 scallion, minced
- 2 tablespoon fresh herbs such as thyme, rosemary, sage or parsley
- As needed Chicken rub
- Lemon juice
- As needed vegetable oil

Directions:

1. In a small cooking bowl, mix the scallions, garlic, butter, minced fresh herbs, 1-1/2 teaspoon of the rub, and lemon juice. Mix with a spoon.
2. Remove any giblets from the cavity of the chicken. Wash the chicken inside and out with cold running water. Dry thoroughly with paper towels.
3. Sprinkle a generous amount of Chicken Rub inside the cavity of the chicken.
4. Gently loosen the skin around the chicken breast and slide in a few tablespoons of the herb butter under the skin and cover.
5. Cover the outside with the remaining herb butter.
6. Insert the chicken wings behind the back. Tie both legs together with a butcher's string. Powder the outside of the chicken with more Chicken Rub then insert sprigs of fresh herbs inside the cavity of the chicken.
7. Set temperature to High and preheat, lid closed for 15 minutes.
8. Oil the grill with vegetable oil. Move the chicken on the grill grate, breast-side up then close the lid.
9. After chicken has cooked for 1 hour, lift the lid. If chicken is browning too quickly, cover the breast and legs with aluminum foil.
10. Close the lid then continue to roast the chicken until an instant-read meat thermometer inserted into the thickest part registers a temperature of 165F
11. Take off chicken from grill and let rest for 5 minutes. Serve, Enjoy!

Nutrition:

Calories 222kcal

Carbohydrates 11g

Protein 29g

Fat 4g

Cholesterol 62mg

Sodium 616mg

Potassium 620mg

110. Grilled Asian Chicken Burgers

Preparation Time: 5 minutes

Cooking Time: 50 minutes

Servings: 4-6

Ingredients:

- 5 Pound chicken, ground
- 1 cup panko breadcrumbs
- 1 cup parmesan cheese
- 1 small jalapeno, diced
- 2 whole scallions, minced
- 2 garlic clove
- ¼ cup minced cilantro leaves

- 2 tablespoon mayonnaise
- 2 tablespoon chili sauce
- 1 tablespoon soy sauce
- 1 tablespoon ginger, minced
- 2 teaspoon lemon juice
- 2 teaspoon lemon zest
- 1 teaspoon salt
- 1 teaspoon ground black pepper
- 8 hamburger buns
- 1 tomato, sliced
- Arugula, fresh
- 1 red onion sliced

Directions:

1. Align a rimmed baking sheet with aluminum foil then spray with nonstick cooking spray.
2. In a large bowl, combine the chicken, jalapeno, scallion, garlic, cilantro, panko, Parmesan, chili sauce, soy sauce ginger, mayonnaise, lemon juice and zest, and salt and pepper.
3. Work the mixture with your fingers until the ingredients are well combined. If the mixture looks too wet to form patties and add additional more panko.
4. Wash your hands under cold running water, form the meat into 8 patties, each about an inch larger than the buns and about ¾" thick. Use your thumbs or a tablespoon, make a wide, shallow depression in the top of each
5. Put them on the prepared baking sheet. Spray the tops with nonstick cooking spray. If not cooking right away, cover with plastic wrap and refrigerate.
6. Set the pellet grill to 350F then preheat for 15 minutes, lid closed.
7. Order the burgers, depression-side down, on the grill grate. Remove and discard the foil on the baking sheet so you'll have an uncontaminated surface to transfer the slider when cooked.
8. Grill the burgers for about 25 to 30 minutes, turning once, or until they release easily from the grill grate when a clean metal spatula is slipped under them. The internal temperature when read on an instant-read meat thermometer should be 160F.
9. Spread mayonnaise and arrange a tomato slice, if desired, and a few arugula leaves on one-half of each bun. Top with a grilled burger and red onions, if using, then replace the top half of the bun. Serve immediately. Enjoy

Nutrition:

Calories 329kcal

Carbohydrates 10g

Protein 21g

Fat 23g

111. Grilled Sweet Cajun Wings

Preparation Time: 10 minutes

Cooking Time: 45 minutes

Servings: 4-6

Ingredients:

- 2-pound chicken wings
- As needed Pork and Poultry rub
- Cajun shake

Directions:

1. Coat wings in Sweet rub and Cajun shake.
2. When ready to cook, set the pellet grill to 350F and preheat, lid closed for 15 minutes.
3. Cook for 30 minutes until skin is brown and center is juicy and an instant-read thermometer reads at least 165F. Serve, Enjoy!

112. The Grilled Chicken Challenge

Preparation Time: 15 minutes

Cooking Time: 1 hour and 10 minutes

Servings: 4-6

Ingredients:

- 1 (4-lbs.) whole chicken
- As needed chicken rub

Directions:

1. When ready to cook, set temperature to 375F then preheat, close the lid for 15 minutes.
2. Rinse and dry the whole chicken (remove and discard giblets, if any). Season the entire chicken, including the inside of the chicken using chicken rub.
3. Place the chicken on the grill and cook for 1 hour and 10 minutes.
4. Remove chicken from grill when internal temperature of breast reaches 160F. Check heat periodically throughout as cook times will vary based on the weight of the chicken.
5. Allow chicken to rest until the internal temperature of breast reaches 165F, 15-20 minutes. Enjoy!

Nutrition:

Calories 212kcal

Carbohydrates 42.6g

Protein 6.1g

Fat 2.4g

Saturated Fat 0.5g

Fiber 3.4g

Sugar 2.9g

113. Classic BBQ Chicken

Preparation Time: 5 minutes

Cooking Time: 1 hour and 45 minutes

Servings: 4-6

Ingredients:

- 4 pounds of your favorite chicken, including legs, thighs, wings, and breasts, skin-on
- Salt
- Olive oil
- 1 cup barbecue sauce, like Hickory Mesquite or Homemade

Directions:

1. Rub the chicken with olive oil and salt.
2. Preheat the grill to high heat.
3. Sear chicken skin side down on the grill for 5-10 minutes.
4. Turn the grill down to medium low heat, tent with foil and cook for 30 minutes.
5. Turn chicken and baste with barbecue sauce.
6. Cover the chicken again and allow to cook for another 20 minutes.
7. Baste, cover and cook again for 30 minutes; repeat basting and turning during this time.
8. The chicken is done when the internal temperature of the chicken pieces are 165°F and juices run clear.
9. Baste with more barbecue sauce to serve!

Nutrition:

Calories: 539

Sodium: 684mg

Dietary Fiber: 0.3g

Fat: 11.6g

Carbs: 15.1g

Protein: 87.6g.

114. Sweet Orange Chili Lime Chicken

Preparation Time: 35 minutes

Cooking Time: 15 minutes

Servings: 4

Ingredients:

- 1/2 cup sweet chili sauce
- 1/4 cup soy sauce
- 1 teaspoon mirin
- 1 teaspoon orange juice, fresh squeezed
- 1 teaspoon orange marmalade
- 2 tablespoons lime juice
- 1 tablespoon brown sugar
- 1 clove garlic, minced
- 4 boneless, skinless chicken breasts
- Sesame seeds, for garnish

Directions:

1. Whisk sweet chili sauce, soy sauce, mirin, orange marmalade, lime and orange juice, brown sugar, and minced garlic together in a small mixing bowl.
2. Set aside 1/4 cup of the sauce.
3. Toss chicken in sauce to coat and marinate 30 minutes.
4. Preheat your grill to medium heat.
5. Put the chicken on the grill and grill each side for 7 minutes.
6. Baste the cooked chicken with remaining marinade and garnish with sesame seeds to serve with your favorite sides.

Nutrition:

Calories: 380

Sodium: 1274mg

Dietary Fiber: 0.5g

Fat: 12g

Carbs:19.7g

Protein: 43.8g.

115. Zesty Chili Lime Chicken

Preparation Time: 8 - 24 hours

Cooking Time: 20 minutes

Servings: 4

Ingredients:

- 2 lbs. Boneless, skinless chicken thighs

For the marinade:

- 1/4 cup fresh lime juice
- 2 teaspoons lime zest
- 1/4 cup honey
- 2 tablespoons olive oil
- 1 tablespoon balsamic vinegar
- 1/2 teaspoon sea salt
- 1/2 teaspoon black pepper
- 2 garlic cloves, minced
- 1/4 teaspoon onion powder

Directions:

1. Whisk together marinade ingredients in a large mixing bowl; reserve 2 tablespoons of the marinade for grilling.
2. Add chicken and marinade to a sealable plastic bag and marinate 8 hours or overnight in the refrigerator.
3. Preheat grill to medium high heat and brush lightly with olive oil.
4. Place chicken on grill and cook 8 minutes per side.
5. Baste each side of chicken with reserved marinade during the last few minutes of cooking; chicken is done when the internal temperature reaches 165 degrees Fahrenheit.
6. Plate chicken, tent with foil, and allow to rest for 5 minutes.
7. Serve and enjoy!

Nutrition:

Calories: 381

Sodium: 337mg

Dietary Fiber: 1.1g

Fat: 20.2g

Carbs: 4.7g

Protein: 44.7g.

116. Chipotle Adobo Chicken

Preparation Time: 1 - 24 hours

Cooking Time: 20 minutes

Servings: 4-6

Ingredients:

- 2 lbs. chicken thighs or breasts (boneless, skinless)
- For the marinade:
- 1/4 cup olive oil
- 2 chipotle peppers in adobo sauce, plus 1 teaspoon adobo sauce from the can
- 1 tablespoon garlic, minced
- 1 shallot, finely chopped
- 1-1/2 tablespoons cumin
- 1 tablespoon cilantro, super-finely chopped or dried
- 2 teaspoons chili powder
- 1 teaspoon dried oregano
- 1/2 teaspoon salt
- Fresh limes, for garnish
- Cilantro, for garnish

Directions:

1. Preheat grill to medium-high.
2. Add marinade ingredients to a food processor or blender and pulse into a paste.
3. Add the chicken and marinade to a sealable plastic bag, and coat well.
4. Place in the refrigerator for 1 hour to 24 hours before grilling.
5. Grill chicken for 7 minutes, turn and grill an additional 7 minutes; or until good grill marks appear.
6. Turn heat to low and continue to grill until chicken is cooked through and internal temperature reaches 165 degrees Fahrenheit.
7. Remove chicken from grill and allow to rest 5 to 10 minutes before serving.
8. Garnish with a squeeze of fresh lime and a sprinkle of cilantro to serve.

Nutrition:

Calories: 561

Sodium: 431mg

Dietary Fiber: 0.3g

Fat: 23.8g

Carbs: 18.7g

Protein: 65.9g.

117. Honey Balsamic Marinated Chicken

Preparation Time: 30 minutes – 4 hours

Cooking Time: 20 minutes

Servings: 4

Ingredients:

- 2 lbs. boneless, skinless chicken thighs
- 1 teaspoon olive oil
- 1/2 teaspoon sea salt
- 1/4 teaspoon black pepper
- 1/2 teaspoon paprika
- 3/4 teaspoon onion powder
- For the Marinade:
- 2 tablespoons honey
- 2 tablespoons balsamic vinegar
- 2 tablespoons tomato paste
- 1 teaspoon garlic, minced

Directions:

1. Add chicken, olive oil, salt, black pepper, paprika, and onion powder to a sealable plastic bag. Seal and toss to coat, covering chicken with spices and oil; set aside.
2. Whisk together balsamic vinegar, tomato paste, garlic, and honey.
3. Divide the marinade in half. Add one half to the bag of chicken and store the other half in a sealed container in the refrigerator.
4. Seal the bag and toss chicken to coat. Refrigerate for 30 minutes to 4 hours.
5. Preheat a grill to medium-high.
6. Discard bag and marinade. Add chicken to the grill and cook 7 minutes per side or until juices run clear and a meat thermometer reads 165 degrees Fahrenheit.
7. During last minute of cooking, brush remaining marinade on top of the chicken thighs.
8. Serve immediately.

Nutrition:

Calories: 485

Sodium: 438mg

Dietary Fiber: 0.5g

Fat: 18.1g

Carbs: 11g

Protein: 66.1g.

118. California Grilled Chicken

Preparation Time: 35 minutes

Cooking Time: 20 minutes

Servings: 4

Ingredients:

- 4 boneless, skinless chicken breasts
- 3/4 cup balsamic vinegar
- 2 tablespoons extra virgin olive oil

- 1 tablespoon honey
- 1 teaspoon oregano
- 1 teaspoon basil
- 1 teaspoon garlic powder
- For Garnish:
- Sea salt
- Black pepper, fresh ground
- 4 slices fresh mozzarella cheese
- 4 slices avocado
- 4 slices beefsteak tomato
- Balsamic glaze, for drizzling

Directions:

1. Whisk together balsamic vinegar, honey, olive oil, oregano, basil and garlic powder in a large mixing bowl.
2. Add chicken to coat and marinate for 30 minutes in the refrigerator.
3. Preheat grill to medium-high. Grill chicken for 7 minutes per side, or until a meat thermometer reaches 165°F.
4. Top each chicken breast with mozzarella, avocado, and tomato and tent with foil on the grill to melt for 2 minutes.
5. Garnish with a drizzle of balsamic glaze, and a pinch of sea salt and black pepper.

Nutrition:

Calories: 883

Sodium: 449mg

Dietary Fiber: 15.2g

Fat: 62.1g

Carbs: 29.8g

Protein: 55.3g.

119. Salsa Verde Marinated Chicken

Preparation Time: 4 hours 35 minutes

Cooking Time: 4 hours and 50 minutes

Servings: 6

Ingredients:

- 6 boneless, skinless chicken breasts
- 1 tablespoon olive oil
- 1 teaspoon sea salt
- 1 teaspoon chili powder
- 1 teaspoon ground cumin
- 1 teaspoon garlic powder
- For the salsa verde marinade:
- 3 teaspoons garlic, minced
- 1 small onion, chopped
- 6 tomatillos, husked, rinsed and chopped
- 1 medium jalapeño pepper, cut in half, seeded
- 1/4 cup fresh cilantro, chopped
- 1/2 teaspoon sugar or sugar substitute

Directions:

1. Add salsa Verde marinade ingredients to a food processor and pulse until smooth.
2. Mix sea salt, chili powder, cumin, and garlic powder together in a small mixing bowl.
3. Season chicken breasts with olive oil and seasoning mix, and lay in glass baking dish.
4. Spread a tablespoon of salsa verde marinade over each chicken breast to cover; reserve remaining salsa for serving.
5. Cover dish with plastic wrap and refrigerate for 4 hours.
6. Preheat grill to medium-high and brush with olive oil.
7. Add chicken to grill and cook 7 minutes per side or until juices run clear and a meat thermometer reads 165°F.
8. Serve each with additional salsa verde and enjoy!

Nutrition:

Calories: 321

Sodium: 444mg

Dietary Fiber: 1.3g

Fat: 13.7g

Carbs: 4.8g

Protein: 43g.

120. Hawaiian Chicken Skewers

Preparation Time: 1 hour and 15 minutes

Cooking Time: 15 minutes

Servings: 4-5

Ingredients:

- 1 lb. boneless, skinless chicken breast, cut into 1-1/2 inch cubes
- 3 cups pineapple, cut into 1-1/2 inch cubes
- 2 large green peppers, cut into 1-1/2 inch pieces
- 1 large red onion, cut into 1-1/2 inch pieces
- 2 tablespoons olive oil, to coat veggies
- For the marinade:
- 1/3 cup tomato paste
- 1/3 cup brown sugar, packed
- 1/3 cup soy sauce
- 1/4 cup pineapple juice
- 2 tablespoons olive oil
- 1-1/2 tablespoon mirin or rice wine vinegar
- 4 teaspoons garlic cloves, minced
- 1 tablespoon ginger, minced
- 1/2 teaspoon sesame oil
- Pinch of sea salt
- Pinch of ground black pepper
- 10 wooden skewers, for assembly

Directions:

1. Combine marinade ingredients in a mixing bowl until smooth. Reserve a 1/2 cup of the marinade in the refrigerator.

2. Add chicken and remaining marinade to a sealable plastic bag and refrigerate for 1 hour.
3. Soak 10 wooden skewer sticks in water for 1 hour.
4. Preheat the grill to medium heat.
5. Add red onion, bell pepper and pineapple to a mixing bowl with 2 tablespoons olive oil and toss to coat.
6. Thread red onion, bell pepper, pineapple and chicken onto the skewers until all of the chicken has been used.
7. Place skewers on grill and grab your reserved marinade from the refrigerator; grill for 5 minutes then brush with remaining marinade and rotate.
8. Brush again with marinade and grill about 5 additional minutes or until chicken reads 165F on a meat thermometer.
9. Serve warm.

Nutrition:

Calories: 311

Sodium: 1116mg

Dietary Fiber: 4.2g

Fat: 8.8g

Carbs: 38.1g

Protein: 22.8g.

121. Maple and Bacon Chicken

Preparation Time: 20 minutes

Cooking Time: 1 and ½ hours

Servings: 7

Ingredients

- 4 boneless and skinless chicken breast
- Salt as needed
- Fresh pepper
- 12 slices bacon, uncooked
- 1 cup maple syrup
- ½ cup melted butter
- 1 teaspoon liquid smoke

Directions:

1. Preheat your smoker to 250 degrees Fahrenheit
2. Season the chicken with pepper and salt
3. Wrap the breast with 3 bacon slices and cover the entire surface
4. Secure the bacon with toothpicks
5. Take a medium-sized bowl and stir in maple syrup, butter, liquid smoke, and mix well
6. Reserve 1/3rd of this mixture for later use
7. Submerge the chicken breast into the butter mix and coat them well
8. Place a pan in your smoker and transfer the chicken to your smoker
9. Smoker for 1 to 1 and a ½ hours
10. Brush the chicken with reserved butter and smoke for 30 minutes more until the internal temperature reaches 165 degrees Fahrenheit
11. Enjoy!

Nutrition:

Calories: 458

Fats: 20g

Carbs: 65g

Fiber: 1g

122. Paprika Chicken

Preparation Time: 20 minutes

Cooking Time: 2 - 4 hours

Servings: 7

Ingredients:

- 4-6 chicken breast
- 4 tablespoons olive oil
- 2 tablespoons smoked paprika
- ½ tablespoon salt
- ¼ teaspoon pepper
- 2 teaspoons garlic powder
- 2 teaspoons garlic salt
- 2 teaspoons pepper
- 1 teaspoon cayenne pepper
- 1 teaspoon rosemary

Directions:

1. Preheat your smoker to 220 degrees Fahrenheit using your favorite wood Pellets
2. Prepare your chicken breast according to your desired shapes and transfer to a greased baking dish
3. Take a medium bowl and add spices, stir well
4. Press the spice mix over chicken and transfer the chicken to smoker
5. Smoke for 1-1 and a ½ hours
6. Turn-over and cook for 30 minutes more
7. Once the internal temperature reaches 165 degrees Fahrenheit
8. Remove from the smoker and cover with foil
9. Allow it to rest for 15 minutes
10. Enjoy!

Nutrition:

Calories: 237

Fats: 6.1g

Carbs: 14g

Fiber: 3g

123. Sweet Sriracha BBQ Chicken

Preparation Time: 30 minutes

Cooking Time: 1 and ½-2 hours

Servings: 5

Ingredients:

- 1 cup sriracha
- ½ cup butter
- ½ cup molasses
- ½ cup ketchup
- ¼ cup firmly packed brown sugar
- 1 teaspoon salt
- 1 teaspoon fresh ground black pepper
- 1 whole chicken, cut into pieces
- ½ teaspoon fresh parsley leaves, chopped

Directions:

1. Preheat your smoker to 250 degrees Fahrenheit using cherry wood
2. Take a medium saucepan and place it over low heat, stir in butter, sriracha, ketchup, molasses, brown sugar, mustard, pepper and salt and keep stirring until the sugar and salt dissolves
3. Divide the sauce into two portions
4. Brush the chicken half with the sauce and reserve the remaining for serving
5. Make sure to keep the sauce for serving on the side, and keep the other portion for basting
6. Transfer chicken to your smoker rack and smoke for about 1 and a ½ to 2 hours until the internal temperature reaches 165 degrees Fahrenheit
7. Sprinkle chicken with parsley and serve with reserved BBQ sauce
8. Enjoy!

Nutrition:

Calories: 148

Fats: 0.6g

Carbs: 10g

Fiber: 1g

124. Smoked Chicken Drumsticks

Preparation Time: 10 minutes

Cooking Time: 2 hours 30 minutes

Servings: 5

Ingredients:

- 10 chicken drumsticks
- 2 tsp garlic powder
- 1 tsp salt
- 1 tsp onion powder
- 1/2 tsp ground black pepper
- ½ tsp cayenne pepper
- 1 tsp brown sugar
- 1/3 cup hot sauce
- 1 tsp paprika
- ½ tsp thyme

Directions:

1. In a large mixing bowl, combine the garlic powder, sugar, hot sauce, paprika, thyme, cayenne, salt, and ground pepper. Add the drumsticks and toss to combine.
2. Cover the bowl and refrigerate for 1 hour.
3. Remove the drumsticks from the marinade and let them sit for about 1 hour until they are at room temperature.
4. Arrange the drumsticks into a rack.
5. Start your pellet grill on smoke, leaving the lid open for 5 minutes for the fire to start.
6. Close the lid and preheat grill to 250°F, using hickory or apple hardwood pellets.
7. Place the rack on the grill and smoke drumsticks for 2 hours, 30 minutes, or until the drumsticks' internal temperature reaches 180°F.
8. Remove drumsticks from heat and let them rest for a few minutes.
9. Serve.

Nutrition:

Calories: 167

Total Fat: 5.4 g

Saturated Fat: 1.4 g

Cholesterol: 81 mg

Sodium: 946 mg

Total Carbohydrate: 2.6 g

Dietary Fiber: 0.5 g

Total Sugars: 1.3 g

Protein: 25.7 g

125. Chicken Cordon Bleu

Preparation Time: 15 minutes

Cooking Time: 40 minutes

Servings: 6

Ingredients:

- 6 boneless skinless chicken breasts
- 6 slices of ham
- 12 slices Swiss cheese
- 1 cup panko breadcrumbs
- ½ cup all-purpose flour
- 1 tsp ground black pepper or to taste
- 1 tsp salt or to taste
- 4 tbsp. grated parmesan cheese
- 2 tbsp. melted butter
- ½ tsp garlic powder

- ½ tsp thyme
- ¼ tsp parsley

Directions:

1. Butterfly the chicken breast with a paring knife. Place the chicken breast in between 2 plastic wraps and pound with a mallet until the chicken breasts are ¼ inch thick.
2. Place a plastic wrap on a flat surface. Place one fat chicken breast on it.
3. Place one slice of Swiss cheese on the chicken. Place one slice of ham over the cheese and place another cheese slice over the ham.
4. Roll the chicken breast tightly. Fold both ends of the roll tightly. Pin both ends of the rolled chicken breast with a toothpick.
5. Repeat step 3 and 4 for the remaining chicken breasts
6. In a mixing bowl, combine the all-purpose flour, ½ tsp salt, and ½ tsp pepper. Set aside.
7. In another mixing bowl, combine breadcrumbs, parmesan, butter, garlic, thyme, parsley, ½ tsp salt, and ½ tsp pepper. Set aside.
8. Break the eggs into another mixing bowl and whisk. Set aside.
9. Grease a baking sheet.
10. Bake one chicken breast roll. Dip into the flour mixture, brush with eggs and dip into breadcrumb mixture. The chicken breast should be coated.
11. Place it on the baking sheet.
12. Repeat steps 9 and 10 for the remaining breast rolls.
13. Preheat your grill to 375°F with the lid closed for 15 minutes.
14. Place the baking sheet on the grill and cook for about 40 minutes, or until the chicken is golden brown.
15. Remove the baking sheet from the grill and let the chicken rest for a few minutes.
16. Slice cordon bleu and serve.

Nutrition:

Calories: 560

Total Fat: 27.4 g

Saturated Fat: 15.9 g

Cholesterol: 156mg

Sodium: 1158 mg

Total Carbohydrate: 23.2 g

Dietary Fiber: 1.1 g

Total Sugars: 1.2 g

Protein: 54.3 g

126. Chicken Fajitas on a Wood Pellet Grill

Preparation Time: 0 minutes

Cooking Time: 20 minutes

Servings: 10

Ingredients:

- Chicken breast - 2 lbs., thin sliced
- Red bell pepper - 1 large
- Onion - 1 large
- Orange bell pepper - 1 large
- Seasoning mix
- Oil - 2 tbsps.
- Onion powder - ½ tbsp.
- Granulated garlic - ½ tbsp.
- Salt - 1 tbsp.

Directions:

1. Preheat the grill to 450 degrees.
2. Mix the seasonings and oil.
3. Add the chicken slices to the mix.
4. Line a large pan with a non-stick baking sheet.
5. Let the pan heat for 10 minutes.
6. Place the chicken, peppers, and other vegetables in the grill.
7. Grill for 10 minutes or until the chicken is cooked.
8. Remove it from the grill and serve with warm tortillas and vegetables.

Nutrition:

Carbohydrates: 5 g

Protein: 29 g

Fat: 6 g

Sodium: 360 mg

Cholesterol: 77 mg

127. Smoked Cornish Chicken in Wood Pellets

Preparation Time: 0 minutes

Cooking Time: 1 hour 10 minutes

Servings: 6

Ingredients:

- Cornish hens - 6
- Canola or avocado oil - 2-3 tbsps.
- Spice mix - 6 tbsps.

Directions:

1. Preheat your wood pellet grill to 275 degrees.
2. Rub the whole hen with oil and the spice mix. Use both of these ingredients liberally.

3. Place the breast area of the hen on the grill and smoke for 30 minutes.
4. Flip the hen, so the breast side is facing up. Increase the temperature to 400 degrees.
5. Cook until the temperature goes down to 165 degrees.
6. Pull it out and leave it for 10 minutes.
7. Serve warm with a side dish of your choice.

Nutrition:

Carbohydrates: 1 g

Protein: 57 g

Fat: 50 g

Sodium: 165 mg

Cholesterol: 337 mg

128. Pellet Smoked Chicken Burgers

Preparation time: 20 minutes

Cooking time: 1 hour and 10 minutes

Servings: 6

Ingredients:

- 2 lb. ground chicken breast
- 2/3 cup of finely chopped onions
- 1 Tbsps. of cilantro, finely chopped
- 2 Tbsp. fresh parsley, finely chopped
- 2 Tbsp. of olive oil
- 1/2 tsp of ground cumin
- 2 Tbsps. of lemon juice freshly squeezed
- 3/4 tsp of salt and red pepper to taste

Directions:

1. In a bowl add all ingredients; mix until combined well.
2. Form the mixture into 6 patties.
3. Start your pellet grill on SMOKE (oak or apple pellets) with the lid open until the fire is established. Set the heat to 350F and preheat, lid closed, for 10 to 15 minutes.
4. Smoke the chicken burgers for 45 - 50 minutes or until cooked through, turning every 15 minutes.
5. Your burgers are ready when internal temperature reaches 165 F
6. Serve hot.

Nutrition:

Calories: 221

Carbohydrates: 2.12g

Fat: 8.5g

Fiber: 0.4g

Protein:32.5g

129. Perfect Smoked Chicken Patties

Preparation time: 20 minutes

Cooking time: 50 minutes

Servings: 6

Ingredients:

- 2 lb. ground chicken breast
- 2/3 cup minced onion
- 1 Tbsps. cilantro (chopped)
- 2 Tbsp. fresh parsley, finely chopped
- 2 Tbsp. olive oil
- 1/8 tsp crushed red pepper flakes
- 1/2 tsp ground cumin
- 2 Tbsps. fresh lemon juice
- 3/4 tsp kosher salt
- 2 tsp paprika
- Hamburger buns for serving

Directions:

1. In a bowl combine all ingredients from the list.
2. Using your hands, mix well. Form mixture into 6 patties. Refrigerate until ready to grill (about 30 minutes).
3. Start your pellet grill on SMOKE with the lid open until the fire is established). Set the temperature to 350F and preheat for 10 to 15 minutes.
4. Arrange chicken patties on the grill rack and cook for 35 to 40 minutes turning once.
5. Serve hot with hamburger buns and your favorite condiments.

Nutrition:

Calories: 258

Carbohydrates: 2.5g

Fat: 9.4g

Fiber: 0.6g

Protein: 39g

130. Smoked Chicken Breasts with Dried Herbs

Preparation time: 15 minutes

Cooking time: 40 minutes

Servings: 4

Ingredients:

- 4 chicken breasts boneless
- 1/4 cup garlic-infused olive oil
- 2 clove garlic minced
- 1/4 tsp of dried sage
- 1/4 tsp of dried lavender
- 1/4 tsp of dried thyme
- 1/4 tsp of dried mint
- 1/2 Tbsps. dried crushed red pepper
- Kosher salt to taste

Directions:

1. Place the chicken breasts in a shallow plastic container.

2. In a bowl, combine all remaining ingredients, and pour the mixture over the chicken breast and refrigerate for one hour.
3. Remove the chicken breast from the sauce (reserve sauce) and pat dry on kitchen paper.
4. Start your pellet grill on SMOKE (hickory pellet) with the lid open until the fire is established). Set the temperature to 250F and preheat for 10 to 15 minutes.
5. Place chicken breasts on the smoker. Close pellet grill lid and cook for about 30 to 40 minutes or until chicken breasts reach 165F.
6. Serve hot with reserved marinade.

Nutrition:

Calories: 391

Carbohydrates: 0.7g

Fat: 3.21g

Fiber: 0.12g

Protein: 20.25g

131. Grilled Chicken with Pineapple

Preparation Time: 1 hour

Cooking time: 1 hr. 15 minutes

Servings: 6

Ingredients:

- 2 lbs. Chicken tenders
- 1 c. sweet chili sauce
- ¼ c. fresh pineapple juice
- ¼ c. honey

Directions:

1. Combine the honey, pineapple juice, and sweet chili sauce in a medium bowl. Whisk together thoroughly.
2. Put ¼ cup of the mixture to one side.
3. Coat the chicken in the sauce.
4. Place a lid over the bowl and leave it in the fridge for 30 minutes to marinate.
5. Heat the grill to high heat.
6. Separate the chicken from the marinade and grill for 5 minutes on each side.
7. Use the reserved sauce to brush over the chicken.
8. Continue to grill for a further 1 minute on each side.
9. Take the chicken off the grill and let it rest for 5 minutes before servings.

Nutrition:

Calories: 270

Fat: 2 g,

Carbohydrates: 25 g,

Protein: 33 g

132. Lemon Chicken Breast

Preparation time: 15 minutes

Cooking time: 30 minutes

Servings: 4

Ingredients:

- 6 chicken breasts, skinless and boneless
- ½ cup oil
- 1-3 fresh thyme sprigs
- 1 teaspoon ground black pepper
- 2 teaspoon salt
- 2 teaspoons honey
- 1 garlic clove, chopped
- 1 lemon, juiced and zested
- Lemon wedges

Directions:

1. Take a bowl and prepare the marinade by mixing thyme, pepper, salt, honey, garlic, lemon zest, and juice. Mix well until dissolved
2. Add oil and whisk
3. Clean breasts and pat them dry, place in a bag alongside marinade and let them sit in the fridge for 4 hours
4. Pre-heat your smoker to 400 degrees F
5. Drain chicken and smoke until the internal temperature reaches 165 degrees, for about 15 minutes
6. Serve and enjoy!

Nutrition:

Calories: 230

Fats: 7g

Carbohydrates: 1g

Fiber: 2g

133. Whole Orange Chicken

Preparation time: 15 minutes + marinate time

Cooking time: 45 minutes

Servings: 4

Ingredients:

- 1 whole chicken, 3-4 pounds' backbone removed
- 2 oranges
- ¼ cup oil
- 2 teaspoons Dijon mustard
- 1 orange, zest
- 2 tablespoons rosemary leaves, chopped
- 2 teaspoons salt

Directions:

1. Clean and pat your chicken dry
2. Take a bowl and mix in orange juice, oil, orange zest, salt, rosemary leaves, Dijon mustard and mix well
3. Marinade chicken for 2 hours or overnight
4. Pre-heat your grill to 350 degrees F

5. Transfer your chicken to the smoker and smoke for 30 minutes' skin down. Flip and smoke until the internal temperature reaches 175 degrees F in the thigh and 165 degrees F in the breast
6. Rest for 10 minutes and carve
7. Enjoy!

Nutrition:

Calories: 290

Fats: 15g

Carbohydrates: 20g

Fiber: 1g

134. Grilled Chicken Fajitas

Preparation time: 30 minutes

Cooking time: 15 minutes

Servings: 4

Ingredients:

- 1 lb. boneless skinless chicken breast
- 1/2 green bell pepper, julienned
- 8 tortillas, flour or corn
- 1/2 red bell pepper, julienned guacamole, sour cream, jalapeños
- 1 avocado, sliced
- Toppings: shredded cheese, salsa,
- 1/2 cup yellow onion, julienned

- 1 tsp kosher salt
- 1 tsp garlic powder
- 1 tsp dried oregano
- 1 tsp chili powder
- 1 tsp cumin
- 1 tsp paprika

Directions:

1. Preheat your pellet grill to 350°F.
2. Mix all rub ingredients in a small bowl.
3. Rinse chicken under water then coat the chicken with the rub mixture, ensuring to coat the chicken breast evenly and thoroughly.
4. Place chicken breast on the pellet grill and cook, flipping after about 5 minutes. Cook for about 10-12 minutes' total, or until no longer pink.
5. After chicken has cooked all the way through, remove from heat and allow to rest for 10 minutes.
6. Add onions, green pepper and red pepper to a stove pan in your kitchen while the chicken rests. Add a splash of olive oil (if desired) and sauté the veggies for about 8 minutes or until they begin to soften.
7. Slice the chicken into thin strips.
8. Serve immediately on corn or flour tortillas. Add onions and avocado slices.
9. Squeeze lime wedges over the steak and add any additional toppings as desired like shredded cheese, salsa, guacamole, sour cream, etc.
10. Chicken fajitas recipe is also well complimented by Spanish rice and beans (pinto, black, or refried).

11. If you want to save a little bit on cooking time, feel free to substitute chicken tenders for chicken breasts.

Nutrition:

Energy517 kcal

Calcium, Ca148 mg

Magnesium, Mg73 mg

Phosphorus, P462 mg

Iron, Fe4.59 mg

Potassium, K841 mg

Sodium, Na1325 mg

Zinc, Zn1.76 mg

135. Mediterranean Style Chicken Kebabs

Preparation time: 30 minutes

Cooking time: 15 minutes

Servings: 3-4

Ingredients:

- 1 1/2 lbs. boneless skinless chicken breasts
- 2 red bell peppers, cut into cubes
- 2 green bell peppers, cut into cubes
- 1 red onion, cut into cubes
- 10-12 bamboo skewers
- 3/4 cup extra virgin olive oil
- 1 lemon, juiced
- 5 garlic cloves, minced
- 2 tsp paprika
- 2 tsp thyme
- 3 tsp oregano
- 3 tsp kosher salt
- 3 tsp ground black pepper

Directions:

1. Cut chicken breasts into 1 inch cubes.
2. Cut bell peppers and onions into similar 1 inch slices.
3. Mix marinade ingredients in a bowl and whisk until combined. Place chicken in a sealable ziplock bag. Pour 1/2 of the marinade into the bag over your chicken.
4. Place bell peppers and onions in a separate ziplock bag.
5. Pour the other 1/2 of the marinade into the bag over your vegetables.
6. Let both bags marinade in refrigerator for 30 minutes.
7. Preheat pellet grill to 375°F.
8. Remove chicken and vegetables from your refrigerator.
9. Thread a combination of chicken, bell pepper, and onions onto your skewers. Make combinations according to your preference, but I usually do 4-5 pieces of chicken per skewer with pepper and onion in between.
10. Place threaded skewers onto grill grate. Cook for about 5-6 minutes per side, or until center is no longer pink.
11. Remove skewers from grill and allow to rest for at least 10 minutes. Serve and enjoy!
12. Depending on the type of skewers you buy, it might be helpful to soak them in water for about 10 minutes before threading them. I've had skewers that do great on the grill without soaking and some that char up if they aren't soaked.

13. Mediterranean skewers go very well with couscous, rice pilaf, orzo, hummus, pita, and other traditional Mediterranean sides.

Nutrition:

Calcium, Ca54 mg

Magnesium, Mg77 mg

Phosphorus, P425 mg

Iron, Fe2.31 mg

Potassium, K955 mg

Sodium, Na2177 mg

Zinc, Zn1.6 mg

136. BBQ Smoked Chicken Thighs

Preparation time: 15 minutes

Cooking time: 45 minutes

Servings: 4

Ingredients:

- 6 chicken thighs
- Olive oil, for basting
- 2 tbsps. paprika
- 1 tbsp. ground black pepper
- 1 tbsp. kosher salt
- 1 tbsp. garlic salt
- 1 tbsp. onion powder
- 1 tbsp. mustard powder
- 1/2 tbsp. cayenne pepper
- 1/2 cup light brown sugar
- Probe meat thermometer

Directions:

1. Preheat your pellet grill to 250F. Turn smoke setting on medium, if applicable.
2. Thoroughly combine rub ingredients in a bowl.
3. Apply a thin outer coat of olive oil to all of the chicken thighs.
4. Apply a generous amount of rub to each chicken thigh. Be sure to coat both sides and under the skin with rub.
5. Put your seasoned thighs on the pellet smoker. Smoke thighs until they reach an internal temperature of 165°F. Measure internal temperature with a probe thermometer. Cooking time will typically between 1 1/2 to 2 hours.
6. Remove from smoker. If you want to get extra crisp the outer skin, place thighs on a baking sheet and place in 400°F oven for 3 to 4 minutes.
7. Let thighs rest at room temperature for 20 minutes. Serve and enjoy!
8. Serve with your favorite BBQ sides. I recommend: coleslaw, potato salad, mac and cheese, cornbread, green beans, baked potato, fries, baked beans.

Nutrition:

Energy672 kcal

Protein48.93 g

Calcium, Ca49 mg

Magnesium, Mg61 mg

Phosphorus, P481 mg

Iron, Fe2.35 mg

Potassium, K691 mg

Sodium, Na2032 mg

Zinc, Zn3.94 mg

137. Buffalo Chicken Burgers

Preparation time: 15 minutes

Cooking time: 20 minutes

Servings: 4

Ingredients:

- 1 lb. ground chicken breast
- 4 slices mozzarella cheese
- 4 tbsp. bread crumbs
- Ranch dressing (or blue cheese)
- 2 tbsps. parmesan cheese
- More wing sauce, to drizzle
- 2 tbsps. buffalo wing sauce
- 4 wheat buns
- 1 tsp kosher salt
- Lettuce leaves
- 1 tsp ground black pepper
- Fresh sliced tomato

Directions:

1. Preheat pellet grill to 350°F.
2. In a bowl, combine ground chicken, bread crumbs, salt, pepper, parmesan cheese, and wing sauce. Mix until combined.
3. Form burger mixture into 4 patties.
4. Place patties on pellet grill and cook for about 10 minutes, flipping halfway through. Place mozzarella cheese slices on top of the burgers for the last minute or so to allow for them to melt.
5. Remove from grill once chicken patties have been cooked all the way through.
6. Allow to rest for at least 10 minutes. Then, place each patty on the bottom half of a bun. Drizzle ranch dressing and buffalo wing sauce. Top with lettuce and fresh sliced tomato. Serve and enjoy!
7. For a simpler variation, you can substitute burger patty for a thin chicken breast. Grill chicken breast according to instructions then drizzle with ranch and wing sauce. Top with tomato and lettuce.
8. If you are worried about not knowing exactly when your chicken patties are cooked all the way through, use a probe thermometer to measure the center of the burger's temperature. They are ready to come off when your patty has reached a minimum internal temperature of 165°F.
9. Serve with fries, carrots, or celery, and extra ranch dressing for dipping.

138. Grilled Cheesy Chicken Quesadillas

Preparation time: 15 minutes

Cooking time: 15 minutes

Servings: 4

Ingredients:

- 1 1/2 lb. boneless skinless chicken breast
- 1 tsp chili powder
- 1 tsp kosher salt
- 12 corn tortillas, 6-8-inch diameter
- 1 tsp dried oregano
- 1 cup Monterey jack cheese
- 1 tsp cumin
- Vegetable oil, to brush
- 1 tsp garlic powder

Directions:

1. Combine kosher salt, oregano, cumin, garlic powder, and chili powder in a small bowl.
2. Rub mixture on chicken breast and let rest for about 20 minutes.
3. Preheat your pellet grill to 350°F.
4. Place chicken breast on grill and cook for about 10 minutes, flipping after 5 minutes. Cook until chicken is no longer pink and thoroughly cooked.
5. Allow to rest for 10 minutes, then slice into small slices.
6. Brush the top and bottom of each tortilla with a light amount of vegetable oil.
7. Top 6 of the tortillas with cheese and chicken slices. Place the other 6 tortillas on top.
8. Grill for 8 minutes, or until the bottom side is lightly browned and crispy.
9. Carefully flip using a wide spatula and cook the other side until it becomes lightly browned and crispy. The second side typically takes about 6 to 8 minutes.
10. Use a knife or pizza cutter to cut each quesadilla into half or quarter wedges.
11. Serve and enjoy!
12. Serve with sour cream, salsa, pico de gallo, guacamole, and chile con queso.
13. If you find it easier, feel free to cook assembled quesadillas on a large skillet.
14. Pellet Flavor Recommendations: Hickory, Mesquite

139. Pellet Grill Beer Can Chicken

Preparation time: 10 minutes

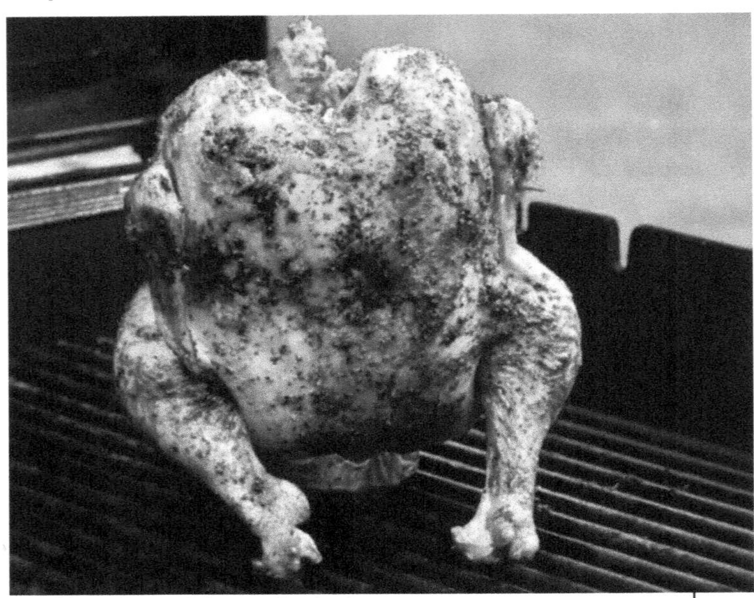

Cooking time: 2 hours 5 minutes

Servings: 4-6

Ingredients:

- 1 whole chicken (3-5 lbs.)
- 1 tbsp. ground black pepper
- 2 tbsps. paprika
- 2 tsp dried thyme
- 2 tbsps. kosher salt
- 2 tsp dried oregano
- 2 tbsps. onion powder
- 2 tsp garlic powder
- 1 tbsp. cayenne pepper
- Vegetable oil, to lightly coat chicken
- 1 tbsp. ground cumin
- 1 can beer (12 oz.)

Directions:

1. Preheat pellet grill to 350°F.
2. Lightly coat chicken with a thin layer of vegetable oil.
3. Mix all other seasoning ingredients in a small bowl.
4. Rub the chicken down thoroughly with seasoning mixture, ensuring to season the cavity.
5. Open beer can and pour out (or drink) 1/4 of the beer. Place opened beer can in the cavity of the chicken, with the very bottom of the can sticking out.
6. Place chicken on a sheet tray with raised edges. You can also utilize a beer can chicken roaster rack instead of a sheet tray. Place sheet tray with chicken onto the center of the cooking grate and cook for approximately 2 hours.
7. The chicken is done once it reaches an internal temperature of 165°F in the centermost point of the breast, regardless of how long it has been on the grill.
8. Allow to rest for 10 minutes. Carve, serve, and enjoy!
9. Beer can chicken roaster racks are widely available online and fairly cheap. They can help out a great deal with this recipe to balance your chicken and ensure juices are captured.
10. Lagers are the most popular type of beer for beer can chicken. You want something that's not too hoppy and not too bitter. Fruit forward sours also work well because the acidity interacts nicely with grilled chicken.

140. Smoke-grilled Chicken breast

Preparation time: 15 minutes

Cooking time: 25 minutes

Servings: 4-6

Ingredients:

- 4 large chicken breasts (boneless & skinless)
- 2 tablespoons brown sugar
- 2 tablespoons paprika
- 2 tablespoons kosher salt
- 2 tablespoons garlic powder
- 2 tablespoons onion powder
- 2 tablespoons turbinado sugar
- 1 tablespoon olive oil
- 1 teaspoon black pepper
- 1 teaspoon cayenne pepper
- 1 teaspoon celery seed

Directions:

1. In a bowl, mix the dry ingredients.
2. Pat dry the boneless skinless breast before drizzling it with olive oil on both sides. Use a little amount of the oil in this task.
3. Generously sprinkle the bowl mixture on the breasts and refrigerate for about 30 minutes.
4. For 5 minutes, heat your smoker on smoke. Increase the smoker heat to 350F, closing down the lid. (do this for 15 minutes)
5. Place the chicken on the grill on one of its spiced side after seasoning. Close the lid and let it cook for about 13 minutes.
6. Flip the chicken to the other side, cooking it for 12 minutes. Alternatively, cook till 165 to 170 F when considering heat.
7. Line your slicing board with foil then place the chicken.
8. Let it cool for 5 minutes before slicing the bird.
9. Enjoy!

Nutrition:

Calories- 327

Fat- 9g

Carbs- 23g

Protein- 40g

Fiber- 4g

Sodium- 3274mg

Cholesterol- 102mg

Sugar- 13g

141. Grilled whole chicken

Preparation time: 10 minutes

Cooking time: 1 hour 20 minutes

Servings: 6

Ingredients:

- 5 lbs. whole chicken
- Chicken rub (of your choice)
- ½ cup oil

Directions:

1. Preheat your smoker on smoke for 5 minutes. (keep lid open)
2. Use baker's twine to tie the chicken legs together. Drizzle the chicken with oil before coating with chicken rub. With the breast side facing up, place the chicken on the grill.
3. Keep the grill closed while your chicken cooks for 70 minutes. Use a thermometer to check the internal temperature. Open when the temperature clocks 165F even before the entire 70 minutes' elapses.
4. Ensure the chicken's internal temperature is about 165F. If not, let it continue to cook for a little while.
5. Omit from the grill and let it sit for 15 minutes before cutting.
6. Enjoy!

Nutrition:

Calories- 935

Fat- 53g

Sat fat- 15g

Carbs- 0g

Protein- 107g

Cholesterol- 346mg

Sugar- 0g

142. Smoke-grilled whole roaster chicken

Preparation time: 10 minutes

Cooking time: 1 hour 50 minutes

Servings: 5

Ingredients:

- 4lb whole chicken
- ¼ cup chicken rub
- 4 cloves garlic (smashed)
- 1/2 red onion (chopped)
- 1/2 lemon (sliced in half)

Chicken rub ingredients:

- 1/2 cup kosher salt
- 1 cup brown sugar
- 4 tablespoons smoked paprika
- 2 tablespoons black pepper
- 1/2 tablespoon cumin
- 1/2 tablespoon garlic powder
- 1/2 tablespoon onion powder
- 1 teaspoon cayenne pepper

Directions:

1. Mix all the chicken rub ingredients in a bowl and set aside.
2. Initial step is preheating your smoker to 225F.
3. Pat dry the chicken and entirely cover it with the chicken rub.
4. Stuff the chicken's cavity with smashed garlic cloves, chopped onion and lemon.
5. Tie the chicken legs and wings.
6. Place the chicken on the smoker for an hour. Thereafter, increase heat to 350F and remove when the chicken's internal temperature is 165F. (might take another hour)
7. Let it cool for about 10 minutes before slicing.
8. Note: You can store the chicken rub in an airtight container for up to a year. You can downsize the amount to a ratio of 1:1 of brown sugar to your flavors of preference.

Nutrition:

Calories- 840

Fat- 27.9g

Sat fat- 7.6g

Carbohydrates- 37.2g

Protein- 106.8g

Fiber- 3.5g

Sodium- 11643mg

Cholesterol- 323mg

Calcium- 124mg

Iron- 7mg

Potassium- 1152mg

143. Brined, glazed and smoked chicken

Preparation time: 10 minutes

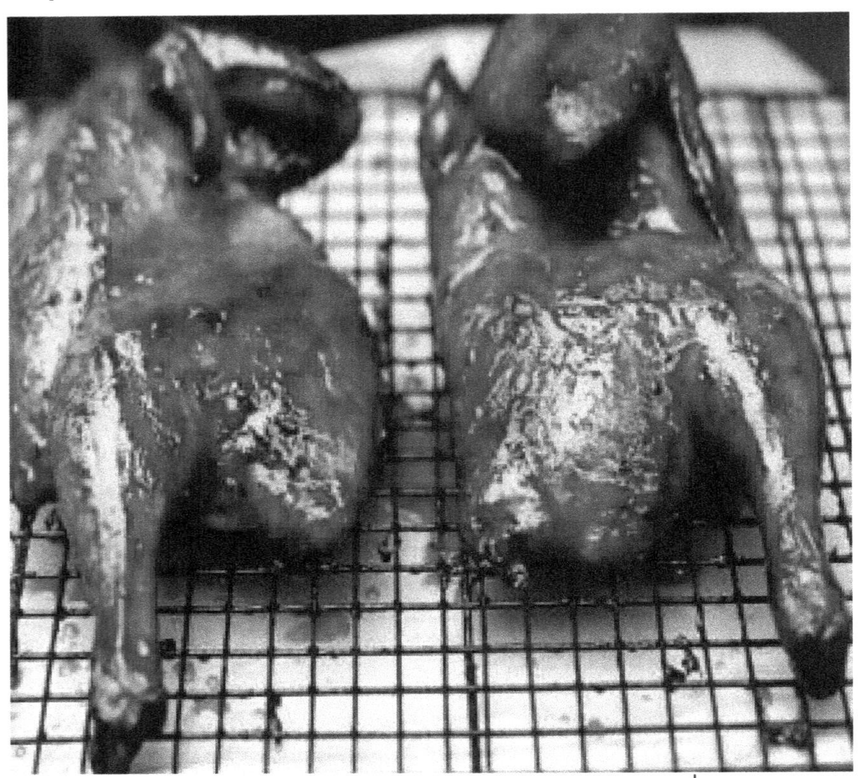

Cooking time: 2 hours

Servings: 5

Ingredients:

- 5lb roaster chicken (halves)
- 1 cup glaze
- 2 tablespoons pepper
- 2 tablespoons salt

Glaze ingredients:

- 2 cups BBQ sauce (of your choice)
- 2/3 cup honey/ agave nectar
- 2 tablespoons Dijon mustard

Directions:

1. Rinse the chicken halves and pat them dry. Season the chicken with pepper and salt and refrigerate for 6 hours.
2. Preheat your smoker to 225F.
3. Take the chicken out of the fridge and place on the smoker. Let it cook till it the bird clocks an internal temperature of 150F. Once it reads this, entirely brush the chicken with the glaze on all sides. Let it continue to cook.
4. Once internal temperature clocks 165F, omit the chicken from the smoker and brush it with the glaze again. Cover it with a foil sheet, letting it sit for 15 minutes.
5. Enjoy!

Nutrition:

Calories- 983

Fat- 14.4g

Saturated fat- 3.9g

Protein- 132.1g

Carbohydrates- 75.5g

Fiber- 1.6g

Sodium- 4269mg

Cholesterol- 349mg

144. Smoked chicken

Preparation time: 2 - 8 hours

Cooking time: 20 minutes

Servings: 8

Ingredients:

- 6 lbs. whole chicken
- 8 cups cold water (divided)
- 2/3 cup Chicken rub
- 1/4 cup + 2 tablespoons Kosher salt

Directions:

1. In a saucepan, bring 1 cup of water to boil.
2. Add the whole amount of kosher salt into the saucepan and stir. Add the residing cups of water (7 cups of water) and stir.
3. In a zip top bag, add in the chicken. Do away with the giblets first.
4. Pour in the salt water into the same bag and seal.
5. Place the bag in a bowl and refrigerate for 2 hours minimum. (8 hours' maximum)
6. Omit the chicken from the fridge once the time elapses and discard the water. Rinse the chicken and pat dry. Generously sprinkle and rub the chicken with the chicken rub. You can remove the skin on the breast to add more chicken rub.
7. Set the chicken aside.
8. Switch on your smoker on 'smoke' on low heat setting. Place the chicken on the grill, inserting the meat thermometer.
9. Increasing heat to 225F, cooking till the internal temperature reads 165F.
10. Omit the bird from the smoker and cover with a foil.
11. Let it sit for 20 minutes then slice.

Nutrition:

Calories- 211

Fat- 11g

Cholesterol- 76mg

Carbohydrates- 2g

Protein- 24g

Fiber- 0g

Sugar- 2g

Cholesterol- 76mg

145. Grilled chicken wings

Preparation time: 10 minutes

Cooking time: 45 minutes

Servings: 6

Ingredients:

- 6 pounds' chicken wings
- 4 tablespoons BBQ rub
- 1/3 cup oil

BBQ rub ingredients

- 1/3 cup brown sugar
- 1 teaspoon salt
- 1 teaspoon paprika
- 1 teaspoon onion salt
- 1 teaspoon onion powder
- 1/2 teaspoon garlic powder
- 1/4 teaspoon cumin
- 1/4 teaspoon cinnamon
- 1/4 teaspoon pepper
- 1/4 teaspoon cayenne

Directions:

1. In a bowl, combine your seasoning and oil.
2. Add in the chicken wings in the bowl and coat well.
3. Preheat your smoker to 350F for just 15 minutes.
4. Put the wings on the grill grate and space them well. Cook the wings for about 45 minutes with the lid closed. (till well cooked with crisp skin)
5. Omit the wings from the grill, tossing with BBQ sauce of your choice.

Nutrition:

Calories- 490

Sat fat- 8g

Protein- 33g

Sodium- 134mg

Cholesterol- 141mg

146. Bourbon smoke-grilled chicken wings

Preparation time: 15 minutes

Cooking time: 2 hours 45 minutes

Servings: 6

Ingredients:

- 4 lbs. chicken wings
- Chicken rub
- 2 tablespoons vegetable oil

Bourbon sauce ingredients

- 2 cups ketchup
- 1/2 cup bourbon
- 1/2 cup brown sugar
- 1/3 cup apple cider vinegar
- 1/4 cup Worcestershire sauce
- 1/4 cup tomato paste
- 5 cloves garlic (minced)
- 1/2 medium yellow onion (minced)
- 2 tablespoons liquid smoke
- 1/2 tablespoon kosher salt
- 1/2 teaspoon cayenne pepper
- 1/2 teaspoon black pepper

Directions:

1. In a saucepan, heat olive oil over medium heat. Add the minced garlic and minced yellow onion to the saucepan, cooking for 5 minutes. Afterwards, add in the bourbon and cook for almost 3 minutes.
2. Add in the tomato sauce and combine well. Include the other unused ingredients and combine.
3. Bring to boil by increasing heat to medium high before lowering to low. Let it simmer for about 20 minutes.
4. Sieve the sauce if you prefer having a smoother sauce.
5. Pat dry the chicken wings before tossing with oil in a bowl. Thereafter, coat with chicken rub.
6. Switch on your smoker on 'smoke' for 5 minutes and keep the lid open.
7. Increase the heat by setting your smoker to 250F.
8. Place the chicken wings onto the grill grate and close the lid. Let the wings cook for 2 hours 30 minutes or till they attain an internal temperature of 165F.
9. Set your smoker on 'high', basting the wings with the bourbon sauce on each side. Cook one side for 5 minutes before

flipping and cooking the other side for a further 5 minutes.
10. Omit from the smoker and let it sit for 10 minutes.

Nutrition:

Calories- 811

Fat- 27.3g

Saturated fat- 7.1g

Carbohydrates- 38g

Protein- 89.7g

Fiber- 1g

Sugars- 33.8g

Sodium- 1859mg

Cholesterol- 269mg

Potassium- 1206mg

Calcium- 83mg

Iron- 5mg

147. Buffalo Chicken drumsticks

Preparation time: 5 minutes

Cooking time: 1 hours 5 minutes

Servings: 6

Ingredients:

- 12 chicken legs
- 1 cup buffalo sauce
- 1/2 teaspoon kosher salt

Directions:

1. Preheat your grill to 325F.
2. Toss the drumsticks with buffalo seasoning and salt in a bowl.
3. Place the drumsticks on the grill and cook for 40 minutes. (flip them twice at most) Thereafter, set at high to cook for 10 minutes. Brush the drumsticks with buffalo sauce and cook for a further 10 minutes.
4. Ensure the internal temperature reaches 165F.
5. Omit from the grill.

Nutrition:

Calories- 956

Fat- 47g

Saturated fat- 13g

Carbohydrates- 1g

Protein- 124g

Sodium- 1750mg

148. Smoked Texas style chicken legs

Preparation time: 15 minutes

Cooking time: 1 hour 15 minutes

Servings: 6

Ingredients:

- 8 chicken legs
- 1 cup Texas spicy BBQ sauce
- Pepper
- Salt

Directions:

1. Use a paper towel to pat dry the chicken drumsticks.
2. Season with pepper and salt.
3. Preheat your smoker to 180F for 15 minutes.
4. Place the drumsticks/ chicken legs on the grill. With the chicken legs equally spaced, smoke for 30 minutes.
5. Increase heat to 350F, cooking for a further 30 minutes.
6. Brush the drumsticks with the sauce before cooking for 15-30 minutes or till internal temperature reads 165F.

Nutrition:

Calories- 433

Total fat- 14.6

Saturated fat- 4g

Carbohydrates- 15.2g

Protein- 56.3g

Cholesterol- 173mg

Sodium- 731mg

Sugars- 10.9g

Dietary fiber- 0.3g

149. Sweet & Spicy Chicken Thighs

Preparation Time: 15 minutes

Cooking Time: 15 minutes

Servings: 4

Ingredients:

- 2 garlic cloves, minced
- ¼ cup honey
- 2 tablespoons soy sauce
- ¼ teaspoon red pepper flakes, crushed
- 4 (5-ounce) skinless, boneless chicken thighs
- 2 tablespoons olive oil
- 2 teaspoons sweet rub
- ¼ teaspoon red chili powder
- Ground black pepper, as required

Method:

1. Preheat the Z Grills Wood Pellet Grill & Smoker on grill setting to 400 degrees F.

2. In a small bowl, add garlic, honey, soy sauce and red pepper flakes and with a wire whisk, beat until well combined.
3. Coat chicken thighs with oil and season with sweet rub, chili powder and black pepper generously.
4. Arrange the chicken drumsticks onto the grill and cook for about 15 minutes per
5. In the last 4-5 minutes of cooking, coat drumsticks with garlic mixture.
6. Serve immediately.

Nutrition:

Calories 309

Total Fat 12.1 g

Saturated Fat 2.9 g

Cholesterol 82 mg

Sodium 504 mg

Total Carbs 18.7 g

Fiber 0.2 g

Sugar 17.6 g

Protein 32.3 g

150. Bacon Wrapped Chicken Breasts

Preparation Time: 0 minute

Cooking Time: 3 hours

Servings: 6

Ingredients:

For Brine:

- ¼ cup brown sugar
- ¼ cup kosher salt
- 4 cups water
  For Chicken:
- 6 skinless, boneless chicken breasts
- ¼ cup chicken rub
- 18 bacon slices
- 1½ cups BBQ sauce

Directions:

1. For brine: in a large pitcher, dissolve sugar and salt in water.
2. Place the chicken breasts in brine and refrigerate for about 2 hours, flipping once in the middle way.
3. Preheat the Z Grills Wood Pellet Grill & Smoker on grill setting to 230 degrees F.
4. Remove chicken breasts from brine and rinse under cold running water.
5. Season chicken breasts with rub generously.
6. Arrange 3 bacon strips of bacon onto a cutting board, against each other.
7. Place 1 chicken breast across the bacon, leaving enough bacon on the left side to wrap it over just a little.
8. Wrap the bacon strips around chicken breast and secure with toothpicks.
9. Repeat with remaining breasts and bacon slices.
10. Arrange the chicken breasts into pellet grill and cook for about 2½ hours.
11. Coat the breasts with BBQ sauce and cook for about 30 minutes more.
12. Serve immediately.

Nutrition:

Calories 481

Total Fat 12.3 g

Saturated Fat 4.2 g

Cholesterol 41 mg

Sodium 3000 mg

Total Carbs 32 g

Fiber 0.4g

Sugar 22.2 g

Protein 55.9 g

151. Glazed Chicken Wings

Preparation Time: 15 minutes

Cooking Time: 2 hours

Servings: 6

Ingredients:

- 2 pounds' chicken wings
- 2 garlic cloves, crushed
- 3 tablespoons hoisin sauce
- 2 tablespoons soy sauce
- 1 teaspoon dark sesame oil
- 1 tablespoon honey
- ½ teaspoon ginger powder
- 1 tablespoon sesame seeds, toasted lightly

Directions:

1. Preheat the Wood Pellet Grill & Smoker on grill setting to 225 degrees F.
2. Arrange the wings onto the lower rack of grill and cook for about 1½ hours.
3. Meanwhile, in a large bowl, mix together remaining all ingredients.
4. Remove wings from grill and place in the bowl of garlic mixture.
5. Coat wings with garlic mixture generously.

6. Now, set the grill to 375 degrees F.
7. Arrange the coated wings onto a foil-lined baking sheet and sprinkle with sesame seeds.
8. Place the pan onto the lower rack of pellet grill and cook for about 25-30 minutes.
9. Serve immediately.

Nutrition:

Calories 336

Total Fat 13 g

Saturated Fat 3.3 g

Cholesterol 135 mg

Sodium 560 mg

Total Carbs 7.6 g

Fiber 0.5 g

Sugar 5.2 g

Protein 44.7 g

152. Chicken Casserole

Preparation Time: 15 minutes

Cooking Time: 55 minutes

Servings: 8

Ingredients:

- 2 (15-ounce) cans cream of chicken soup
- 2 cups milk
- 2 tablespoons unsalted butter
- ¼ cup all-purpose flour
- 1 pound skinless, boneless chicken thighs, chopped
- ½ cup hatch chiles, chopped
- 2 medium onions, chopped
- 1 tablespoon fresh thyme, chopped
- Salt and ground black pepper, as required
- 1 cup cooked bacon, chopped
- 1 cup tater tots

Directions:

1. Preheat the Wood Pellet Grill & Smoker on grill setting to 400 degrees F.
2. In a large bowl, mix together chicken soup and milk.
3. In a skillet, melt butter over medium heat.
4. Slowly, add flour and cook for about 1-2 minutes or until smooth, stirring continuously.
5. Slowly, add soup mixture, beating continuously until smooth.
6. Cook until mixture starts to thicken, stirring continuously.
7. Stir in remaining ingredients except bacon and simmer for about 10-15 minutes.
8. Stir in bacon and transfer mixture into a 2½-quart casserole dish.
9. Place tater tots on top of casserole evenly.
10. Arrange the pan onto the grill and cook for about 30-35 minutes.
11. Serve hot.

Nutrition:

Calories 440

Total Fat 25.8 g

Saturated Fat 9.3 g

Cholesterol 86 mg

Sodium 1565 mg

Total Carbs 22.2 g

Fiber 1.5 g

Sugar 4.6 g

Protein 28.9 g

153. Delicious Grilled BBQ Chicken Breasts

Preparation time: 15 minutes

Cooking time: 30 minutes

Servings: 6

Ingredients:

- 4 chicken breasts
- 1/4 cup Olive oil
- 2 clove garlic minced
- 1 cup BBQ sauce
- 1/2 cup BBQ hot sauce
- 2 tbsp. Worcestershire sauce

Directions:

1. In a deep container place the chicken breasts.
2. In a separate bowl, combine olive oil, garlic, BBQ sauces and Worcestershire sauce.
3. Cover the chicken breasts evenly with BBQ sauce.
4. Start pellet grill on, lid open, until the fire is established (4-5 minutes). Increase the temperature to 350F and allow to pre-heat, lid closed, for 10 - 15 minutes.
5. Remove the chicken breast from the sauce (reserve sauce) and place chicken breasts direct on the hot grill and cook 15 - 20 minutes, depending on breast size (or to taste).
6. Ten minutes before the chicken is done, sprinkle on your BBQ sauce mixture.
7. Serve hot.

Nutrition:

Calories 390,19

Total Fat 13,71g

Saturated Fat 2,2g

Cholesterol 103,67mg

Sodium 1423,04mg

Potassium 705,01mg

Total Carbohydrates 27,92g

Fiber 1,2g

Sugar 20,98g

Protein 35,34g

154. Grilled Chicken Breast with Coriander-Lime Marinade

Preparation time: 4 – 5 hours

Cooking time: 20 minutes

Servings: 6

Ingredients:

- 4 chicken fillets
- 1/2 cup chopped coriander
- 1/2 cup lime juice (3-4 limes)
- 1 cup of honey
- 4 cloves of garlic minced
- 2 tbsps. olive oil
- Salt and pepper

Directions:

1. Place your chicken breast in a "zip" freezer bag.
2. In a bowl, combine coriander, lime juice, honey, garlic, olive oil and salt and pepper.
3. Pour the coriander-lime mixture in a bag with chicken.
4. Marinate in refrigerator for 4 - 5 hours.
5. Remove the chicken from the bag and pat dry on paper towel.
6. Start pellet grill on, lid open, until the fire is established (4-5 minutes). Increase the temperature to 350F and allow to pre-heat, lid closed, for 10 - 15 minutes.
7. Arrange chicken breasts on the hot grill and cook 10 - 20 minutes, depending on breast size.
8. Five minutes before ready, splash the marinade over the chicken.
9. Serve hot.

Nutrition:

Calories 440,85

Total Fat 16,22g

Saturated Fat 1,94g

Cholesterol 100,69mg

Sodium 199,48mg

Potassium 1171,87mg

Total Carbohydrates 49,22g

Fiber 18,15g

Sugar 23,56g

Protein 39g

155. Grilled Chicken Breast with Lemon and Honey Rub

Preparation time: 5 minutes

Cooking time: 55 minutes

Servings: 5

Ingredients:

- 4 chicken breasts
- 3 tbsps. of fresh butter
- 1/2 cup chicken broth
- Juice of 1 lemon
- 1 tbsp. of honey
- 1 clove of crushed garlic
- Fresh rosemary chopped to taste
- Salt and pepper

Directions:

1. In a pan melt the butter and sauté the chicken breasts for 2-3 minutes on each side until they get good color.
2. Remove from heat and let rest for 5 -10 minutes.
3. In a small bowl, stir the broth, lemon juice, honey, garlic, rosemary and salt, and pepper.
4. Rub the chicken breast generously with lemon/honey mixture.
5. Start pellet grill on, lid open, until the fire is established (4-5 minutes). Increase the temperature to 350F and allow to pre-heat, lid closed, for 10 - 15 minutes.
6. Place chicken breasts on the hot grill and cook 10 – 20 minutes, depending on breast size.
7. Serve hot.

Nutrition:

Calories 293,82

Total Fat 11,94g

Saturated Fat 5,49g

Cholesterol 139,15mg

Sodium 293,66mg

Potassium 725,83mg

Total Carbohydrates 3,76g

Fiber 0,02g

Sugar 3,53g

Protein 40,69g

156. Grilled Chicken Breasts with Herbed Coffee Sauce

Preparation time: 2 hours

Cooking time: 20 minutes

Servings: 4

Ingredients:

- 4 boneless skinless chicken breast halves
- 2 tbsps. melted butter or olive oil
- 1/4 cup packed dark brown sugar
- 1/2 cup chicken broth
- 4 slices lemon (1/4 inch thick)
- 1 tsp black peppercorns
- 1 tsp mustard seeds
- 1 tsp coriander seeds
- 3/4 cup strong brewed coffee
- Salt to taste

Directions:

1. Brush your chicken breast with oil and sprinkle with salt.
2. In a large container combine all remaining ingredients and submerge your chicken breast.
3. Cover and refrigerate for 2 hours.
4. Start pellet grill on, lid open, until the fire is established (4-5 minutes). Increase the temperature to 350F and allow to pre-heat, lid closed, for 10 - 15 minutes.
5. Grill chicken, without turning, 10 minutes for boneless chicken and 10 to 15 minutes for bone-in (or to taste).
6. Serve hot.

Nutrition:

Calories 277,11

Total Fat 10,38g

Saturated Fat 1,89g

Cholesterol 73,1mg

Sodium 161,45mg

Potassium 369,8mg

Total Carbohydrates 18,7g

Fiber 0,83g

Sugar 14,92g

Protein 27,77g

157. Grilled Chicken Thighs with Red Pepper Marinade

Preparation time: 4 hours

Cooking time: 30 minutes

Servings: 6

Ingredients:

2 lbs. chicken thighs

1/2 cup chicken broth

1 tsp red pepper flakes

1 tsp sweet paprika

1 tsp freshly ground black pepper

1 tsp dried oregano

1 tsp curry powder

1 tbsp. garlic powder

2 tbsps. olive oil

Directions:

1. Place the chicken thighs in a large flat dish so they are in a single layer.
2. In a bowl, combine broth, red pepper flakes, paprika, black pepper, oregano, curry and garlic powder and olive oil.
3. Pour the mixture over chicken thighs.
4. Cover and refrigerate for 4 hours.
5. Start pellet grill on, lid open, until the fire is established (4-5 minutes). Increase the temperature to 450F and allow to pre-heat, lid closed, for 10 - 15 minutes.
6. Remove chicken tights from marinade and pat dry.
7. Place marinated chicken thighs on the grill grate, skin side down. Cook for 10 minutes, flip, and cook another 10 minutes.
8. Serve hot.

Nutrition:

Calories 230,18

Total Fat 10,64g

Saturated Fat 5,49g

Cholesterol 125,5mg

Sodium 192,51mg

Potassium 398,7mg

Total Carbohydrates 1,84g

Fiber 0,45g

Sugar 0,12g

Protein 30,48g

158. Grilled Chicken Tights in Spicy Marinade

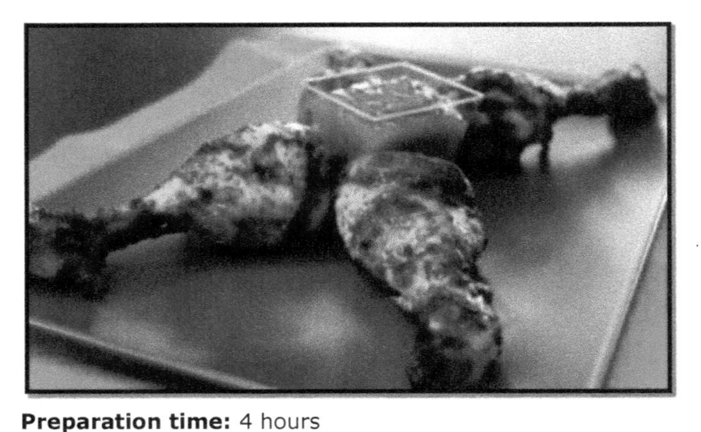

Preparation time: 4 hours

Cooking time: 30 minutes

Servings: 6

Ingredients:

- 6 chicken tights
- 2 cloves garlic minced
- 1/3 cup balsamic vinegar
- 1/3 cup olive oil
- 2 tbsps. mustard
- Salt and ground pepper
- 1 tbsp. oregano
- 1 tsp coriander
- 1 tbsp. BBQ dry spice mix

Directions:

1. Place the chicken tights in a shallow dish in a single layer.
2. In a bowl, combine the garlic, balsamic vinegar, oil, mustard, salt and pepper, oregano coriander and BBQ dry spice mix.
3. Pour the mixture over chicken thighs evenly.
4. Marinate in refrigerator for 4 hours.
5. Start pellet grill on, lid open, until the fire is established (4-5 minutes). Increase the temperature to 350F and allow to pre-heat, lid closed, for 10 - 15 minutes.
6. Remove the chicken tights from marinade and par dry on kitchen towel.
7. Place marinated chicken thighs on the grill grate, skin side down. Cook for 10 minutes, flip, and cook another 10 minutes.
8. Serve hot.

Nutrition:

Calories 438,7

Total Fat 32,54g

Saturated Fat 7,38g

Cholesterol 138,61mg

Sodium 195,02mg

Potassium 371,1mg

Total Carbohydrates 3,7g

Fiber 0,64g

Sugar 2,2g

Protein 30,78g

159. Grilled Light Turkey Burgers

Preparation time: 10 minutes

Cooking time: 40 minutes

Servings: 6

- 2 lbs. ground turkey
- 1 small red bell pepper
- 1 onion finely chopped
- 1/2 bunch fresh chopped parsley
- 1 large egg
- Salt and pepper to taste
- 1/2 tsp dry thyme
- 1/2 tsp dry oregano

Directions:

1. Place the ground turkey meat along with all remaining ingredients in a deep ball.
2. Using your hands, knead the mixture well.
3. Wet your hands with water and make patties.
4. Start pellet grill on, lid open, until the fire is established (4-5 minutes). Increase the temperature to 350F and allow to pre-heat, lid closed, for 10 - 15 minutes.
5. Place the turkey burgers on the grill and cook for 5 - 7 minutes, covered, until nice grill marks form. Flip and continue to cook, covered, for 3-5 minutes more.
6. The internal temperature for food safety for ground turkey as recommended by the USDA is 165°F.
7. Serve hot.

Nutrition:

Calories 252,06

Total Fat 12,48g

Saturated Fat 3,34g

Cholesterol 135,33mg

Sodium 101,51mg

Potassium 454,13mg

Total Carbohydrates 3,59g

Fiber 0,96g

Sugar 1,92g

Protein 31,26g

160. Grilled Turmeric Chicken Breast

Preparation time: 5 minutes

Cooking time: 45 minutes

Servings: 4

- 4 chicken breasts, boneless, skinless
- 4 cloves garlic, finely diced
- 1/2 cup chicken fat
- 1 tsp turmeric powder, or to taste
- Table salt to taste

Directions:

1. Cut the chicken lengthwise into pieces.
2. Combine the chicken fat, turmeric, diced garlic and rub evenly the chicken breast.
3. Start pellet grill on, lid open, until the fire is established (4-5 minutes). Increase the temperature to 350F and allow to pre-heat, lid closed, for 10 - 15 minutes.
4. Place chicken breasts on the hot grill and cook 10 - 15 minutes, depending on breast size.
5. Serve hot.

Nutrition:

Calories 477,14

Total Fat 31,7g

Saturated Fat 8,98g

Cholesterol 172,82mg

Sodium 274,27mg

Potassium 885,23mg

Total Carbohydrates 0,99g

Fiber 0,06g

Sugar 0,03g

Protein 50,29g

161. Festive Whole Chicken

Preparation Time: 15 minutes

Cooking Time: 5 hours

Servings: 6

Ingredients:

- ¾ cup dark brown sugar
- ½ cup ground espresso beans
- 1 tablespoon ground cumin
- 1 tablespoon ground cinnamon
- 1 tablespoon garlic powder
- 1 tablespoon cayenne pepper
- Salt and black pepper
- 1 (4-pound) giblets removed whole chicken

Directions:

1. Preheat the pallet grill to 200-225 degrees F.
2. Mix together all ingredients except chicken.
3. Rub the chicken with spice mixture generously.
4. Place the chicken in pallet grill and cook, covered for about 3-5 hours.
5. Remove chicken from pallet grill and transfer onto a cutting board for about 10 minutes before carving.
6. Cut the chicken in desired sized pieces and serve.

Nutrition:

Calories:658

Fat: 22.8g

Carbs: 20.7g

Protein: 88.1g

162. Entrée Chicken

Preparation Time: 8 hours

Cooking Time: 3 hours

Servings: 4

Ingredients:

For Brine:

- 1 cup brown sugar
- ½ cup kosher salt
- 16 cups water

For Chicken:

- 1 (3-5-pound) whole chicken
- 1 tablespoon crushed garlic
- 1 teaspoon onion powder
- Salt and ground black pepper
- 1 quartered medium yellow onion
- 3 peeled whole garlic cloves
- 1 quartered lemon
- 4-5 fresh thyme sprigs

Directions:

1. For brine: in a bucket, dissolve brown sugar and kosher salt in water. Place the chicken in brine and refrigerate overnight. Preheat the pallet grill to 225 degrees F. Remove the chicken from brine and with paper towels, pat it dry.
2. In a small bowl, mix together crushed garlic, onion powder, salt and black pepper. Rub chicken with garlic mixture evenly. Fill the chicken with onion, garlic cloves, lemon and thyme.
3. With kitchen strings, tie the legs together. Place the chicken in pallet grill and cook, covered for about 2½-3 hours. Remove chicken from pallet grill and transfer onto a cutting board for about 10 minutes before carving.
4. Cut the chicken desired sized pieces and serve.

Nutrition:

Calories: 804

Fat: 25.3g

Carbs: 40.3g

Protein: 99.1g

163. Super-Tasty Chicken Drumsticks

Preparation Time: 15 minutes

Cooking Time: 2 hours

Servings: 6

Ingredients:

- 1 cup fresh orange juice
- ¼ cup honey
- 2 tablespoons sweet chili sauce
- 2 tablespoons hoisin sauce
- 2 tablespoons finely grated fresh ginger
- 2 tablespoons minced garlic
- 1 teaspoon Sriracha
- ½ teaspoon sesame oil
- 6 chicken drumsticks

Directions:

1. Preheat the pallet grill to 225 degrees F. In a bowl, mix together all ingredients except chicken drumsticks.
2. Reserve half of honey mixture as a sauce. Coat the chicken drumsticks with remaining honey mixture.
3. Arrange the chicken drumsticks in pallet grill and cook for about 2 hours, coating with remaining honey mixture occasionally.
4. Serve drumsticks with reserved honey mixture as sauce.

Nutrition

Calories: 385

Fat: 10.5g

Carbs: 22.7g

Protein: 47.6g

164. Divine Chicken Drumsticks

Preparation Time: 20 minutes

Cooking Time: 2 hours

Servings: 8

Ingredients:

- 8 chicken drumsticks
- Salt and black pepper
- 6-ounce spicy BBQ sauce

Directions:

1. With kitchen shears, trim half of the top and bottom knuckle of each chicken drumstick to release the tendons and ligaments.
2. Season each drumstick with salt and black pepper generously and keep aside for about 20 minutes. Preheat the pallet grill to 275 degrees F.
3. Arrange the chicken drumsticks in pallet grill and cook for about 30 minutes per side. Remove drumsticks from the grate and place in a baking dish.
4. Cover the baking dish with a piece of foil, cook for about 45 minutes. Remove the foil and coat the drumsticks with BBQ sauce evenly. Cook for about 15 minutes more. Serve immediately.

Nutrition:

Calories: 319

Fat: 9.8g

Carbs: 7.7g

Protein: 46.8g

165. Decadent Chicken Drumsticks

Preparation Time: 10 minutes

Cooking Time: 2 hours

Servings: 6

Ingredients:

- 1 teaspoon dried thyme
- 1 tablespoon paprika
- 1 tablespoon cayenne pepper
- 1 teaspoon ground cumin
- 1 teaspoon garlic powder
- 1 teaspoon onion powder
- Salt and black pepper
- 6 chicken drumsticks
- 1 cup olive oil

Directions:

1. Preheat the pallet grill to 220 degrees F. In a bowl, mix together thyme, spices, salt and balk pepper.
2. Coat chicken drumsticks with oil generously and rub with spice mixture evenly.
3. Arrange the chicken drumsticks in pallet grill and cook for about 2 hours, flipping occasionally.

Nutrition:

Calories: 586

Fat: 43.7g

Carbs: 2.1g

Protein: 47.3g

166. Drunken Drumsticks

Preparation Time: 3 hours

Cooking Time: 60 minutes

Servings: 8

Ingredients:

For Brine:

- ½ cup brown sugar
- ½ cup kosher salt
- 5 cups water
- 2 (12-ounce) bottles beer
- 8 chicken drumsticks

For Coating:

- ¼ cup olive oil
- ½ cup BBQ rub
- 1 tablespoon minced fresh parsley
- 1 tablespoon minced fresh chives
- ¾ cup BBQ sauce
- ¼ cup beer

Directions:

1. For brine: in a bucket, dissolve brown sugar and kosher salt in water and beer. Place the chicken drumsticks in brine and refrigerate, covered for about 3 hours. Preheat the pallet grill to 275 degrees F.
2. Remove chicken drumsticks from brine and rinse under cold running water. With paper towels, pat dry chicken drumsticks. Coat drumsticks with olive oil and rub with BBQ rub evenly.
3. Sprinkle drumsticks with parsley and chives. Arrange the chicken drumsticks in pallet grill and cook for about 45 minutes. Meanwhile, in a bowl, mix together BBQ sauce and beer.
4. Remove from grill and coat the drumsticks with BBQ sauce evenly. Cook for about 15 minutes more. Serve immediately.

Nutrition:

Calories: 601

Fat: 21.4g

Carbs: 27.6g

Protein: 63g

CHAPTER 17. TURKEY RECIPES

167. Spatchcock Turkey

Preparation Time: 20 Minutes

Cooking Time: 1 Hour & 20 Minutes

Servings: 12

Ingredients

For The Turkey

- 1 whole turkey (roughly 15 pounds), thawed
- Salt to taste

For Turkey Stock Ingredients

- 4 carrots, sliced
- 1 onion, chopped
- 5 springs fresh thyme
- 1-quart unsalted chicken stock
- 5 springs fresh sage
- 1-quart water
- 4 stalks of celery, chopped

Directions:

1. Remove the giblet packet and neck from inside the turkey; set aside.
2. Cut out the back bone using kitchen shears or a sharp knife & set aside.
3. three. Lay the turkey flat, on a metallic rack & generously practice the dry brine on both sides (salt). Place in a refrigerator for in a single day to air dry.
4. Next, put the whole elements for turkey inventory in a large-sized roasting pan. Place the roasting pan over the pellet grill & placed the top shelf in its place (putting the turkey over the top shelf).
5. Grill the turkey until the inner temperature displays a hundred and sixty F, at 350 F.
6. Strain the turkey stock & sense free to apply it in gravy. Serve warm and enjoy.

Nutrition:

837 Calories

290 Calories from Fat

32g Total Fat

8.4g Saturated Fat

0.3g Trans Fat

8.4g Polyunsaturated Fat

10g Monounsaturated Fat

413mg Cholesterol 686mg Sodium

1417mg Potassium

4.8g Total Carbohydrates

1.1g Dietary Fiber

2.3g Sugars 125g Protein

168. Tequila Lime Roasted Turkey

Preparation Time: 25 Minutes

Cooking Time: 2 Hours & 35 Minutes

Servings: 12

Ingredients

- 9 garlic cloves
- 1 bone-in whole turkey (roughly 15 pounds), thawed
- 3 jalape ño chiles, cut in half & seeded
- 1 ¼ cups gold tequila
- 3 ounces' olive oil
- 1 ½ teaspoons pepper
- 3 limes, cut into wedges
- 1 ¼ cups lime juice, fresh
- ¾ cups each of orange juice & chicken broth
- 3 tablespoon chili powder
- 1 tablespoon salt

Directions

1. Preheat your smoker to 325 F in advance. Place the turkey breast in a shallow roasting pan, preferably pores and skin aspect up.
2. Place the jalapeno & garlic in a mini meals processor. Cover & process on high strength until chopped finely. Add the chili powder observed by using three oz. of tequila, three oz. of lime juice, oil, pepper and salt. Cover & method on high electricity again till the aggregate is completely smooth.
3. Next, the usage of spoon or fingers; loosen the turkey pores and skin & rub the organized garlic aggregate over and underneath the turkey pores and skin; calmly pour the leftover blend on top of the turkey. Insert an ovenproof meat thermometer into the thickest part of the breast & make certain that it doesn't' t touch the bone.
4. Pour the broth and orange juice observed by using the leftover lime juice and tequila into a roasting pan.
5. Roast until the thermometer displays an analyzing of one hundred 65 F, uncovered.
6. Place the turkey on a warm platter and then, cover with aluminum foil. Let stand for 12 to 15 minutes before carving. Spoon the pan juices on pinnacle of the turkey & garnish your dish with some clean lime wedges. Enjoy.

Nutrition:

517 Calories

341 Calories from Fat

38g Total Fat

17g Saturated Fat
1.8g Polyunsaturated Fat
18g Monounsaturated Fat
154mg Cholesterol
118mg Sodium
558mg Potassium
0.3g Total Carbohydrates
0g Dietary Fiber
0g Sugars
44g Protein

169. Grilled Stuffed Turkey Breast

Preparation Time: 10 Minutes

Cooking Time: 52 Minutes

Servings: 6

Ingredients:

- 5 pounds (2.3 kg) turkey breasts, cooked
- 5 slices bacon, cut into small pieces
- ¾ cup fresh mushrooms
- 1 bunch scallion, chopped
- 1/2 cup white wine
- 3 tablespoons panko bread crumbs
- Salt, to taste
- Black pepper, to taste

Directions:

1. When ready to cook, set temperature to 375F (191C) and preheat, lid closed for 15 minutes.
2. Slice the breast horizontally, making sure not to slice all the way through. Lay the breast open flat.
3. In a skillet cook the bacon for 5 minutes, or until crispy. Remove the bacon and set aside. Sauté the mushrooms in the bacon grease for 5 minutes, or until browned. Add the scallions and cook for an additional 2 minutes. Put in the wine and cook down until no wine remains. Stir in the bread crumbs and bacon and season with salt and pepper.
4. Set the filling in the refrigerator to cool for 15 to 20 minutes.
5. Once chilled, spread the filling over the breast, pressing lightly to make sure it adheres. Roll the turkey breast tightly and tie with cooking twine at about 1-inch intervals. put the ends of the turkey breast under and tie with twine lengthwise.
6. Season the outside of the turkey breast with salt and pepper. Move the turkey on the grill and cook for 40 minutes.
7. Remove the turkey from the grill and let cool for 10 minutes before slicing. Serve warm.

Nutrition:
Calcium, Ca61 mg
Magnesium, Mg99 mg
Phosphorus, P762 mg
Iron, Fe4.98 mg
Potassium, K1220 mg
Sodium, Na417 mg
Zinc, Zn6.33 mg

170. Cheesy Turkey Burger

Preparation Time: 1 hour 40 minutes

Cooking Time: 1 hour 20 minutes

Servings: 8

Ingredients:

- 3 lb. ground turkey
- Burger seasoning
- 7 oz. brie cheese, sliced into cubes
- 8 burger buns, sliced
- Blueberry jam
- 2 roasted bell peppers, sliced

Directions:

1. Season the turkey with the burger seasoning.
2. Mix well.
3. Form 8 patties from the mixture.
4. Press cheese into the patties.
5. Cover the top with more turkey.
6. Preheat your wood pellet grill to 350 degrees F.
7. Cook the turkey burgers for 30 to 40 minutes per side.
8. Spread the burger buns with blueberry jam.
9. Add the turkey burger on top.
10. Top with the bell peppers.

Nutrition:

Calcium, Ca104 mg
Magnesium, Mg34 mg
Phosphorus, P281 mg
Iron, Fe4.63 mg
Potassium, K517 mg
Sodium, Na1470 mg
Zinc, Zn4.14 mg

171. Turkey Sandwich

Preparation Time: 20 minutes

Cooking Time: 20 minutes

Servings: 4

Ingredients:

- 8 bread slices
- 1 cup gravy
- 2 cups turkey, cooked and shredded

Directions:

1. Set your wood pellet grill to smoke.
2. Preheat it to 400 degrees F.
3. Place a grill mat on top of the grates.
4. Add the turkey on top of the mat.
5. Cook for 10 minutes.

15. Toast the bread in the flame broiler.
16. Top the bread with the gravy and shredded turkey.

Nutrition:

Calcium, Ca390 mg
Magnesium, Mg40 mg
Phosphorus, P317 mg
Iron, Fe5.5 mg
Potassium, K490 mg
Sodium, Na631 mg
Zinc, Zn7.46 mg

172. Smoked Turkey

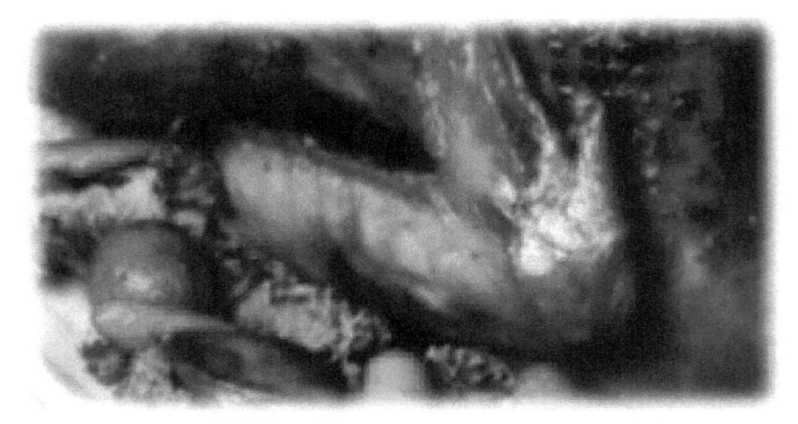

Preparation Time: 1 hour

Cooking Time: 6 hours

Servings: 8

Ingredients:

- 1 cup butter
- 1/2 cup maple syrup
- 2 tablespoons chicken seasoning
- 1 whole turkey

Directions:

1. Add the butter to a pan over low heat.
2. Stir in the maple syrup.
3. Simmer for 5 minutes, stirring.
4. Turn off the stove and let cool.
5. Add to a marinade injection.
17. Inject into the turkey.
18. Add the turkey to the wood pellet grill.
19. Set it smoke.
20. Smoke at 275 degrees F for 6 hours.

Nutrition:

Calcium, Ca54 mg
Magnesium, Mg64 mg
Phosphorus, P523 mg
Iron, Fe3.65 mg
Potassium, K655 mg
Sodium, Na390 mg
Zinc, Zn3.79 mg

173. Texas Turkey

Preparation Time: 1 hour

Cooking Time: 4 hours

Servings: 6

Ingredients:

- 1 pre-brined turkey

- Salt and pepper to taste
- 1 lb. butter

Directions:

1. Preheat your wood pellet grill to 300 degrees F.
2. Season the turkey with the salt and pepper.
3. Grill for 3 hours.
4. Add the turkey to a roasting pan.
5. Cover the turkey with the butter.

21. Cover with foil.
22. Add to the grill and cook for another 1 hour.
23. Let rest for 20 minutes before carving and serving.

Nutrition:
Calcium, Ca40 mg
Magnesium, Mg13 mg
Phosphorus, P108 mg
Iron, Fe1.29 mg
Potassium, K145 mg
Sodium, Na515 mg
Zinc, Zn1.44 mg

174. Teriyaki Turkey

Preparation Time: 25 Minutes

Cooking Time: 4 hours 5 minutes

Servings: 10

Ingredients:

Glaze

- 1/4 cup melted butter
- 1/2 cup apple cider
- 2 cloves garlic, minced
- 1/2 teaspoon ground ginger
- 2 tablespoons soy sauce
- 2 tablespoons honey

Turkey

- 2 tablespoons chicken seasoning
- 1 whole turkey

Thickener

- 1 tablespoon cold water
- 1 teaspoon cornstarch

Directions:

1. Add the glaze ingredients to a pan over medium heat.
2. Bring to a boil and then simmer for 5 minutes.
3. Reserve 5 tablespoons of the mixture.
4. Add the remaining to a marinade injection.
5. Place the turkey in a baking pan.
6. Season with the chicken seasoning.
7. Turn on the wood pellet grill.
8. Set it to 300 degrees F.
9. Add the turkey to the grill.
10. Cook for 3 hours.
11. Add the thickener to the reserved mixture.
12. Brush the turkey with this sauce.
13. Cook for another 1 hour.

Nutrition:
Calcium, Ca8 mg
Magnesium, Mg8 mg
Phosphorus, P57 m
Iron, Fe1.05 mg
Potassium, K80 mg
Sodium, Na165 mg
Zinc, Zn0.59 mg

175. Homemade Turkey Gravy

Cooking Time: 3 hours 20 minutes

Servings: 8-12

Ingredients:

- 1 turkey, neck
- 2 large Onion, eight
- 4 celeries, stalks
- 4 large carrots, fresh
- 8 clove garlic, smashed
- 8 thyme sprigs
- 4 cup chicken broth
- 1 teaspoon chicken broth
- 1 teaspoon salt
- 1 teaspoon cracked black pepper
- 1 butter, sticks

- 1 cup all-purpose flour

Directions:

1. When ready to cook, set the temperature to 350F and preheat the wood pellet grill with the lid closed, for 15 minutes.
2. Place turkey neck, celery, carrot (roughly chopped), garlic, onion and thyme on a roasting pan. Add four cups of chicken stock then season with salt and pepper.
3. Move the prepped turkey on the rack into the roasting pan and place in the wood pellet grill.
4. Cook for about 3-4 hours until the breast reaches 160F. The turkey will continue to cook and it will reach a finished internal temperature of 165F.
5. Strain the drippings into a saucepan and simmer on low.
6. In a saucepan, mix butter (cut into 8 pieces) and flour with a whisk stirring until golden tan. This takes about 8 minutes, stirrings constantly.
7. Whisk the drippings into the roux then cook until it comes to a boil. Season with salt and pepper.

Nutrition:

Calories 160kcal

Carbohydrate 27g

Protein 55g

Fat 23g

Saturated Fat 6.1g

176. Bacon Wrapped Turkey Legs

Preparation Time: 10 minutes

Cooking Time: 3 hours

Servings: 4-6

Ingredients:

- Gallon water
- To taste rub
- ½ cup pink curing salt
- ½ cup brown sugar
- 6 whole peppercorns
- 2 whole dried bay leaves
- ½ gallon ice water
- 8 whole turkey legs
- 16 sliced bacon

Directions:

1. In a large stockpot, mix one gallon of water, the rub, curing salt, brown sugar, peppercorns and bay leaves.
2. Boil it to over high heat to dissolve the salt and sugar granules. Take off the heat then add in ½ gallon of ice and water.
3. The brine must be at least to room temperature, if not colder.
4. Place the turkey legs, completely submerged in the brine.
5. After 24 hours, drain the turkey legs then remove the brine.
6. Wash the brine off the legs with cold water, then dry thoroughly with paper towels.
7. When ready to cook, start the wood pellet grill according to grill instructions. Set the heat to 250F and preheat, lid closed for 10 to 15 minutes.
8. Place turkey legs directly on the grill grate.
9. After 2 ½ hours, wrap a piece of bacon around each leg then finish cooking them for 30 to 40 minutes of smoking.
10. The total smoking time for the legs will be 3 hours or until the internal temperature reaches 165F on an instant-read meat thermometer. Serve, Enjoy!

Nutrition:

Calories 390kcal

Total Fat 14g

Saturated Fat 0g

Cholesterol 64mg

Sodium 738mg

Carbohydrates 44g

177. Smoked Turkey Patties

Preparation time: 20 minutes

Cooking time: 40 minutes

Servings: 6

Ingredients:

- 2 lbs. turkey minced meat
- 1/2 cup of parsley finely chopped
- 2/3 cup of onion finely chopped
- 1 red bell pepper finely chopped
- 1 large egg at room temperature
- Salt and pepper to taste
- 1/2 tsp dry oregano
- 1/2 tsp dry thyme

Directions:

1. In a bowl, combine well all ingredients.
2. Make from the mixture patties.
3. Start pellet grill on (recommended apple or oak pellet) lid open, until the fire is established (4-5 minutes). Increase the temperature to 350F and allow to pre-heat, lid closed, for 10 - 15 minutes.
4. Place patties on the grill racks and cook with lid covered for 30 to 40 minutes.
5. Your turkey patties are ready when you reach a temperature of 130F
6. Serve hot.

Nutrition:

Calories: 251

Carbohydrates: 3.4g

Fat: 12.5

Fiber: 0.9g

Protein: 31.2g

178. Apple Smoked Turkey

Preparation time: 30 Minutes

Cooking time: 3 Hours

Servings: 5

Ingredients:

- 4 Cups Applewood chips
- 1 Fresh or frozen turkey of about 12 pounds
- 3 Tablespoons of extra-virgin olive oil
- 1 tablespoon of chopped fresh sage
- 2 and ½ teaspoons of kosher salt
- 2 Teaspoons of freshly ground black pepper
- 1 and ½ teaspoons of paprika
- 1 Teaspoon of chopped fresh thyme
- 1 Teaspoon of chopped fresh oregano
- 1 Teaspoon of garlic powder
- 1 Cup of water
- ½ Cup of chopped onion
- ½ Cup of chopped carrot
- ½ Cup of chopped celery

Directions:

1. Soak the wood chips into the water for about 1 hour; then drain very well.
2. Remove the neck and the giblets from the turkey; then reserve and discard the liver. Pat the turkey dry; then trim any excess of fat and start at the neck's cavity
3. Loosen the skin from the breast and the drumstick by inserting your fingers and gently push it between the meat and skin and lift the wingtips, then over back and tuck under the turkey
4. Combine the oil and the next 7 ingredients in a medium bowl and rub the oil under the skin; then rub it over the breasts and the drumsticks
5. Tie the legs with the kitchen string.
6. Pour 1 cup of water, the onion, the carrot, and the celery into the bottom of an aluminum foil roasting pan
7. Place the roasting rack into a pan; then arrange the turkey with the breast side up over a roasting rack; then let stand at the room temperature for about 1 hour
8. Remove the grill rack; then preheat the charcoal smoker grill to medium-high heat.
9. After preheating the smoker to a temperature of about 225°F
10. Place 2 cups of wood chips on the heating element on the right side.
11. Replace the grill rack; then place the roasting pan with the turkey over the grill rack over the left burner.
12. Cover and smoke for about 3 hours and turn the chicken halfway through the cooking time; then add the remaining 2 cups of wood chips halfway through the cooking time.
13. Place the turkey over a cutting board; then let stand for about 30 minutes
14. Discard the turkey skin; then serve and enjoy your dish!

Nutrition:

Calories: 530,

Fat: 22g,

Carbohydrates: 14g,

Protein: 41g,

Dietary Fiber 2g

179. Buttered Turkey

Preparation Time: 15 minutes

Cooking Time: 4 hours

Servings: 16

Ingredients:

- ½ pound butter, softened
- 2 tablespoons fresh thyme, chopped
- 2 fresh rosemaries, chopped
- 6 garlic cloves, crushed
- 1 (20-pound) whole turkey, neck and giblets removed
- Salt and ground black pepper, as required

Directions:

1. Preheat the Z Grills Wood Pellet Grill & Smoker on smoke setting to 300 degrees F, using charcoal.
2. In a bowl, place butter, fresh herbs, garlic, salt and black pepper and mix well.
3. With your fingers, separate the turkey skin from breast to create a pocket.
4. Stuff the breast pocket with ¼-inch thick layer of butter mixture.
5. Season the turkey with salt and black pepper evenly.
6. Arrange the turkey onto the grill and cook for 3-4 hours.
7. Remove turkey from pallet grill and place onto a cutting board for about 15-20 minutes before carving.
8. With a sharp knife, cut the turkey into desired-sized pieces and serve.

Nutrition:

Calories 965

Total Fat 52 g

Saturated Fat 19.9 g

Cholesterol 385 mg

Sodium 1916 mg

Total Carbs 0.6 g

Fiber 0.2 g

Sugar 0 g

Protein 106.5 g

180. Glazed Turkey Breast

Preparation Time: 15 minutes

Cooking Time: 4 hours

Servings: 6

Ingredients:

- ½ cup honey
- ¼ cup dry sherry
- 1 tablespoon butter
- 2 tablespoons fresh lemon juice
- Salt, as required
- 1 (3-3½-pound) skinless, boneless turkey breast

Directions:

1. In a small pan, place honey, sherry and butter over low heat and cook until the mixture becomes smooth, stirring continuously.
2. Remove from heat and stir in lemon juice and salt. Set aside to cool.
3. Transfer the honey mixture and turkey breast in a sealable bag.
4. Seal the bag and shake to coat well.
5. Refrigerate for about 6-10 hours.
6. Preheat the Wood Pellet Grill & Smoker on grill setting to 225-250 degrees F.
7. Place the turkey breast onto the grill and cook for about 2½-4 hours or until desired doneness.
8. Remove turkey breast from pallet grill and place onto a cutting board for about 15-20 minutes before slicing.
9. With a sharp knife, cut the turkey breast into desired-sized slices and serve.

Nutrition:

Calories 443

Total Fat 11.4 g

Saturated Fat 4.8 g

Cholesterol 159 mg

Sodium 138 mg

Total Carbs 23.7 g

Fiber 0.1 g

Sugar 23.4 g

Protein 59.2 g

181. Herb Roasted Turkey

Preparation Time: 15 Minutes

Cooking Time: 3 Hours 30 Minutes

Servings: 12

Ingredients:

- 14 pounds' turkey, cleaned
- 2 tablespoons chopped mixed herbs
- Pork and poultry rub as needed
- ¼ teaspoon ground black pepper
- 3 tablespoons butter, unsalted, melted
- 8 tablespoons butter, unsalted, softened
- 2 cups chicken broth

Directions:

1. Clean the turkey by removing the giblets, wash it inside out, pat dry with paper towels, then place it on a roasting pan and tuck the turkey wings by tiring with butcher's string.
2. Switch on the grill, fill the grill hopper with Hickory flavored wood pellets, power the grill on by using the control panel, select 'smoke' on the temperature dial, or set the temperature to 325 degrees F and let it preheat for a minimum of 15 minutes.
3. Meanwhile, prepared herb butter and for this, take a small bowl, place the softened butter in it, add black pepper and mixed herbs and beat until fluffy.
4. Place some of the prepared herb butter underneath the skin of turkey by using a handle of a wooden spoon and massage the skin to distribute butter evenly.
5. Then rub the turkey's exterior with melted butter, season with pork and poultry rub, and pour the broth in the roasting pan.
6. When the grill has preheated, open the lid,

place roasting pan containing turkey on the grill grate, shut the grill and smoke for 3 hours and 30 minutes until the internal temperature reaches 165 degrees F and the top has turned golden brown.
7. When done, transfer turkey to a cutting board, rest for 30 minutes, then carve it into slices and serve.

Nutrition:

Calories: 154.6

Fat: 3.1 g

Carbs: 8.4 g

Protein: 28.8 g

182. Turkey Legs

Preparation Time: 10 Minutes

Cooking Time: 5 Hours

Servings: 4

Ingredients:

- 4 turkey legs
- For the Brine:
- ½ cup curing salt
- 1 tablespoon whole black peppercorns
- 1 cup BBQ rub
- ½ cup brown sugar
- 2 bay leaves
- 2 teaspoons liquid smoke
- 16 cups of warm water
- 4 cups ice
- 8 cups of cold water

Directions:

1. Prepare the brine and for this, take a large stockpot, place it over high heat, pour warm water in it, add peppercorn, bay leaves, and liquid smoke, stir in salt, sugar, and BBQ rub and bring it to a boil.
2. Remove pot from heat, bring it to room temperature, then pour in cold water, add ice cubes and let the brine chill in the refrigerator.
3. Then add turkey legs in it, submerge them completely, and let soak for 24 hours in the refrigerator.
4. After 24 hours, remove turkey legs from the brine, rinse well and pat dry with paper towels.
5. When ready to cook, switch on the grill, fill the grill hopper with hickory flavored wood pellets, power the grill on by using the control panel, select 'smoke' on the temperature dial, or set the temperature to 250 degrees F and let it preheat for a minimum of 15 minutes.
6. When the grill has preheated, open the lid, place turkey legs on the grill grate, shut the grill, and smoke for 5 hours until nicely browned and the internal temperature reaches 165 degrees F. Serve immediately.

Nutrition:

Calories: 416

Fat: 13.3 g

Carbs: 0 g

Protein: 69.8 g

183. Turkey Breast

Preparation Time: 12 Hours

Cooking Time: 8 Hours

Servings: 6

Ingredients:

FOR THE BRINE:

- 2 pounds' turkey breast, deboned
- 2 tablespoons ground black pepper
- ¼ cup salt
- 1 cup brown sugar
- 4 cups cold water

FOR THE BBQ RUB:

- 2 tablespoons dried onions
- 2 tablespoons garlic powder
- ¼ cup paprika
- 2 tablespoons ground black pepper
- 1 tablespoon salt
- 2 tablespoons brown sugar
- 2 tablespoons red chili powder
- 1 tablespoon cayenne pepper
- 2 tablespoons sugar
- 2 tablespoons ground cumin

Directions:

1. Prepare the brine and for this, take a large bowl, add salt, black pepper, and sugar in it, pour in water, and stir until sugar has dissolved.
2. Place turkey breast in it, submerge it completely and let it soak for a minimum of 12 hours in the refrigerator.
3. Meanwhile, prepare the BBQ rub and for this, take a small bowl, place all of its ingredients in it and then stir until combined, set aside until required.
4. Then remove turkey breast from the brine and season well with the prepared BBQ rub.
5. When ready to cook, switch on the grill, fill the grill hopper with apple-flavored wood pellets, power the grill on by using the control panel, select 'smoke' on the temperature dial, or set the temperature to 180 degrees F and let it preheat for a minimum of 15 minutes.
6. When the grill has preheated, open the lid, place turkey breast on the grill grate, shut the grill, change the smoking temperature to 225 degrees F, and smoke for 8 hours until the internal temperature reaches 160 degrees F.
7. When done, transfer turkey to a cutting board, let it rest for 10 minutes, then cut it into slices and serve.

Nutrition:

Calories: 250

Fat: 5 g

Carbs: 31 g;

Protein: 18 g

184. Apple Wood-Smoked Whole Turkey

Preparation Time: 10 minutes

Cooking Time: 5 hours

Servings: 6

Ingredients:

- 1 (10- to 12-pound) turkey, giblets removed
- Extra-virgin olive oil, for rubbing
- ¼ cup poultry seasoning
- 8 tablespoons (1 stick) unsalted butter, melted
- ½ cup apple juice
- 2 teaspoons dried sage
- 2 teaspoons dried thyme

Directions:

1. Supply your smoker with wood pellets and follow the manufacturer's specific start-up procedure. Preheat, with the lid closed, to 250°F.
2. Rub the turkey with oil and season with the poultry seasoning inside and out, getting under the skin.
3. In a bowl, combine the melted butter, apple juice, sage, and thyme to use for basting.
4. Put the turkey in a roasting pan, place on the grill, close the lid, and grill for 5 to 6 hours, basting every hour, until the skin is brown and crispy, or until a meat thermometer inserted in the thickest part of the thigh reads 165°F.
5. Let the turkey meat rest for about 15 to 20 minutes before carving.

Nutrition:

Calories: 180

Carbs: 3g

Fat: 2g

Protein: 39g

185. Savory-Sweet Turkey Legs

Preparation Time: 10 minutes

Cooking Time: 5 hours

Servings: 4

Ingredients:

- 1-gallon hot water
- 1 cup curing salt (such as Morton Tender Quick)
- ¼ cup packed light brown sugar
- 1 teaspoon freshly ground black pepper
- 1 teaspoon ground cloves
- 1 bay leaf
- 2 teaspoons liquid smoke
- 4 turkey legs
- Mandarin Glaze, for serving

Directions:

1. In a huge container with a lid, stir together the water, curing salt, brown sugar, pepper, cloves, bay leaf, and liquid smoke until the salt and sugar are dissolved; let come to room temperature.
2. Submerge the turkey legs in the seasoned brine, cover, and refrigerate overnight.
3. When ready to smoke, remove the brine's turkey legs and rinse them; discard the brine.
4. Supply your smoker with wood pellets and follow the manufacturer's specific start-up procedure. Preheat, with the lid closed, to 225F.
5. Arrange the turkey legs on the grill, close the lid, and smoke for 4 to 5 hours, or until dark brown and a meat thermometer inserted in the thickest part of the meat reads 165F.
6. Serve with Mandarin Glaze on the side or drizzled over the turkey legs.

Nutrition:

Calories: 190

Carbs: 1g

Fat: 9g

Protein: 24g

186. Marinated Smoked Turkey Breast

Preparation Time: 15 minutes

Cooking Time: 4 hours

Servings: 6

Ingredients:

- 1 (5 pounds) boneless chicken breast
- 4 cups water
- 2 tablespoons kosher salt
- 1 teaspoon Italian seasoning
- 2 tablespoons honey
- 1 tablespoon cider vinegar
- Rub:
- ½ teaspoon onion powder
- 1 teaspoon paprika
- 1 teaspoon salt
- 1 teaspoon ground black pepper
- 1 tablespoon brown sugar
- ½ teaspoon garlic powder
- 1 teaspoon oregano

Directions:

7. In a huge container, combine the water, honey, cider vinegar, Italian seasoning and salt.
8. Add the chicken breast and toss to combine. Cover the bowl and place it in the refrigerator and chill for 4 hours.
9. Rinse the chicken breast with water and pat dry with paper towels.
10. In another mixing bowl, combine the brown sugar, salt, paprika, onion powder, pepper, oregano and garlic.
11. Generously season the chicken breasts with the rub mix.
12. Preheat the grill to 225°F with lid closed for 15 minutes. Use cherry wood pellets.
13. Arrange the turkey breast into a grill rack. Place the grill rack on the grill.
14. Smoke for about 3 to 4 hours or until the internal temperature of the turkey breast reaches 165°F.
15. Remove the chicken breast from heat and let them rest for a few minutes. Serve.

Nutrition:

Calories 903

Fat: 34g;

Carbs: 9.9g

Protein 131.5g

187. Maple Bourbon Turkey

Preparation Time: 15 minutes

Cooking Time: 3 hours

Servings: 8

Ingredients:

- 1 (12 pounds) turkey
- 8 cup chicken broth
- 1 stick butter (softened)
- 1 teaspoon thyme
- 2 garlic cloves (minced)
- 1 teaspoon dried basil
- 1 teaspoon pepper
- 1 teaspoon salt
- 1 tablespoon minced rosemary
- 1 teaspoon paprika
- 1 lemon (wedged)
- 1 onion
- 1 orange (wedged)
- 1 apple (wedged)
- Maple Bourbon Glaze:
- ¾ cup bourbon
- 1/2 cup maple syrup
- 1 stick butter (melted)
- 1 tablespoon lime

Directions:

16. Wash the turkey meat inside and out under cold running water.
17. Insert the onion, lemon, orange and apple into the turkey cavity.

18. In a mixing bowl, combine the butter, paprika, thyme, garlic, basil, pepper, salt, basil and rosemary.
19. Brush the turkey generously with the herb butter mixture.
20. Set a rack into a roasting pan and place the turkey on the rack. Put a 5 cups of chicken broth into the bottom of the roasting pan.
21. Preheat the grill to 350°F with lid closed for 15 minutes, using maple wood pellets.
22. Place the roasting pan in the grill and cook for 1 hour.
23. Meanwhile, combine all the maple bourbon glaze ingredients in a mixing bowl. Mix until well combined.
24. Baste the turkey with glaze mixture. Continue cooking, basting turkey every 30 minutes and adding more broth as needed for 2 hours, or until the internal temperature of the turkey reaches 165°F.

11. Take off the turkey from the grill and let it rest for a few minutes. Cut into slices and serve.

Nutrition:

Calories 1536

Fat 58.6g

Carbs: 24g

Protein 20.1g

CHAPTER 18. SEAFOOD RECIPES

188. Jerk Shrimp

Preparation time: 15 minutes

Cooking time: 6

Servings: 12

Ingredients:

- 2 pounds' shrimp, peeled, deveined
- 3 tablespoons olive oil
- For the Spice Mix:
- 1 teaspoon garlic powder
- 1 teaspoon of sea salt
- 1/4 teaspoon ground cayenne
- 1 tablespoon brown sugar
- 1/8 teaspoon smoked paprika
- 1 tablespoon smoked paprika
- 1/4 teaspoon ground thyme
- 1 lime, zested

Directions:

1. Switch on the grill, fill the grill hopper with flavored wood pellets, power the grill on by using the control panel, select 'smoke' on the temperature dial, or set the temperature to 450 degrees F and let it preheat for a minimum of 5 minutes.
2. Meanwhile, prepare the spice mix and for this, take a small bowl, place all of its ingredients in it and stir until mixed.
3. Take a large bowl, place shrimps in it, sprinkle with prepared spice mix, drizzle with oil and toss until well coated.
4. When the grill has preheated, open the lid, place shrimps on the grill grate, shut the grill, and smoke for 3 minutes per side until firm and thoroughly cooked.
5. When done, transfer shrimps to a dish and then serve.

Nutrition

Calories: 131 Cal

Fat: 4.3 g

Carbs: 0 g

Protein: 22 g

Fiber: 0 g

189. Spicy Shrimps Skewers

Preparation time: 10 minutes

Cooking time: 6 minutes

Servings: 4

Ingredients:

- 2 pounds' shrimp, peeled, and deveined
- For the Marinade:
- 6 ounces Thai chilies
- 6 cloves of garlic, peeled
- 1 ½ teaspoon sugar
- 2 tablespoons Napa Valley rub
- 1 ½ tablespoon white vinegar
- 3 tablespoons olive oil

Directions:

1. Prepare the marinade and for this, place all of its ingredients in a food processor and then pulse for 1 minute until smooth.
2. Take a large bowl, place shrimps on it, add prepared marinade, toss until well coated, and let marinate for a minimum of 30 minutes in the refrigerator.
3. When ready to cook, switch on the grill, fill the grill hopper with apple-flavored wood pellets, power the grill on by using the control panel, select 'smoke' on the temperature dial, or set the temperature to 450 degrees F and let it preheat for a minimum of 5 minutes.
4. Meanwhile, remove shrimps from the marinade and then thread onto skewers.
5. When the grill has preheated, open the lid, place shrimps' skewers on the grill grate, shut the grill, and smoke for 3 minutes per side until firm.
6. When done, transfer shrimps' skewers to a dish and then serve.

Nutrition

Calories: 187.2 Cal

Fat: 2.7 g

Carbs: 2.7 g

Protein: 23.2 g

Fiber: 0.2 g

190. Tuna Tacos

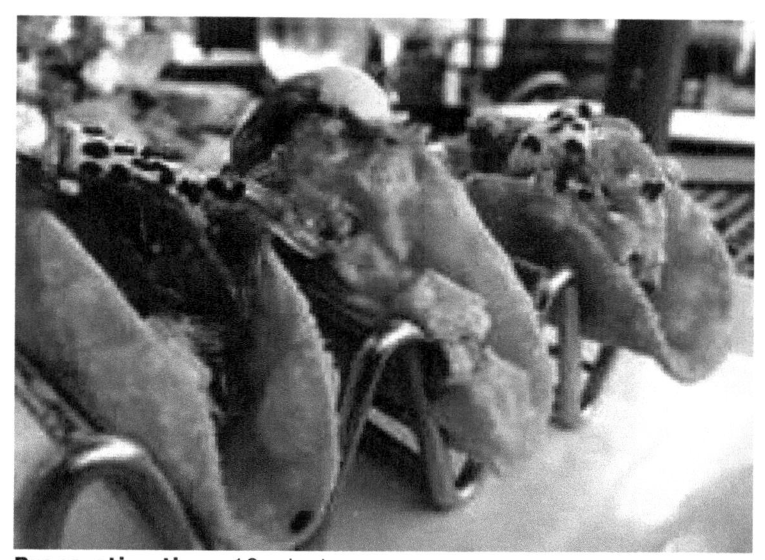

Preparation time: 10 minutes

Cooking time: 35 minutes

Servings: 4

Ingredients:

- 1.5 kg of tuna
- 3 tablespoons of olive oil
- 1/4 cup of spices for fish
- 1 piece of grated ginger root
- 3 tablespoons of vinegar
- 1 tablespoon of honey
- 1 teaspoon of red pepper flakes
- 1/2 teaspoon of salt
- 1/4 teaspoon ground black pepper
- 1 fresh anna (already cleaned and finely chopped)
- 1 cabbage (grated)
- 2 carrots (grated)
- 12 tortillas (you can also use the piadina)
- 3 spoons of cilantro (chopped)

Directions:

1. Preheat the barbecue to 230 ° C and prepare it for the grill, close the lid, and leave it for about 15 minutes.
2. Brush the tuna with a light layer of olive oil and then cover it with a layer of spice for fish, let the tuna marinate for 10 minutes while preparing the cabbage salad.
3. For the salad, mix ginger, vinegar, honey, the pepper flakes, salt, and pepper, then in a large bowl combined with the pineapple, carrots, and cabbage.
4. Grate the tuna for 3 minutes on each side, then remove it from the grill and let it rest for 5 minutes before continuing to fray it. At this point you can fill the tortillas (or piadina) with tuna and coleslaw, the tacos are ready to serve them!!

Nutrition

Calories: 290cal

Fat: 22 g

Carbs: 1 g

Protein: 20 g

Fiber: 0.3 g

191. Lemon Garlic Scallops

Preparation time: 10 minutes

Cooking time: 5 minutes

Servings: 6

Ingredients:

- 1 dozen scallops
- 2 tablespoons chopped parsley
- Salt as needed
- 1 tablespoon olive oil
- 1 tablespoon butter, unsalted
- 1 teaspoon lemon zest
- For the Garlic Butter:
- ½ teaspoon minced garlic
- 1 lemon, juiced
- 4 tablespoons butter, unsalted, melted

Directions:

1. Switch on the grill, fill the grill hopper with alder flavored wood pellets, power the grill on by using the control panel, select 'smoke' on the temperature dial, or set the temperature to 400 degrees F and let it preheat for a minimum of 15 minutes.
2. Meanwhile, remove the grill from scallops, pat dry with paper towels, and then season with salt and black pepper.
3. When the grill has preheated, open the lid, place a skillet on the grill grate, add butter and oil, and when the butter melts, place seasoned scallops on it and then cook for 2 minutes until seared.
4. Meanwhile, prepare the garlic butter and for this, take a small bowl, place all of its ingredients in it and then whisk until combined.
5. Flip the scallops, top with some of the prepared garlic butter, and cook for another minute.
6. When done, transfer scallops to a dish, top with remaining garlic butter, sprinkle with parsley and lemon zest and then serve.

Nutrition

Calories: 184 Cal Fat: 10 g

Carbs: 1 g Protein: 22 g

Fiber: 0.2 g

192. Halibut in Parchment

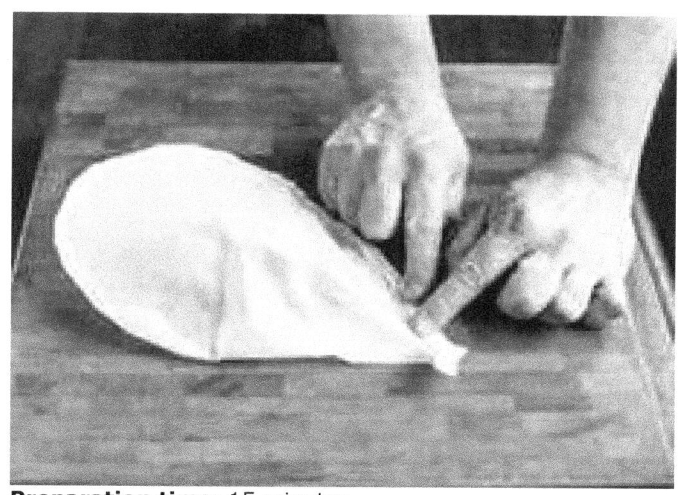

Preparation time: 15 minutes

Cooking time: 15 minutes

Servings: 4

Ingredients:

- 16 asparagus spears, trimmed, sliced into 1/2-inch pieces
- 2 ears of corn kernels
- 4 ounces' halibut fillets, pin bones removed
- 2 lemons, cut into 12 slices
- Salt as needed
- Ground black pepper as needed
- 2 tablespoons olive oil
- 2 tablespoons chopped parsley

Directions:

1. Switch on the grill, fill the grill hopper with flavored wood pellets, power the grill on by using the control panel, select 'smoke' on the temperature dial, or set the temperature to 450 degrees F and let it preheat for a minimum of 5 minutes.
2. Meanwhile, cut out 18-inch long parchment paper, place a fillet in the center of each parchment, season with salt and black pepper, and then drizzle with oil.
3. Cover each fillet with three lemon slices, overlapping slightly, sprinkle one-fourth of asparagus and corn on each fillet, season with some salt and black pepper, and seal the fillets and vegetables tightly to prevent steam from escaping the packet.
4. When the grill has preheated, open the lid, place fillet packets on the grill grate, shut the grill, and smoke for 15 minutes until packets have turned slightly brown and puffed up.
5. When done, transfer packets to a dish, let them stand for 5 minutes, then cut 'X' in the center of each packet, carefully uncover the fillets and vegetables, sprinkle with parsley, and then serve.

Nutrition:

Calories: 186.6 Cal

Fat: 2.8 g

Carbs: 14.2 g

Protein: 25.7 g

Fiber: 4.1 g

193. Chilean Sea Bass

Preparation time: 30 minutes

Cooking time: 40 minutes

Servings: 6

Ingredients:

- 4 sea bass fillets, skinless, each about 6 ounces
- Chicken rub as needed
- 8 tablespoons butter, unsalted
- 2 tablespoons chopped thyme leaves
- Lemon slices for serving
- For the Marinade:
- 1 lemon, juiced
- 4 teaspoons minced garlic
- 1 tablespoon chopped thyme
- 1 teaspoon blackened rub
- 1 tablespoon chopped oregano
- 1/4 cup oil

Directions:

1. Prepare the marinade and for this, take a small bowl, place all of its ingredients in it, stir until well combined, and then pour the mixture into a large plastic bag.
2. Add fillets in the bag, seal it, turn it upside down to coat fillets with the marinade and let it marinate for a minimum of 30 minutes in the refrigerator.
3. When ready to cook, switch on the grill, fill the grill hopper with apple-flavored wood pellets, power the grill on by using the control panel, select 'smoke' on the temperature dial, or set the temperature to 325 degrees F and let it preheat for a minimum of 15 minutes.
4. Meanwhile, take a large baking pan and place butter on it. When the grill has preheated, open the lid, place the baking pan on the grill grate, and wait until butter melts.
5. When done, transfer fillets to a dish, sprinkle with thyme, then serve with lemon slices.

Nutrition

Calories: 232 Cal

Fat: 12.2 g

Carbs: 0.8 g

Protein: 28.2 g

Fiber: 0.1 g

194. Sriracha Salmon

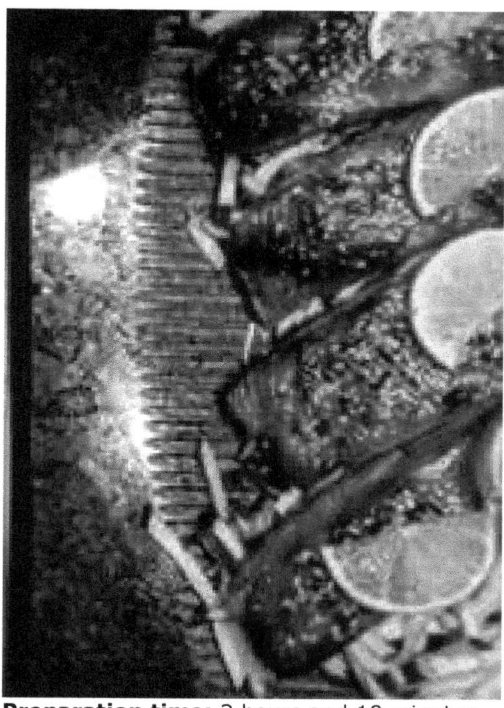

Preparation time: 2 hours and 10 minutes

Cooking time: 25 minutes

Servings: 4

Ingredients:

- 3-pound salmon, skin on
- For the Marinade:
- 1 teaspoon lime zest
- 1 tablespoon minced garlic
- 1 tablespoon grated ginger
- Sea salt as needed
- Ground black pepper as needed
- 1/4 cup maple syrup
- 2 tablespoons soy sauce
- 2 tablespoons Sriracha sauce
- 1 tablespoon toasted sesame oil
- 1 tablespoon rice vinegar
- 1 teaspoon toasted sesame seeds

Directions:

1. Prepare the marinade and for this, take a small bowl, place all of its ingredients in it, stir until well combined, and then pour the mixture into a large plastic bag.
2. Add salmon in the bag, seal it, turn it upside down to coat salmon with the marinade and let it marinate for a minimum of 2 hours in the refrigerator.
3. When ready to cook, switch on the Wood Pellet grill, fill the grill hopper with flavored wood pellets, power the grill on by using the control panel, select 'smoke' on the temperature dial, or set the temperature to 450 degrees F and let it preheat for a minimum of 5 minutes.
4. Meanwhile, take a large baking sheet, line it with parchment paper, place salmon on it skin-side down and then brush with the marinade.
5. When the grill has preheated, open the lid, place a baking sheet containing salmon on the grill grate, shut the grill, and smoke for 25 minutes until thoroughly cooked.
6. When done, transfer salmon to a dish and then serve.

Nutrition

Calories: 360 Cal

Fat: 21 g

Carbs: 28 g

Protein: 16 g

Fiber: 1.5 g

195. Grilled Rainbow Trout

Preparation time: 1 hour

Cooking time: 2 hours

Servings: 6

Ingredients:

- 6 rainbow trout, cleaned, butterfly
- For the Brine:
- 1/4 cup salt
- 1 tablespoon ground black pepper
- 1/2 cup brown sugar
- 2 tablespoons soy sauce
- 16 cups water

Directions:

1. Prepare the brine and for this, take a large container, add all of its ingredients in it, stir until sugar has dissolved, then add trout and let soak for 1 hour in the refrigerator.
2. When ready to cook, switch on the Wood pellet grill, fill the grill hopper with oak flavored wood pellets, power the grill on by using the control panel, select 'smoke' on the temperature dial, or set the temperature to 225 degrees F and let it preheat for a minimum of 15 minutes.
3. Meanwhile, remove trout from the brine and pat dry with paper towels.
4. When the grill has preheated, open the lid, place trout on the grill grate, shut the grill, and smoke for 2 hours until thoroughly cooked and tender.
5. When done, transfer trout to a dish and then serve.

Nutrition

Calories: 250 Cal

Fat: 12 g

Carbs: 1.4 g

Protein: 33 g

Fiber: 0.3 g

196. Grilled Salmon Kyoto

Preparation time: 10 minutes

Cooking time: 10 minutes

Servings: 4

Ingredients:

- 1/3 Cup soy sauce
- ¼ cup orange juice concentrate
- Two tablespoons vegetable oil
- Two tablespoons tomato sauce
- One clove garlic
- Half teaspoon minced fresh ginger root
- One teaspoon lemon juice
- Four steaks salmon steaks
- One tablespoon olive oil
- Half teaspoon prepared mustard
- One tablespoon green onion, minced

Directions:

1. Take a deep glass baking dish and merge orange juice concentrate, mustard, tomato sauce, soy sauce, green onion, ginger, lemon juice, oil, and garlic.
2. Put salmon in the marinade and turn it and cover it, keep in the freezer for a half -hour to one hour.
3. Now, preheat the grill for elevate heat.
4. Eliminate the salmon from the marinade. Pour the marinade in the little saucepan. Allow to boil and cook for one minute.
5. Now, lightly oil the grill grate and brush or sprinkle salmon with olive oil. Cook on the grill for five to ten minutes until it fish flakes with the fork.
6. Now turn the salmon and brush with boiled marinade halfway.

Nutrition:

Calcium, Ca44 mg
Magnesium, Mg57 mg
Phosphorus, P134 mg
Iron, Fe1.34 mg

197. Best Halibut Soft Tacos

Preparation time: 25 minutes

Cooking time: 5 minutes

Servings: 4

Ingredients:

- One mango, diced
- Half cup diced avocado
- ¼ cup chopped red onion
- Two medium tomatoes, chopped
- Two medium jalapeno peppers
- One teaspoon olive oil
- Half teaspoon salt
- Two teaspoons olive oil
- Two tablespoons minced fresh parsley
- One-pound halibut steaks
- One teaspoon lemon juice
- One teaspoon honey
- ¼ teaspoon ground black pepper
- ¼ teaspoon garlic salt
- Four large leaves Bibb lettuce leaves
- Four flour tortillas
- Four teaspoons taco sauce

Directions:

1. First, preheat the grill for high flame and softly oil the grate.
2. Blend avocado, mango, parsley, tomatoes, onion, two tablespoons olive oil, honey, jalapeno pepper, and lemon juice in the little bowl.
3. Brush halibut steaks with one tablespoon olive oil and season with garlic salt, salt, and black pepper.
4. Keep halibut on the grill and cover the lid and cook until it gets flakes easily with the help of a fork for three to five minutes.
5. Keep Bibb lettuce leaves on the top of every tortilla. Split halibut into four parts and then nestle in the lettuce leaves.
6. Top with the mixture of mango and sprinkle with taco sauce

Nutrition:
Calcium, Ca363 mg
Magnesium, Mg234 mg
Phosphorus, P1312 mg
Iron, Fe14.31 mg
Potassium, K3684 mg
Sodium, Na3019 mg
Zinc, Zn24.69 mg

198. Acapulco Margarita Grouper

Preparation time: 20 minutes

Cooking time: 12 minutes

Servings: 4

Ingredients:

- Four grouper fillets
- 1/3 Cup tequila
- Half cup orange liqueur
- ¾ cup fresh lime juice
- Four tablespoons olive oil
- One teaspoon salt
- Three large cloves garlic
- One intermediate jalapeno, seeded and minced
- Three intermediate tomatoes
- One medium onion
- Four tablespoons chopped fresh cilantro
- One tablespoon olive oil
- One teaspoon ground black pepper
- One pinch white sugar
- One teaspoon salt

Direction:

1. Put fish in the deep baking dish. Take a bowl and stir lime juice, garlic, tequila, one teaspoon salt, garlic, Orange liqueur, and olive oil.
2. Pour the mixture over the fillets and then rub in the fish. Coat and keep in the freezer for half an hour and then turning fillets for one time.
3. After, preheat the grill for high temperature.
4. Take an intermediate bowl and then toss onion, cilantro, sugar, tomatoes, and jalapeno and then season with salt and keep salsa aside.
5. Eliminate the fillets from the marinade and then dry them. Brush the fillets with oil and drizzle with ground black pepper. Take a little saucepan and boil the marinade for few a minutes.
6. Now, eliminate from the flame and then strain out the garlic cloves. Keep aside to chill.
7. Now, Grill fish for four minutes each side until fish gets flaked with the help of a fork
8. Move fillets to many dishes. Move the fish to plate and spoon salsa over the fish and sprinkle with cooked marinade for serving.

Nutrition:
Calcium, Ca165 mg
Magnesium, Mg146 mg
Phosphorus, P545 mg
Iron, Fe3.82 mg
Potassium, K440 mg
Sodium, Na1558 mg
Zinc, Zn0.9 mg

Potassium, K2503 mg
Sodium, Na5308 mg
Zinc, Zn1.94 mg

199. Grilled Oyster Shooters

Preparation time: 5 minutes

Cooking time: 10 minutes

Servings: 4

Ingredients

- Eight medium fresh oysters in shells
- 1/3 cup Fresh lemon juice
- One dash hot pepper sauce to taste
- One pinch salt
- Three tablespoons Worcestershire sauce

Directions:

1. First, preheat the grill for elevated heat and collect all ingredients.
2. Put the whole oyster on the warm grill and cook until it gets open for five to ten minutes.
3. Eliminate the oyster from the grill and snoop the shell top. Slide a sharp knife among the shell and oyster to separate.
4. Top each with salt, one tablespoon Worcestershire sauce, two tablespoon lemon juice, and warm pepper sauce.
5. Serve in the shell while still hot.

Nutrition:
Calcium, Ca35 mg
Magnesium, Mg29 mg
Phosphorus, P118 mg
Iron, Fe4.06 mg
Potassium, K456 mg
Sodium, Na224 mg
Zinc, Zn8.52 mg

200. Spicy Marinated Tuna Steak

Preparation time: 10 minutes

Cooking time: 11 minutes

Servings: 4

Ingredients:

- ¼ cup of orange juice
- ¼ cup of soy sauce
- Two tablespoons olive oil
- One clove garlic, minced
- Half teaspoon chopped fresh oregano
- Half teaspoon ground black pepper
- One tablespoon lemon juice
- Two tablespoons chopped fresh parsley
- Four tuna steaks

Directions:

1. Take a big non-reactive dish and merge soy sauce, lemon juice, oregano, orange juice, parsley, pepper, garlic, olive oil, and pepper.
2. Put the tuna steaks in the marinade and coat. Cover and keep in the freezer for a half-hour.
3. First, preheat the grill for elevated heat and lightly oil the grate.
4. Cook the tuna steak for five to six minutes and then discard leftover marinade.

Nutrition:

Calcium, Ca107 mg

Magnesium, Mg99 mg
Phosphorus, P503 mg
Iron, Fe5.26 mg
Potassium, K1059 mg
Sodium, Na1078 mg
Zinc, Zn9.8 mg

201. Tasty Grilled Shrimp

Preparation time: 15 minutes

Cooking time 6 minutes

Servings: 6

Ingredients:

- One large clove garlic
- One teaspoon coarse salt
- Two tablespoons olive oil
- Two teaspoons lemon juice
- Two pounds' large shrimp
- Eight wedges lemon
- Half teaspoon cayenne pepper
- One teaspoon paprika

Directions:

1. First, preheat the grill for intermediate heat. Take a little bowl and grind the garlic with salt.
2. Merge paprika and cayenne pepper and then stir in the lemon juice and olive oil to make a paste.
3. Take a big bowl and toss shrimp with a paste of garlic until it gets coated.
4. Now, lightly oil the grate on the grill. Cook the shrimp for two to three minutes per side until it gets opaque.
5. Move to the serving dish and decorate with lemon wedges and serve.

Nutrition:
Calcium, Ca263 mg
Magnesium, Mg111 mg
Phosphorus, P1128 mg
Iron, Fe1.77 mg
Potassium, K669 mg
Sodium, Na4896 mg

202. Simple Grilled Salmon with lemon pepper

Preparation time: 15 minutes

Cooking time: 16 minutes

Servings: 6

Ingredients:

- One and a half pounds' salmon fillet
- Half teaspoon lemon pepper
- ¼ teaspoon garlic powder
- 1/3 Cup brown sugar
- 1/3 Cup water
- ¼ cup of vegetable oil
- Half teaspoon salt to taste
- 1/3 Cup soy sauce

Directions:

1. First, season salmon fillets with salt, lemon pepper, and garlic powder.
2. Take a little bowl and stir brown sugar, vegetable oil, soy sauce, and water until sugar is completely dissolved.
3. Add fish in the big plastic bag with a mixture of soy sauce and seal it and then turn to coat.
4. Keep in the freezer for two hours. Now, preheat the grill for intermediate heat.
5. Now, lightly oil the grate and put salmon on the preheated grill and remove the marinade.
6. Cook salmon for six to eight minutes each side until fish easily flakes with a fork.

Nutrition:
Calcium, Ca540 mg
Magnesium, Mg120 mg
Phosphorus, P836 mg
Iron, Fe2.74 mg
Potassium, K1076 mg
Sodium, Na4613 mg
Zinc, Zn2.31 mg

203. Grilled Garlic with Herb Shrimp

Preparation time: 10 minutes

Cooking time: 5 minutes

Servings: 4

Ingredients:

- Two teaspoons ground paprika
- Two teaspoons Italian seasoning blend
- Half teaspoon ground black pepper
- Two tablespoons fresh minced garlic
- Two teaspoons dried basil leaves
- Two tablespoons brown sugar, packed
- Two pounds' large shrimp
- Two tablespoons fresh lemon juice
- ¼ cup olive oil

Directions:

1. First of all, take a bowl whisk lemon juice, pepper, Italian seasoning, garlic, brown sugar, olive oil, and basil until blended.
2. After, stir in the shrimp and toss it coat with marinade. Coat and keep in the freezer for two hours, turning for one time.
3. Now, preheat the grill for medium to high heat and lightly oil grill grate and put four inches from the heat source.
4. Eliminate the shrimp from the marinade and drain it and then remove marinade.
5. Keep shrimp on the preheated grill and cook it until it gets opaque in the middle for five to six minutes and serve instantly.

Nutrition:
Calcium, Ca473 mg
Magnesium, Mg143 mg
Phosphorus, P1160 mg
Iron, Fe4.84 mg
Potassium, K1108 mg
Sodium, Na2846 mg
Zinc, Zn4.86 mg

204. Grilled Cilantro Salmon

Preparation time: 10 minutes

Cooking time: 20 minutes

Servings: 8

Ingredients

- Three pounds' salmon
- One fresh jalapeno pepper,
- One teaspoon Old Bay Seasoning TM
- ¼ cup butter
- One cup chopped cilantro

Directions:

1. First, preheat the grill for elevated heat. After, lightly grease to 1 side of a big sheet of aluminum foil and put salmon on the greased side of the foil.
2. Take a saucepan and liquefy the butter in the saucepan over intermediate heat.
3. Eliminate from the heat and merge jalapeno and cilantro.
4. Cilantro is wilted and sprinkles the mixture of butter over the salmon.

5. Keep the foil with salmon on the grill and season with old bay. Cook for fifteen minutes until fish easily flakes with the fork.
   Nutrition:
   Calcium, Ca929 mg
   Magnesium, Mg144 mg
   Phosphorus, P1482 mg
   Iron, Fe3.17 mg
   Potassium, K1627 mg
   Sodium, Na2337 mg
   Zinc, Zn3.21 m

205. Yummy Maui Wowie Shrimp

Preparation time: 15 minutes

Cooking time: 10 minutes

Servings: 6

Ingredients:

- Two pounds uncooked medium shrimp, peeled and deveined
- One pinch garlic salt
- One pinch ground black pepper
- ¼ teaspoon cayenne pepper
- One cup mayonnaise
- One lemon, cut into wedges

Directions:

1. First, preheat the grill for intermediate heat and lightly oil the grate.
2. After, thread the shrimp on the skewers and season with black pepper and garlic salt
3. Coat equally sides of shrimp with mayonnaise.
4. Fry shrimp on the grilled until shrimp gets bright pink on the outer side and opaque on the inner side, mayonnaise gets golden brown for five to ten minutes on every side. Serve with lemon wedges.
   Nutrition:
   Calcium, Ca386 mg
   Magnesium, Mg240 mg
   Phosphorus, P1252 mg
   Iron, Fe2.23 mg
   Potassium, K887 mg
   Sodium, Na4427 mg

206. Wine Infused Salmon

Preparation time: 15 minutes

Cooking time: 5 hours

Servings: 4

Ingredients:

- 2 C. low-sodium soy sauce
- 1 C. dry white wine
- 1 C. water
- ½ tsp. Tabasco sauce
- 1/3 C. sugar
- ¼ C. salt
- ½ tsp. garlic powder
- ½ tsp. onion powder
- Freshly ground black pepper, to taste
- 4 (6-oz.) salmon fillets

Directions:

1. In a large bowl, add all ingredients except salmon and stir until sugar is dissolved.
2. Add salmon fillets and coat with brine well.
3. Refrigerate, covered overnight.
4. Remove salmon from bowl and rinse under cold running water.
5. With paper towels, pat dry the salmon fillets.
6. Arrange a wire rack in a sheet pan.
7. Place the salmon fillets onto wire rack, skin side down and set aside to cool for about 1 hour.
8. Set the temperature of Wood Pellet Grill to 165 degrees F and preheat with closed lid for 15 minutes, using charcoal.
9. Place the salmon fillets onto the grill, skin side down and cook for about 3-5 hours or until desired doneness.
10. Remove the salmon fillets from grill and serve hot.

Nutrition:

Calories per serving: 377;

Carbohydrates: 26.3g;

Protein: 41.1g;

Fat: 10.5g;

Sugar: 25.1g;

Sodium: 14000mg;

Fiber: 0g

207. Citrus Salmon

Preparation time: 15 minutes

Cooking time: 30 minutes

Servings: 6

Ingredients:

- 2 (1-lb.) salmon fillets
- Salt and freshly ground black pepper, to taste

- 1 tbsp. seafood seasoning
- 2 lemons, sliced
- 2 limes, sliced

Directions:

1. Set the temperature of Wood Pellet Grill to 225 degrees F and preheat with closed lid for 15 minutes.
2. Season the salmon fillets with salt, black pepper and seafood seasoning evenly.
3. Place the salmon fillets onto the grill and top each with lemon and lime slices evenly.
4. Cook for about 30 minutes.
5. Remove the salmon fillets from grill and serve hot.

Nutrition:

Calories per serving: 327

Carbohydrates: 1g

Protein: 36.1g

Fat: 19.8g

Sugar: 0.2g

Sodium: 237mg

Fiber: 0.3g

208. Omega-3 Rich Salmon

Preparation time: 15 minutes

Cooking time: 20 minutes

Servings: 6

Ingredients:

- 6 (6-oz.) skinless salmon fillets
- 1/3 C. olive oil
- ¼ C. spice rub
- ¼ C. honey
- 2 tbsp. Sriracha
- 2 tbsp. fresh lime juice

Directions:

1. Set the temperature of Wood Pellet Grill to 300F and preheat with closed lid for 15 minutes.
2. Coat salmon fillets with olive oil and season with rub evenly.
3. In a small bowl, mix together remaining ingredients.
4. Arrange salmon fillets onto the grill, flat-side up and cook for about 7-10 minutes per side, coating with honey mixture once halfway through.
5. Serve hot alongside remaining honey mixture.

Nutrition:

Calories per serving: 384

Carbohydrates: 15.7g

Protein: 33g

Fat: 21.7g

Sugar: 11.6g

Sodium: 621mg

Fiber: 0g

209. Enticing Mahi-Mahi

Preparation time: 10 minutes

Cooking time: 10 minutes

Servings: 4

Ingredients:

- 4 (6-oz.) mahi-mahi fillets
- 2 tbsp. olive oil
- Salt and freshly ground black pepper, to taste

Directions:

1. Set the temperature of Wood Pellet Grill to 350F and preheat with closed lid for 15 minutes.
2. Coat fish fillets with olive oil and season with salt and black pepper evenly.
3. Place the fish fillets onto the grill and cook for about 5 minutes per side.
4. Remove the fish fillets from grill and serve hot.

Nutrition:

Calories per serving: 195

Carbohydrates: 0g

Protein: 31.6g

Fat: 7g

Sugar: 0g

Sodium: 182mg

Fiber: 0g

210. Super-Tasty Trout

Preparation time: 15 minutes

Cooking time: 5 hours

Servings: 2

Ingredients:

- 1 (7-lb.) whole lake trout, butterflied
- ½ C. kosher salt
- ½ C. fresh rosemary, chopped
- 2 tsp. lemon zest, grated finely

Directions:

1. Rub the trout with salt generously and then, sprinkle with rosemary and lemon zest.
2. Arrange the trout in a large baking dish and refrigerate for about 7-8 hours.
3. Remove the trout from baking dish and rinse under cold running water to remove the salt.
4. With paper towels, pat dry the trout completely.
5. Arrange a wire rack in a sheet pan.
6. Place the trout onto the wire rack, skin side down and refrigerate for about 24 hours.
7. Set the temperature of Wood Pellet Grill to 180F and preheat with closed lid for 15 minutes, using charcoal.
8. Place the trout onto the grill and cook for about 2-4 hours or until desired doneness.
9. Remove the trout from grill and place onto a cutting board for about 5 minutes before serving.

Nutrition:

Calories per serving: 633

Carbohydrates: 2.4g

Protein: 85.2g

Fat: 31.8g

Sugar: 0g

Sodium: 5000mg

Fiber: 1.6g

211. No-Fuss Tuna Burgers

Preparation time: 15 minutes

Cooking time: 15 minutes

Servings: 6

Ingredients:

- 2 lb. tuna steak
- 1 green bell pepper, seeded and chopped
- 1 white onion, chopped
- 2 eggs
- 1 tsp. soy sauce
- 1 tbsp. blackened Saskatchewan rub
- Salt and freshly ground black pepper, to taste

Directions:

1. Set the temperature of the Wood Pellet Grill to 500 degrees F and preheat with closed lid for 15 minutes.
2. In a bowl, add all the ingredients and mix until well combined.
3. With greased hands, make patties from mixture.
4. Place the patties onto the grill close to the edges and cook for about 10-15 minutes, flipping once halfway through.
5. Serve hot.

Nutrition:

Calories per serving: 313

Carbohydrates: 3.4g

Protein: 47.5g

Fat: 11g

Sugar: 1.9g

Sodium: 174mg

Fiber: 0.7g

212. Lively Flavored Shrimp

Preparation time: 15 minutes

Cooking time: 30 minutes

Servings: 6

Ingredients:

- 8 oz. salted butter, melted
- ¼ C. Worcestershire sauce
- ¼ C. fresh parsley, chopped
- 1 lemon, quartered
- 2 lb. jumbo shrimp, peeled and deveined
- 3 tbsp. BBQ rub

Directions:

1. In a metal baking pan, add all ingredients except for shrimp and BBQ rub and mix well.
2. Season the shrimp with BBQ rub evenly.
3. Add the shrimp in the pan with butter mixture and coat well.

4. Set aside for about 20-30 minutes.
5. Set the temperature of the Wood Pellet Grill to 250 degrees F and preheat with closed lid for 15 minutes.
6. Place the pan onto the grill and cook for about 25-30 minutes.
7. Remove the pan from grill and serve hot.

Nutrition:

Calories per serving: 462

Carbohydrates: 4.7g

Protein: 34.9g

Fat: 33.3g

Sugar: 2.1g

Sodium: 485mg

Fiber: 0.2g

213. Flavor-Bursting Prawn Skewers

Preparation time: 15 minutes

Cooking time: 8 minutes

Servings: 5

Ingredients:

- ¼ C. fresh parsley leaves, minced
- 1 tbsp. garlic, crushed
- 2½ tbsp. olive oil
- 2 tbsp. Thai chili sauce
- 1 tbsp. fresh lime juice
- 1½ pounds prawns, peeled and deveined

Instructions:

1. In a large bowl, add all ingredients except for prawns and mix well.
2. In a resalable plastic bag, add marinade and prawns.
3. Seal the bag and shake to coat well
4. Refrigerate for about 20-30 minutes.
5. Set the temperature of Wood Pellet Grill to 450 degrees F and preheat with closed lid for 15 minutes.
6. Remove the prawns from marinade and thread onto metal skewers.
7. Arrange the skewers onto the grill and cook for about 4 minutes per side.
8. Remove the skewers from grill and serve hot.

Nutrition:

Calories per serving: 234

Carbohydrates: 4.9g

Protein: 31.2g

Fat: 9.3g

Sugar: 1.7g

Sodium: 562mg

Fiber: 0.1g

214. Yummy Buttery Clams

Preparation time: 15 minutes

Cooking time: 8 minutes

Servings: 6

Ingredients:

- 24 littleneck clams
- ½ C. cold butter, chopped
- 2 tbsp. fresh parsley, minced
- 3 garlic cloves, minced
- 1 tsp. fresh lemon juice

Directions:

1. Set the temperature of Wood Pellet Grill to 450 degrees F and preheat with closed lid for 15 minutes.
2. Scrub the clams under cold running water.
3. In a large casserole dish, mix together remaining ingredients.
4. Place the casserole dish onto the grill.
5. Now, arrange the clams directly onto the grill and cook for about 5-8 minutes or until they are opened. (Discard any that fail to open).
6. With tongs, carefully transfer the opened clams into the casserole dish and remove from grill.
7. Serve immediately.

Nutrition:

Calories per serving: 306

Carbohydrates: 6.4g

Protein: 29.3g

Fat: 7.6g

Sugar: 0.1g

Sodium: 237mg

Fiber: 0.1g

215. Crazy Delicious Lobster Tails

Preparation time: 15 minutes

Cooking time: 25 minutes

Servings: 4

Ingredients:

- ½ C. butter, melted
- 2 garlic cloves, minced
- 2 tsp. fresh lemon juice
- Salt and freshly ground black pepper, to taste
- 4 (8-oz.) lobster tails

Directions:

1. Set the temperature of Wood Pellet Grill to 450 degrees F and preheat with closed lid for 15 minutes.
2. In a metal pan, add all ingredients except for lobster tails and mix well.
3. Place the pan onto the grill and cook for about 10 minutes.
4. Meanwhile, cut down the top of the shell and expose lobster meat.
5. Remove pan of butter mixture from grill.
6. Coat the lobster meat with butter mixture.
7. Place the lobster tails onto the grill and cook for about 15 minutes, coating with butter mixture once halfway through.
8. Remove from grill and serve hot.

Nutrition:

Calories per serving: 409;

Carbohydrates: 0.6g;

Protein: 43.5g;

Fat: 24.9g;

Sugar: 0.1g;

Sodium: 1305mg;

Fiber: 0g

CHAPTER 19. VEGETABLE RECIPES

216. Smoked Turkey Leg with Green Beans

Preparation time: 10 minutes

Cooking Time: 3 Hours

Servings: 4

Ingredients:

- 2 pounds fresh green beans
- 3 cups of chicken stock
- 1 pound smoked turkey legs, boneless
- 2 tablespoons of apple cider vinegar
- Salt and pepper, to taste

Directions:

1. Preheat the smoker grill to 220 degrees F for 40 minutes.
2. Wash the beans and trim the edges.
3. Pat dry the green beans.
4. Place green beans onto the aluminum foil and then add stock and turkey leg.
5. Place it on the smoker grill and cook for 3 hours.
6. Once done, drain the extra stock.
7. Season it with salt, pepper, and a drizzle of apple cider vinegar.
8. Serve and Enjoy.

Nutrition:

Calories 442

Total Fat 8.8g

Saturated Fat 2.5g

Cholesterol 47mg

217. Lemon & Garlic Asparagus

Preparation time: 10 minutes

Cooking Time: 2 Hours

Servings: 2

Ingredients:

- 2 cups of asparagus
- Olive oil, for greasing
- Salt and pepper, to taste
- 4 tablespoons of butter
- 4 garlic cloves, minced
- 1 lemon, zest

Directions:

1. Preheat the electric smoker grill for 20 minutes at 200 degrees F.
2. Put the trimmed asparagus in boiling water for one minute.
3. Take out the asparagus and pat dry with a paper towel.
4. Sprinkle the vegetables with salt, pepper, and oil.
5. Melt butter along with garlic, and lemon zest in the microwave and pour over the asparagus
6. Transfer the asparagus to aluminum foil pan.
7. Put a pan on the grill grate and set the temperature of the electric smoker to 225 degrees F.
8. Cook the asparagus for 2 hours.
9. Once the asparagus is cooked, it to the serving plate and serve and enjoy.

Nutrition:

Calories 543

Total Fat 7.9g

Saturated Fat 6.1g

Cholesterol 21mg

218. Smoked Paprika Cauliflower

Preparation time: 10 minutes

Cooking Time: 2 Hours

Servings: 4

Ingredients:

- 1 large head of Cauliflower, cut into florets
- 6 tablespoons olive oil
- 1 tablespoon white pepper
- 1 teaspoon of smoked paprika

Directions:

1. Preheat the smoker grill for 220 degrees F.
2. In a mixing bowl, add olive oil, paprika, pepper and cauliflower.
3. Toss ingredients well.
4. Smoke cauliflower for 2 hours.
5. Once done, serve.

Nutrition:

Calories 235

Total Fat 3.9g

Saturated Fat 2.5g

Cholesterol 13mg

219. Cabbage

Preparation time: 10 minutes

Cooking Time: 2 Hours

Servings: 2

Ingredients:

- 2 large cups of red cabbage
- 3 tablespoons of steak seasoning
- 1 stick butter
- 1 vegetable bouillon cube

Directions:

1. Preheat the electric smoker for 20 minutes at 250 degrees F.
2. Place the cabbage onto the tin foil pan and add butter.
3. Sprinkle vegetable bouillon cubes and then season it with steak seasoning.
4. Wrap the tin foil leaving the top slightly open.
5. Cook on the grill grate for 2 hours at 200 degrees F.
6. Once done, serve.

Nutrition:

Calories 223

Total Fat 4.2g

Saturated Fat 1.5g

Cholesterol 51mg

220. Eggplant

Preparation time: 10 minutes

Cooking Time: 1 Hour

Servings: 6

Ingredients:

- 4 cloves of garlic, minced
- 2 tablespoons of balsamic vinegar
- Salt and pepper, to taste
- 6 eggplants
- 6 tablespoons of olive oil

Directions:

1. Preheat the smoker for 50 minutes at 220 degrees F.
2. Cut the eggplant in circles.
3. Marinate the eggplant in garlic, pepper, salt, vinegar, and olive oil mixture.
4. After one hour, place the eggplant onto smoker grill and a smoker for 60 minutes.
5. Once done, serve.

Nutrition:

Calories 142

Total Fat 7.2g

Saturated Fat 3.5g

Cholesterol 71mg

221. Potatoes

Preparation time: 10 minutes

Cooking Time: 2 Hours

Servings: 1

Ingredients:

- A ½ cup of olive oil - 6 large potatoes
- Salt and pepper, to taste
- 2 tablespoons of onion powder
- ½ teaspoon of garlic powder
- 1 teaspoon of dried thyme

Directions:

1. Preheat the electric smoker grill at 200 degrees F for 2 hours.
2. Cut the potatoes and brush with olive oil.
3. Season it with salt, garlic powder, thyme, pepper, and onion powder.
4. Smoke on the grill for 2 hours at 220 degrees F.
5. Then, serve and enjoy.

Nutrition:

Calories 213

Total Fat 8.7g

Saturated Fat 2.5g

Cholesterol 5.6mg

222. Blueberry Crumble

Preparation time: 10 minutes

Cooking Time: 3 Hours

Servings: 2

Ingredients:

Filling Ingredients

- 1 cup of Blueberries
- ¾ cup dark brown sugar
- ½ cup self-rising flour
- 1 teaspoon lemon zest, grated
- 1 tablespoon lemon juice
- Ingredients for Crumble
- 2 cups quick-cooking oats
- 1/2 cup all-purpose flour
- 1/2 cup packed brown sugar
- 1 teaspoon cinnamon
- 1cup butter

Directions:

1. Take a mixing bowl, and combine sugar, lemon zest, lemon juice, and flour.
2. Next, add the blueberry and mix all ingredients well.
3. Take an aluminum pan and coat it generously with oil separator.
4. Pour this mixture into the aluminum pan.
5. In a separate bowl, combine all the crumble ingredients.
6. Pour the crumb Ingredients to the blueberry mixture in an aluminum pan.
7. Preheat the smoker grill at 260 degrees Fahrenheit until the smoke form.
8. Once the smoker grill is preheated, put the aluminum pan onto the grill and pocket for 3 hours at 250 degrees Fahrenheit.
9. Once done, serve and enjoy.

Nutrition:

Calories 523

Total Fat 8.9g

Saturated Fat 2.5g

Cholesterol 76mg

223. Baked Peach Cobbler

Preparation time: 10 minutes

Cooking Time: 3 Hours

Servings: 3

Ingredients:

- 4 teaspoons of butter, melted
- 2 pounds of peaches, sliced
- ½ cup maple syrup
- 1 cup flour, self-raising flour
- 3/4 teaspoon baking powder
- 1 pinch cinnamon
- 1 pinch salt
- 1/2 cup unsalted butter, cut into small cubes
- 1/2 cup white sugar
- 4 eggs
- 1/3 teaspoon vanilla

Directions:

1. Preheat the smoker grill at 220 degrees Fahrenheit until the smoke started to form.
2. Take a heatproof pan and coat it with melted butter.
3. In an aluminum pan, combine peaches along with maple syrup.
4. In a separate bowl, combine flour, baking powder, salt, and cinnamon.
5. In a small glass bowl mixed with sugar and butter, then add whisk eggs and vanilla into the butter.
6. Fold this mixture into the flour mixture.
7. Place the aluminum pan onto the smoker grill grate and cook 3 hours at 250 degrees Fahrenheit.
8. Once done, serve.

Nutrition:

Calories 477

Total Fat 8.8g

Saturated Fat 8.5g

Cholesterol 45mg

224. Chocolate Pudding

Preparation time: 10 minutes

Cooking Time: 1 Hour

Servings: 2

Ingredients:

- 1 cup chocolate, chopped
- 1 cup Whipping cream, side serving (topping)
- Cobbler Topping Ingredients
- 2 cups all-purpose flour
- 8 tablespoons of sugar
- 2 teaspoons of baking powder
- 1 tablespoon of cocoa powder
- 1 cup sour cream

Directions:

1. The first step is to preheat the smoker grill at 350 degrees Fahrenheit until the smoke establish.
2. Take a medium bowl and combine sugar, flour, baking soda, and cocoa powder.
3. Mix sour cream to the bowl.
4. Mix the ingredients well.
5. Now add in the chocolate and pour it into the aluminum pan.
6. Put the aluminum pan on top of the grill grate and close the lid.
7. Smoke it for 60 minutes or until the top gets brown and bubbly.
8. Served with whipping cream.

Nutrition:

Calories 784

Total Fat 8.9g

Saturated Fat 3.5g

Cholesterol 56mg

225. Twice-smoked Potatoes

Cooking Time: 1 hour 35 minutes

Servings: 16

Ingredients:

- 8 Idaho, Russet, or Yukon Gold potatoes
- 1 (12-ounce) can evaporated milk, heated
- 1 cup (2 sticks) butter, melted
- ½ cup sour cream, at room temperature
- 1 cup grated Parmesan cheese
- ½ pound bacon, cooked and crumbled
- ¼ cup chopped scallions
- Salt
- Freshly ground black pepper
- 1 cup shredded Cheddar cheese

Directions:

1. Supply your smoker with wood pellets and follow the manufacturer's specific start-up procedure. Preheat, with the lid closed, to 400°F.
2. Poke the potatoes all over with a fork. Arrange them directly on the grill grate, close the lid, and smoke for 1 hour and 15 minutes, or until cooked through and they have some give when pinched.

3. Let the potatoes cool for 10 minutes, then cut in half lengthwise.
4. Into a medium bowl, scoop out the potato flesh, leaving ¼ inch in the shells; place the shells on a baking sheet.
5. Use an electric mixer then set on medium speed to beat the potatoes, milk, butter, and sour cream until smooth.
6. Stir in the Parmesan cheese, bacon, and scallions, and season with salt and pepper.
7. Generously stuff each shell with the potato mixture and top with Cheddar cheese.
8. Move the baking sheet on the grill grate, close the lid, and smoke for 20 minutes, or until the cheese is melted.

226. Bacon-wrapped Jalapeno Poppers

Cooking Time: 20 minutes

Servings: 6

Ingredients:

- 6 jalapenos, Fresh
- 1/2 cup shredded cheddar cheese
- 4 oz. soft cream cheese
- 1-1/2 tbsp. veggie rub
- 12 bacon slices, thin cut

Directions:

1. Preheat your Wood Pellet grill to 375F.
2. Halve the jalapenos lengthwise then scrape membrane and seeds using a spoon. rinse them and set aside.
3. Meanwhile, combine cheddar cheese, cream cheese, and veggie rub in a bowl, medium stirring until incorporated fully.
4. Fill the jalapenos with your cheese mixture then wrap each half with a bacon slice.
5. Place on your grill and grill for about 15-20 minutes until bacon becomes crispy and peppers are soft.
6. Serve and enjoy.

Nutrition:

Calories 329

Total fat 25.7g

Saturated fat 11.4g

Total carbs 5g

Net carbs 4.6g

Protein 18.1g

Sugars 0.6g

Fiber 0.4g

Sodium 1667mg

Potassium 277mg

227. Grilled Potato Salad

Preparation Time: 5 minutes

Cooking Time: 10 minutes

Servings: 8

Ingredients:

- 1 ½ pound fingerling potatoes, halved lengthwise
- 1 small jalapeno, sliced
- 10 scallions
- 2 teaspoons salt
- 2 tablespoons rice vinegar
- 2 teaspoons lemon juice
- 2/3 cup olive oil, divided

Directions:

1. Switch on the Wood Pellet Grill, fill the grill hopper with pecan flavored wood pellets, power the grill on by using the control panel, select 'smoke' on the temperature dial, or set the temperature to 450 degrees F and let it preheat for a minimum of 5 minutes.
2. Meanwhile, prepare scallions, and for this, brush them with some oil.
3. When the grill has preheated, open the lid, place scallions on the grill grate, shut the grill and smoke for 3 minutes until lightly charred.
4. Then transfer scallions to a cutting board, let them cool for 5 minutes, then cut into slices and set aside until required.
5. Brush potatoes with some oil, season with some salt and black pepper, place potatoes on the grill grate, shut the grill and smoke for 5 minutes until thoroughly cooked.
6. Then take a large bowl, pour in remaining oil, add salt, lemon juice, and vinegar and stir until combined.
7. Add grilled scallion and potatoes, toss until well mixed, taste to adjust seasoning and then serve.

Nutrition:

Calories: 223.7 Cal

Fat: 12 g

Carbs: 27 g

Protein: 1.9 g

Fiber: 3.3 g

228. Smoked Pickles

Cooking Time: 15 minutes

Servings: 6

Ingredients:

- 1-quart water
- ¼ cup sugar
- ½ quart white vinegar
- ½ cup salt
- ½ teaspoon peppercorns
- 1 ½ teaspoons celery seeds
- 1 ½ teaspoons coriander seeds
- 1 teaspoon mustard seeds
- 8 cloves of garlic, minced
- 1 bunch dill weed
- 12 small cucumbers

Directions:

1. Place the water, sugar, vinegar, salt, and peppercorns in a saucepan. Bring to a boil over medium flame.
2. Move to a bowl and allow to cool. Add in the rest of the ingredients.
3. Allow the cucumber to soak in the brine for at least 3 days.
4. When ready to cook, fire the Wood Pellet Grill to 500F. Use desired wood pellets when cooking. Close lid then heat for 15 minutes.
5. Pat dry the cucumber with paper towel and place on the grill grate. Smoke for 15 minutes.

Nutrition:

Calories per serving: 67

Protein: 2.4g

Carbs: 12.9g

Fat: 1.1g

Sugar:8.5 g

229. Grilled Scallions

Preparation Time: 15 minutes

Cooking Time: 20 minutes

Servings: 6

Ingredients:

- 10 whole scallions, chopped
- ¼ cup olive oil
- Salt and pepper to taste
- 2 tablespoons rice vinegar
- 1 whole jalapeno, sliced into rings

Directions:

1. Fire the Wood Pellet Grill to 500F. Use desired wood pellets when cooking. Close lid then heat for 15 minutes.
2. Place on a bowl all ingredients and toss to coat. Transfer to a parchment-lined baking tray.
3. Move the scallions on the grill grate and cook for 20 minutes or until the scallions char.

Nutrition:

Calories per serving: 135

Protein: 2.2 g

Carbs: 9.7 g

Fat: 10.1

Sugar: 4.6g

230. Shiitake Smoked Mushrooms

Preparation Time: 10 minutes

Cooking Time: 45 minutes

Servings: 4 -5

Ingredients:

- 4 Cup Shiitake Mushrooms
- 1 tbsp. canola oil
- 1 tsp onion powder
- 1 tsp granulated garlic
- 1 tsp salt
- 1 tsp pepper

Directions:

1. Combine all the ingredients together
2. Apply the mix over the mushrooms generously.
3. Preheat the smoker at 180°F. Add wood chips and half a bowl of water in the side tray.
4. Place it in the smoker and smoke for 45 minutes.
5. Serve warm and enjoy.

Nutrition:

Calories: 301 Cal

Fat: 9 g

Carbohydrates: 47.8 g

Protein: 7.1 g

Fiber: 4.8 g

231. Stuffed Mini Peppers

Preparation Time: 20 minutes

Cooking Time: 15 minutes

Servings: 4

Ingredients:

- 4 mini paprika's
- 1 to 2 spring onions

- Fresh peppers (chili)
- Garlic (fresh or dried)
- 4 anchovy fillets (cut into fine pieces)
- 1 tomato
- Olives
- Parsley
- Capers or caper apple
- Chapelure, breadcrumbs or panko
- 100 gr goat cheese or feta

Directions:

1. Set the wood pellet grill to maximum heat
2. Prepare the filling in advance: Finely chop everything, mix together to a grainy filling.
3. Cut the vegetables in half lengthwise, remove the seeds. Spread the edges with a little oil and place it on the concave side on the hot spot in the grill. (usually at the back of the grill)
4. Lightly color the edges of the vegetables. Then take it back from the grill and fill it with the filling.
5. Place the stuffed peppers back on the grill and cook for about 5-10 minutes. (does not have to be well done)

Nutrition:

Calories: 115

Protein: 4 g

Carbohydrates: 25 g

Sugar: 13 g

Fat: 1 g

Calories from Fat: 5%

Fiber: 5 g

Sodium: 429 mg

232. Baked Tomato with Herb Butter

Preparation Time: 10 minutes

Cooking Time: 12 minutes

Servings: 4

Ingredients:

- 1 tomato per person (not too big)
- Pepper and salt
- Herb butter
- Breadcrumbs or panko (Chinese breadcrumbs / fine bread flakes)
- Sprinkle cheese
- Aluminum shell

Directions:

1. Remove the crown and halve the tomatoes.
2. Season with salt and pepper.
3. Place a slice of herb butter both each half tomato.
4. Finish with breadcrumbs.
5. Place in an aluminum bowl.
6. Set heat to 176 C and place the aluminum tray on the grill.
7. Bake for 8 to 12 minutes (according to the size of the tomatoes and the number of tomatoes in the aluminum dish)

Nutrition:

Calories: 115

Protein: 4 g

Carbohydrates: 25 g

Sugar: 13 g

Fat: 1 g

Calories from Fat: 5%

Fiber: 5 g

Sodium: 429 mg

233. Grilled Asparagus

Preparation Time: 5 minutes

Cooking Time: 3 minutes

Servings: 4

Ingredients:

- Water - 1 glass
- Fresh asparagus - 450 g
- BBQ sauce - 1/4 cup

Directions:

1. In a big skillet, bring 1 cup water to a boil. Put the asparagus in boiling water, cover the pan with a lid and blanch the asparagus for about 4-6 minutes, until completely soft. Remove the asparagus from the water and transfer to a paper towel, blot well to remove all liquid.
2. Soak wooden skewers in cold water for 5 minutes so that they do not burn during frying. Turn on the grill to preheat to medium heat.
3. String the cooled asparagus on wooden skewers (as shown in the photo).
4. Place the asparagus on the grill rack and cook, uncovered, for about 1 minute on each side. Then brush the asparagus with barbecue sauce and cook for about 2 minutes more, turn over, grease the other side with the sauce and cook for about 1 minute.
5. Serve the asparagus immediately.

Nutrition:

Calories: 111

Protein: 5 g

Carbohydrates: 26 g

Fat: 2 g

Calories from Fat: 5%

Fiber: 5 g

Sodium: 429 mg

234. Grilled Stuffed Bell Pepper

Preparation Time: 5 minutes

Cooking Time: 15 minutes

Servings: 4

Ingredients:

- Olive oil - 1/2 cup + 2 tsp.
- Parmesan cheese (shredded on a greater) - 3/4 cup
- Fresh basil leaves - 2 cups
- Sunflower seeds (kernels) or walnuts (kernels) - 2 tbsp.
- Garlic - 4 cloves
- Bulgarian pepper (seeded and finely chopped) - 1/2 cup
- Corn grains (canned) - 4 cups
- Medium sized Bulgarian pepper - 4 pcs.
- Parmesan cheese (grated) (for serving) - 1/4 cup

Directions:

1. Switch on the grill to preheat to medium temperature.
2. Prepare the pesto sauce. Pour 1/2 cup olive oil inside the bowl of a food processor or blender, add 3/4 cup cheese, basil, seeds (or nuts) and garlic, pulsate until smooth.
3. In a large skillet, heat the remaining olive oil; add the chopped bell pepper and fry, stirring occasionally, until soft. Add corn and pesto to the pan and stir well.
4. Cut a whole bell pepper into halves, remove seeds and stalks. Place the halves on a preheated grill, slices down. Place the lid on the grill and cook the peppers for about 8 minutes. Then stuff the pepper halves with the corn mixture and grill for another 4-6 minutes, until the pepper is soft.
5. Serve the finished dish sprinkled with Parmesan.

Nutrition:

Calcium, Ca496 mg

Magnesium, Mg495 mg

Phosphorus, P1131 mg

Iron, Fe11.34 mg

Potassium, K1472 mg

Sodium, Na1046 mg

Zinc, Zn10.3 mg

235. Zucchini Cutlets

Preparation Time: 30 minutes
Cooking Time: 30 minutes
Servings: 4
Ingredients:

- Zucchini - 750 g
- Salt and black pepper
- Egg (slightly beaten) - 1 pc.
- Coarse flour - 2/3 cup (60 g)
- Chopped nutmeg - 1/4 tsp.

For the sauce:

- Lemon zest - 1 tsp
- Lemon juice - 1 tbsp.
- Mint (chopped) - 3-4 tbsp.
- Fat-free yogurt (natural) - 150 g

Directions:

1. Grind the zucchini with a blender or on a fine grater, season with salt, leave for 30 minutes at room temperature. Then rinse inside a colander under running cold water. Squeeze well with your hands and put on a paper towel, blot.
2. Transfer the chopped zucchini to a bowl and add the egg, flour, nutmeg and pepper. Mix everything well and let it brew at room temperature for 20 minutes.
3. Prepare the sauce. In a separate bowl, combine lemon, zest, mint and yogurt. Cover and refrigerate.
4. Heat a skillet or skillet over medium heat. Spoon the zucchini mixture (1 tablespoon each) into the pan and gently form the patties. Fry for 3-4 minutes on each side. Serve with yoghurt sauce.

Nutrition:

Calories: 115

Protein: 4 g

Carbohydrates: 25 g

Sugar: 13 g

Fat: 1 g

Calories from Fat: 5%

Fiber: 5 g

Sodium: 429 mg

236. Orzo Pasta with Grilled Shrimps and Vegetables

Preparation Time: 5 minutes

Cooking Time: 18 minutes

Servings: 4

Ingredients:

- Orzo pasta - 230 g

- Zucchini or yellow zucchini (cut into 0.5 cm slices) - 2 pcs. (about 260 g)
- Bulgarian red or yellow pepper (seeded and cut into quarters) - 1 pc.
- Pesto sauce - 3 tbsp., Fresh lime juice - 2 tablespoons
- Fresh or frozen shrimp (uncooked) (peeled) - 450 g
- Fresh tomatoes (peeled and cut into 1 cm cubes) - 250 g
- Extra virgin olive oil - 6.5 tbsp., Red wine vinegar - 4 tbsp.
- Fresh basil leaves (cut into strips) - ½ cup
- Mozzarella cheese (cut into 1 cm cubes) - 230 g
- Fresh basil leaves for serving

Directions:

1. Prepare the orzo pasta in salted water, according to the instructions on the package. Dry the paste, rinse under running cold water, dry again. Transfer to a large bowl and mix with 1 tablespoon of olive oil.
2. Turn on the grill to preheat to medium temperature. In a small bowl, combine 2 tablespoons of oil and 2 tablespoons of vinegar.
3. Grease the zucchini and pepper with an oil mixture, sprinkle with salt and pepper. Mix pesto, lime juice, 3.5 tablespoons oil, and 2 tablespoons vinegar separately. Place the shrimps inside a medium bowl and drizzle with 2 tablespoons of pesto vinegar, stir.
4. Place the zucchini and peppers on the grill rack and fry until crispy, about 3-4 minutes on each side.
5. Transfer vegetables to a cutting board. Sprinkle the shrimps with salt and pepper, place on the grill and cook for about 2-3 minutes on each side. Put the fried shrimp inside a bowl with orzo.
6. Cut the zucchini including bell pepper into cubes and place in a bowl with orzo. Add remaining pesto vinegar, tomatoes, chopped basil and cheese. Season it with salt including pepper to taste, mix well.
7. Serve the dish sprinkled with basil leaves immediately or chill in the refrigerator.
   Nutrition:
   Calcium, Ca708 mg
   Magnesium, Mg1121 mg
   Phosphorus, P4043 mg
   Iron, Fe65.74 mg
   Potassium, K29581 mg
   Sodium, Na6450 mg
   Zinc, Zn19.56 mg

237. Fried Eggplant with Tomato Sauce

Preparation Time: 15 minutes

Cooking Time: 18 minutes

Servings: 4

Ingredients:

- Eggplant - 2 pcs.
- Olive oil - 4 tbsp.
- Garlic - 2 cloves
- Paprika - ½ tsp.
- Sea salt
- Black pepper, freshly ground
- Tomatoes (canned, cut into pieces) - 400 g

Directions:

1. Preheat a barbecue or cast iron grill pan with ribbed bottom. Cut the eggplants into 1 cm circles and place in a colander. Sprinkle with salt, press down with a plate and let sit for 15 minutes. Rinse and pat dry with a paper towel.
2. Preheat 1 tbsp. l. butter in a skillet over low heat. Add the sliced garlic and paprika. Cook it for a few seconds, salt and pepper. Stir in the tomato pulp, bring to a boil over high heat, reduce heat and simmer for 15 minutes.
3. Brush the eggplant with the remaining oil and grill on a barbecue or skillet for 3 minutes on each side, until golden brown. Pour over cooked tomato sauce and serve.
4. Enjoy your meal!

Nutrition:

Calcium, Ca2527 mg

Magnesium, Mg2788 mg

Phosphorus, P6046 mg

Iron, Fe68.23 mg

Potassium, K59613 mg

Sodium, Na1243 mg

Zinc, Zn42.78 mg

238. Mexican Street Corn with Chipotle Butter

Preparation time: 10 Minutes

Cooking time: 12 to 14 Minutes

Servings: 4

Ingredients:

- 4 ears corn
- ½ cup sour cream
- ½ cup mayonnaise
- ¼ cup chopped fresh cilantro, plus more for garnish

- Chipotle Butter, for topping
- 1 cup grated Parmesan cheese

Directions:

1. Supply your smoker with wood pellets and follow the manufacturer's specific start-up procedure. Preheat, with the lid closed, to 450°F.
2. Shuck the corn, removing the silks and cutting off the cores.
3. Tear four squares of aluminum foil large enough to cover an ear of corn completely.
4. In a medium bowl, combine the sour cream, mayonnaise, and cilantro. Slather the mixture all over the ears of corn.
5. Wrap each ear of corn in a piece of foil, sealing tightly. Place on the grill, close the lid, and smoke for 12 to 14 minutes.
6. Remove the corn from the foil and place in a shallow baking dish. Top with chipotle butter, the Parmesan cheese, and more chopped cilantro.
7. Serve immediately.
8. Smoking Tip After the initial 12- to 14-minute cook time, move the corn to indirect heat to keep warm as you cook the rest of your meal. It's very difficult to burn corn on the cob.

Nutrition:

Calories: 150

Carbohydrates: 15 g

Protein: 79 g

Sodium: 45 mg

Cholesterol: 49 mg

239. Twice-Smoked Potatoes

Preparation time: 10 Minutes

Cooking time: 14 Minutes

Servings: 4

Ingredients:

- 8 Idaho, Russet, or Yukon Gold potatoes
- 1 (12-ounce) can evaporated milk, heated
- 1 cup (2 sticks) butter, melted
- ½ cup sour cream, at room temperature
- 1 cup grated Parmesan cheese
- ½ pound bacon, cooked and crumbled
- ¼ cup chopped scallions
- Salt
- Freshly ground black pepper
- 1 cup shredded Cheddar cheese

Directions:

1. Supply your smoker with wood pellets and follow the manufacturer's specific start-up procedure. Preheat, with the lid closed, to 400F.
2. Poke the potatoes all over with a fork. Arrange them directly on the grill grate, close the lid, and smoke for 1 hour and 15 minutes, or until cooked through and they have some give when pinched.
3. Let the potatoes cool for 10 minutes, then cut in half lengthwise.
4. Into a medium bowl, scoop out the potato flesh, leaving ¼ inch in the shells; place the shells on a baking sheet.
5. Using an electric mixer on medium speed, beat the potatoes, milk, butter, and sour cream until smooth.
6. Stir in the Parmesan cheese, bacon, and scallions, and season with salt and pepper.
7. Generously stuff each shell with the potato mixture and top with Cheddar cheese.
8. Place the baking sheet on the grill grate, close the lid, and smoke for 20 minutes, or until the cheese is melted.
9. Technique Tip One extra step can give your potato a salty crust. Before baking, cover the raw potato with your choice of oil, bacon grease (YAASS!), or butter, then coat the spud with sea salt.

Nutrition:

Calories: 150

Carbohydrates: 15 g

Protein: 79 g

Sodium: 45 mg

Cholesterol: 49 mg

240. Roasted Okra

Preparation time: 10 Minutes

Cooking time: 30 Minutes

Servings: 4

Ingredients:

- 1-pound whole okra
- 2 tablespoons extra-virgin olive oil
- 2 teaspoons seasoned salt
- 2 teaspoons freshly ground black pepper

Directions:

1. Supply your smoker with wood pellets and follow the manufacturer's specific start-up procedure. Preheat, with the lid closed, to 400°F. Alternatively, preheat your oven to 400°F.
2. Line a shallow rimmed baking pan with aluminum foil and coat with cooking spray.
3. Arrange the okra on the pan in a single layer. Drizzle with the olive oil, turning to coat. Season on all sides with the salt and pepper.
4. Place the baking pan on the grill grate, close the lid, and smoke for 30 minutes, or until crisp and slightly charred. Alternatively, roast in the oven for 30 minutes.
5. Serve hot.
6. Smoking Tip: Whether you make this okra in the oven or in your wood pellet grill, be sure to fully preheat the oven or cook chamber for the best results.

Nutrition:

Calories: 150

Carbohydrates: 15 g

Protein: 79 g

Sodium: 45 mg

Cholesterol: 49 mg

241. Sweet Potato Chips

Preparation time: 10 Minutes

Cooking time: 12 to 15 Minutes

Servings: 4

Ingredients:

- 2 sweet potatoes
- 1-quart warm water
- 1 tablespoon cornstarch, plus 2 teaspoons
- ¼ cup extra-virgin olive oil
- 1 tablespoon salt
- 1 tablespoon packed brown sugar
- 1 teaspoon ground cinnamon
- 1 teaspoon freshly ground black pepper
- ½ teaspoon cayenne pepper

Directions:

1. Using a mandoline, thinly slice the sweet potatoes.
2. Pour the warm water into a large bowl and add 1 tablespoon of cornstarch and the potato slices. Let soak for 15 to 20 minutes.
3. Supply your smoker with wood pellets and follow the manufacturer's specific start-up procedure. Preheat, with the lid closed, to 375°F.
4. Drain the potato slices, then arrange in a single layer on a perforated pizza pan or a baking sheet lined with aluminum foil. Brush the potato slices on both sides with the olive oil.
5. In a small bowl, whisk together the salt, brown sugar, cinnamon, black pepper, cayenne pepper, and the remaining 2 teaspoons of cornstarch. Sprinkle this seasoning blend on both sides of the potatoes.
6. Place the pan or baking sheet on the grill grate, close the lid, and smoke for 35 to 45 minutes, flipping after 20 minutes, until the chips curl up and become crispy.
7. Store in an airtight container.
8. Ingredient Tip: Avoid storing your sweet potatoes in the refrigerator's produce bin, which tends to give them a hard center and an unpleasant flavor. What, you don't have a root cellar? Just keep them in a cool, dry area of your kitchen.

Nutrition:

Calories: 150

Carbohydrates: 15 g

Protein: 79 g

Sodium: 45 mg

Cholesterol: 49 mg

242. Broccoli-Cauliflower Salad

Preparation time: 10 Minutes

Cooking time: 12 to 25 Minutes

Servings: 4

Ingredients:

- 1½ cups mayonnaise
- ½ cup sour cream
- ¼ cup sugar
- 1 bunch broccoli, cut into small pieces
- 1 head cauliflower, cut into small pieces
- 1 small red onion, chopped
- 6 slices bacon, cooked and crumbled (precooked bacon works well)
- 1 cup shredded Cheddar cheese

Directions:

1. In a small bowl, whisk together the mayonnaise, sour cream, and sugar to make a dressing.
2. In a large bowl, combine the broccoli, cauliflower, onion, bacon, and Cheddar cheese.
3. Pour the dressing over the vegetable mixture and toss well to coat.
4. Serve the salad chilled.
5. Ingredient Tip: I like using precooked bacon for barbecue recipes. First of all, it saves a lot of time; second of all, grilling bacon is just a pain.

Nutrition:

Calories: 150

Carbohydrates: 15 g

Protein: 79 g

Sodium: 45 mg

Cholesterol: 49 mg

243. Wood Pellet Smoked Mushrooms

Preparation time: 15 minutes

Cooking time: 45 minutes

Servings: 5

Ingredients:

- 4 cup Portobello, whole and cleaned
- 1 tbsps. canola oil
- 1 tbsps. onion powder
- 1 tbsps. granulated garlic

1 tbsps. salt

1 tbsps. pepper

Directions:

1. Add all the ingredients and mix well.

2. Set the wood pellet temperature to 180°F then place the mushrooms directly on the grill.
3. Smoke the mushrooms for 30 minutes.
4. Increase the temperature to high and cook the mushrooms for a further 15 minutes.
5. Serve and enjoy.

Nutrition:

Calories 1680

Total fat 30g

Saturated fat 2g

Total Carbs 10g

Net Carbs 10g

Protein 4g, Sugar 0g

Fiber 0g, Sodium: 514mg

Potassium 0mg

244. Wood Pellet Grilled Zucchini Squash Spears

Preparation time: 5 minutes

Cooking time: 10 minutes

Servings: 5

Ingredients:

- 4 zucchinis, cleaned and ends cut
- 2 tbsps. olive oil
- 1 tbsps. sherry vinegar
- 2 thymes, leaves pulled
- Salt and pepper to taste

Directions:

1. Cut the zucchini into halves then cut each half thirds.

2. Add the rest of the ingredients in a zip lock bag with the zucchini pieces. Toss to mix well.

3. Preheat the wood pellet temperature to 350°F with the lid closed for 15 minutes.

4. Remove the zucchini from the bag and place them on the grill grate with the cut side down.

5. Cook zucchini for 4 minutes per side or until tender.

6. Remove from grill and serve with thyme leaves. Enjoy.

Nutrition:

Calories 74

Total fat 5.4g

Saturated fat 0.5g

Total Carbs 6.1g

Net Carbs 3.8g

Protein 2.6g

Sugar 3.9g

Fiber 2.3g

Sodium: 302mg

Potassium 599mg

245. Smoked Deviled Eggs

Preparation time: 15 minutes

Cooking time: 30 minutes

Servings: 5

Ingredients:

- 7 hard-boiled eggs, peeled
- 3 tbsps. mayonnaise
- 3 tbsps. chives, diced
- 1 tbsps. brown mustard
- 1 tbsps. apple cider vinegar
- Dash of hot sauce
- Salt and pepper
- 2 tbsps. cooked bacon, crumbled
- Paprika to taste

Directions:

1. Preheat the wood pellet to 180°F for 15 minutes with the lid closed.
2. Place the eggs on the grill grate and smoke the eggs for 30 minutes. Remove the eggs from the grill and let cool.
3. Half the eggs and scoop the egg yolks into a zip lock bag.
4. Add all other ingredients in the zip lock bag except bacon and paprika. Stir until smooth.
5. Tube the mixture into the egg whites then top with bacon and paprika.
6. Let rest then serve and enjoy.

Nutrition:

Calories 140

Total fat 12g

Saturated fat 3g

Total Carbs 1g

Net Carbs 1g

Protein 6g

Sugar 0g

Fiber 0g

Sodium: 210mg

Potassium 100mg

246. Wood Pellet Grilled Vegetables

Preparation time: 5 minutes

Cooking time: 15 minutes

Servings: 18

Ingredients:

- 1 veggie tray
- 1/4 cup vegetable oil
- 2 tbsp. veggie seasoning

Directions:

1. Preheat the wood pellet grill to 375°F
2. Toss the vegetables in oil then place on a sheet pan.
3. Sprinkle with veggie seasoning then place on the hot grill.
4. Grill for 15 minutes or until the veggies are cooked.
5. Let rest then serve. Enjoy.

Nutrition:

Calories 44

Total fat 5g

Saturated fat 0g

Total Carbs 1g

Net Carbs 1g

Protein 0g

Sugar 0g

Fiber 0g

Sodium: 36mg

Potassium 10mg

247. Wood Pellet Smoked Asparagus

Preparation time: 5 minutes

Cooking time: 1 hour

Servings: 4

Ingredients:

- 1 bunch fresh asparagus, ends cut
- 2 tbsp. olive oil
- Salt and pepper to taste

Directions:

1. Fire up your wood pellet smoker to 230°F
2. Put the asparagus in a bowl then drizzle with olive oil. Season with salt and pepper.
3. Place the asparagus in a tinfoil sheet and fold the sides such that you create a basket.
4. Smoke the asparagus for 1 hour or until soft turning after half an hour.
5. Remove from the grill and serve. Enjoy.

Nutrition:

Calories 43

Total fat 2g

Saturated fat 0g

Total Carbs 4g

Net Carbs 2g

Protein 3g

Sugar 2g

Fiber 2g

Sodium: 148mg

248. Wood Pellet Smoked Acorn Squash

Preparation time: 10 minutes

Cooking time: 2 hours

Servings: 6

Ingredients:

- 3 tbsp. olive oil
- 3 acorn squash, halved and seeded
- 1/4 cup unsalted butter
- 1/4 cup brown sugar
- 1 tbsp. cinnamon, ground
- 1 tbsp. chili powder
- 1 tbsp. nutmeg, ground

Directions:

1. Brush olive oil on the acorn squash cut sides then cover the halves with foil. Poke holes on the foil to allow steam and smoke through.
2. Fire up the wood pellet to 225°F and smoke the squash for 1 ½-2 hours.
3. Remove the squash from the smoker and allow it to sit.
4. Meanwhile, melt butter, sugar and spices in a saucepan. Stir well to combine.
5. Remove the foil from the squash and spoon the butter mixture in each squash half. Enjoy.

Nutrition:

Calories 149

Total fat 10g

Saturated fat 5g

Total Carbs 14g

Net Carbs 12g

Protein 2g

Sugar 0g

Fiber 2g

Sodium: 19mg

Potassium 0mg

249. Vegan Smoked Carrot Dogs

Preparation time: 25 minutes

Cooking time: 35 minutes

Servings: 4

Ingredients:

- 4 thick carrots
- 2 tbsp. avocado oil
- 1 tbsp. liquid smoke
- 1/2 tbsp. garlic powder
- Salt and pepper to taste

Directions:

1. Preheat the wood pellet grill to 425°F and line a baking sheet with parchment paper.
2. Peel the carrots and round the edges.
3. In a mixing bowl, mix oil, liquid smoke, garlic, salt, and pepper. Place the carrots on the baking dish then pour the mixture over.
4. Roll the carrots to coat evenly with the mixture and use fingertips to massage the mixture into the carrots.
5. Place in the grill and grill for 35 minutes or until the carrots are fork-tender ensuring to turn and brush the carrots every 5 minutes with the marinade.
6. Remove from the grill and place the carrots in hot dog bun. Serve with your favorite toppings and enjoy.

Nutrition:

Calories 149

Total fat 1.6g

Saturated fat 0.3g

Total Carbs 27.9g

Net Carbs 24.3g

Protein 5.4g

Sugar 5.6g

Fiber 3.6g

Sodium: 516mg

Potassium 60mg

250. Baked Sweet and Savory Yams

Preparation time: 15 minutes

Cooking time: 55 minutes

Servings: 6

Ingredients:

- 3 pounds' yams, scrubbed
- 3 tablespoons extra virgin olive oil
- Honey to taste
- Goat cheese as needed
- ½ cup brown sugar
- ½ cup pecans, chopped

Directions:

8. Fire the Grill to 350F. Use desired wood pellets when cooking. Close the lid and preheat for 15 minutes.
9. Poke holes on the yams using a fork. Wrap yams in foil and place on the grill grate. Cook for 45 minutes until tender.
10. Remove the yams from the grill and allow to cool. Once cooled, peel the yam and slice to ¼" rounds.
11. Place on a parchment-lined baking tray and brush with olive oil. Drizzle with honey, cheese, brown sugar, and pecans.
12. Place in the grill and cook for another 10 minutes.

Nutrition:

Calories per serving: 421

Protein: 4.3g

Carbs: 82.4g

Fat: 9.3g

Sugar:19.3 g

251. Feisty Roasted Cauliflower

Preparation time: 10 minutes

Cooking time: 10 minutes

Servings: 4

Ingredients:

- 1cauliflower head, cut into florets
- 1tablespoon oil
- 1cup parmesan, grated
- 2garlic cloves, crushed
- ½ teaspoon pepper
- ½ teaspoon salt
- ¼ teaspoon paprika

Directions:

1. Preheat your Smoker to 180 degrees F
2. Transfer florets to smoker and smoke for 1 hour
3. Take a bowl and add all ingredients except cheese
4. Once smoking is done, remove florets
5. Increase temperature to 450 degrees F, brush florets with the brush and transfer to grill
6. Smoke for 10 minutes more
7. Sprinkle cheese on top and let them sit (Lid closed) until cheese melts
8. Serve and enjoy!

Nutrition:

Calories: 45

Fats: 2g

Carbs: 7g

Fiber: 1g

252. Smoked 3-bean Salad

Preparation time: 15 minutes

Cooking time: 20 minutes

Servings: 6

Ingredients:

- 1 can Great Northern Beans, rinsed and drained
- 1 can Red Kidney Beans, rinsed and drained
- 1pound fresh green beans, trimmed
- 2 tablespoons olive oil
- Salt and pepper to taste
- 1 shallot, sliced thinly
- 2 tablespoons red wine vinegar
- 1 teaspoon Dijon mustard

Directions:

1. Fire the Grill to 500F. Use desired wood pellets when cooking. Close the lid and preheat for 15 minutes.
2. Place the beans in a sheet tray and drizzle with olive oil. Season with salt and pepper to taste.
3. Place in the grill and cook for 20 minutes. Make sure to shake the tray for even cooking.
4. Once cooked, remove the beans and place in a bowl. Allow to cool first.
5. Add the shallots and the rest of the ingredients. Season with more salt and pepper if desired. Toss to coat the beans with the seasoning.

Nutrition:

Calories per serving: 179

Protein: 8.2 g

Carbs: 23.5g

Fat: 6.5g

Sugar: 2.2g

253. Cauliflower with Parmesan and Butter

Preparation time: 15 minutes

Cooking time: 45 minutes

Servings: 4

Ingredients:

- 1 medium head of cauliflower
- 1 teaspoon minced garlic
- 1 teaspoon salt
- ½ teaspoon ground black pepper
- 1/4 cup olive oil
- 1/2 cup melted butter, unsalted
- 1/2 tablespoon chopped parsley
- 1/4 cup shredded parmesan cheese

Directions:

13. Switch on the grill, fill the grill hopper with flavored wood pellets, power the grill on by using the control panel, select 'smoke' on the temperature dial, or set the temperature to 450 degrees F and let it preheat for a minimum of 15 minutes.
14. Meanwhile, brush the cauliflower head with oil, season with salt and black pepper and then place in a skillet pan.
15. When the grill has preheated, open the lid, place prepared skillet pan on the grill grate, shut the grill and smoke for 45 minutes until golden brown and the center has turned tender.
16. Meanwhile, take a small bowl, place melted butter in it, and then stir in garlic, parsley, and cheese until combined.
17. Baste cheese mixture frequently in the last 20 minutes of cooking and, when done, remove the pan from heat and garnish cauliflower with parsley.
18. Cut it into slices and then serve.

Nutrition:

Calories: 128Cal

Fat: 7.6 g

Carbs: 10.8 g

Protein: 7.4 g

Fiber: 5 g

254. Bacon-wrapped Jalapeño Poppers

Preparation time: 20 minutes

Cooking time: 20 minutes

Servings: 8 - 12

Ingredients:

- 12 large jalapeño peppers
- 8 oz. cream cheese, softened
- 1cup pepper jack cheese, shredded
- Juice of 1 lemon1/2 tsp garlic powder
- 1/4 tsp kosher salt
- 1/4 tsp ground black pepper
- 12 bacon slices, cut in half

Directions:

19. Preheat pellet grill to 400°F.

20. Slice jalapeños in half lengthwise. Remove seeds and scrape sides with a spoon to remove the membrane.
21. In a medium bowl, mix cream cheese, pepper jack cheese, garlic powder, salt, and pepper until thoroughly combined.
22. Use a spoon or knife to place the cream cheese mixture into each jalapeño half. Make sure not to fill over the sides of the jalapeño half.
23. Wrap each cheese-filled pepper with a half slice of bacon. If you can't get a secure wrap, then hold bacon and pepper together with a toothpick.
24. Place assembled poppers on the grill and cook for 15-20 minutes or until bacon is crispy.
25. Remove from grill, allow to cool, then serve and enjoy!

Nutrition:

Calories: 78.8

Fat: 7.2 g

Cholesterol: 19.2 mg

Carbohydrate: 1 g

Fiber: 0.2 g

Sugar: 0.7 g

Protein: 2.5 g

255. Potluck Salad with Smoked Cornbread

Preparation time: 10 minutes

Cooking time: 45 minutes

Servings: 6

Ingredients:

- 1 cup all-purpose flour
- 1 cup yellow cornmeal
- 1 tablespoon sugar
- 2 teaspoons baking powder
- 1 teaspoon salt
- 1 cup milk
- 1 egg, beaten, at room temperature
- 4 tablespoons (½ stick) unsalted butter, melted and cooled
- Nonstick cooking spray or butter, for greasing
- ½ cup milk
- ½ cup sour cream
- 2 tablespoons dry ranch dressing mix
- 1-pound bacon, cooked and crumbled
- 3 tomatoes, chopped
- 1 bell pepper, chopped
- 1 cucumber, seeded and chopped
- 2 stalks celery, chopped (about 1 cup)
- ½ cup chopped scallions

Directions:

1. For the cornbread:
2. In a medium bowl, combine the flour, cornmeal, sugar, baking powder, and salt.
3. In a small bowl, whisk together the milk and egg. Pour in the butter, then slowly fold this mixture into the dry ingredients.
4. Supply your smoker with wood pellets and follow the manufacturer's specific start-up procedure. Preheat, with the lid closed, to 375°F.
5. Coat a cast iron skillet with cooking spray or butter.
6. Pour the batter into the skillet, place on the grill grate, close the lid, and smoke for 35 to 45 minutes, or until the cornbread is browned and pulls away from the side of the skillet.
7. Remove the cornbread from the grill and let cool, then coarsely crumble.
8. For the salad:
9. In a small bowl, whisk together the milk, sour cream, and ranch dressing mix.
10. In a medium bowl, combine the crumbled bacon, tomatoes, bell pepper, cucumber, celery, and scallions.
11. In a large serving bowl, layer half of the crumbled cornbread, half of the bacon-veggie mixture, and half of the dressing. Toss lightly.
12. Repeat the layering with the remaining cornbread, bacon-veggie mixture, and dressing. Toss again.
13. Refrigerate the salad for at least 1 hour. Serve cold.

Nutrition:

Calcium, Ca225 mg

Magnesium, Mg54 mg

Phosphorus, P349 mg

Iron, Fe4.28 mg

Potassium, K769 mg

Sodium, Na1647 mg

256. Grilled Artichokes

Preparation time: 15 minutes

Cooking time: 15 minutes

Servings: 6

Ingredients:

- 3 large artichokes, blanched and halved
- 3 + 3 tablespoons olive oil
- Salt and pepper to taste
- 1 cup mayonnaise
- 1 cup yogurt
- 2 tablespoons parsley, chopped
- 2 tablespoons capers
- Lemon juice to taste

Directions:

26. Fire the Grill to 500F. Use desired wood pellets when cooking. Close the lid and preheat for 15 minutes.
27. Brush the artichokes with 3 tablespoons of olive oil. Season with salt and pepper to taste.
28. Place on the grill grate and cook for 15 minutes.
29. Allow to cool before slicing.
30. Once cooled, slice the artichokes and place in a bowl.
31. In another bowl, mix together the mayonnaise, yogurt, parsley, capers, and lemon juice. Season with salt and pepper to taste. Mix until well-combined.
32. Pour sauce over the artichokes.
33. Toss to coat.

Nutrition:

Calories per serving: 257

Protein: 6.7g

Carbs: 13.2 g

Fat: 20.9g

Sugar: 3.7g

257. Butter Braised Green Beans

Preparation time: 15 minutes

Cooking time: 20 minutes

Servings: 6

Ingredients:

- 24 ounces Green Beans, trimmed
- 8 tablespoons butter, melted
- Salt and pepper to taste

Directions:

34. Fire the Grill to 500F. Use desired wood pellets when cooking. Close the lid and preheat for 15 minutes.
35. Place all ingredients in a bowl and toss to coat the beans with the seasoning.
36. Place the seasoned beans in a sheet tray.
37. Cook in the grill for 20 minutes.

Nutrition:

Calories per serving: 164

Protein: 1.6g

Carbs: 5.6 g

Fat: 15.8g

Sugar: 1.3g

258. Smoked Acorn Squash

Preparation time: 10 minutes

Cooking time: 2 hours

Servings: 6

Ingredients:

- 3 acorn squash, seeded and halved
- 3 tbsp. olive oil
- 1/4 cup butter, unsalted
- 1 tbsp. cinnamon, ground
- 1 tbsp. chili powder
- 1 tbsp. nutmeg, ground
- 1/4 cup brown sugar

Directions:

38. Brush the cut sides of your squash with olive oil then cover with foil poking holes for smoke and steam to get through.
39. Preheat your Wood Pellet Grill to 225F.
40. Place the squash halves on the grill with the cut side down and smoke for about 1½- 2 hours.
41. Let it sit while you prepare spiced butter. Melt butter in a saucepan then add spices and sugar stirring to combine.
42. Remove the foil form the squash halves.
43. Place 1 tbsp. of the butter mixture onto each half.
44. Serve and enjoy!

Nutrition:

Calories 149

Total 10g

Saturated fat 5g

Total carbs 14g

Net carbs 12g

Protein 2g

Sugars 2g

Fiber 2g

Sodium 19mg

Potassium 101m

CHAPTER 20. DESSERT RECIPES

259. Bacon and Chocolate Cookies

Preparation Time:20 minutes

Cooking Time: 10 - 12 minutes

Servings: 2

Ingredients:

- 2¾ cups all-purpose flour
- 1½ teaspoons baking soda
- ½ teaspoon salt
- 12 tablespoons (1½ sticks) unsalted butter, softened
- 1 cup light brown sugar
- 1 cup granulated sugar
- 2 eggs, at room temperature
- 2½ teaspoons apple cider vinegar
- 1 teaspoon vanilla extract
- 2 cups semisweet chocolate chips
- 8 slices bacon, cooked and crumbled

Directions:

1. In a large bowl, combine the flour, baking soda, and salt, and mix well.
2. In a separate large bowl, using an electric mixer on medium speed, cream the butter and sugars. Reduce the speed to low and mix in the eggs, vinegar, and vanilla.
3. With the mixer speed still on low, slowly incorporate the dry ingredients, chocolate chips, and bacon pieces.
4. Supply your smoker with wood pellets and follow the manufacturer's specific start-up procedure. Preheat, with the lid closed, to 375°F (191°C).
5. Line a large baking sheet with parchment paper.
6. Drop rounded teaspoonful of cookie batter onto the prepared baking sheet and place on the grill grate. Close the lid and smoke for 10 to 12 minutes, or until the cookies are browned around the edges.

Nutrition:

Calcium, Ca416 mg

Magnesium, Mg154 mg

Phosphorus, P1121 mg

Iron, Fe25.7 mg

Potassium, K2165 mg

Sodium, Na4364 mg

Zinc, Zn7.38 mg

260. Fast S'Mores Dip Skillet

Preparation Time: 5 minutes

Cooking Time: 6 – 8 minutes

Servings: 4 - 6

Ingredients:

- 2 tablespoons salted butter, melted
- ¼ cup milk
- 12 ounces (340 g) semisweet chocolate chips
- 16 ounces (454 g) Jet-Puffed marshmallows
- Graham crackers and apple wedges, for serving

Directions:

1. Supply your smoker with wood pellets and follow the manufacturer's specific start-up procedure. Preheat, with the lid closed, to 450ºF (232ºC).
2. Place a cast iron skillet on the preheated grill grate and pour in the melted butter and milk, stirring for about 1 minute.
3. Once the mixture starts to heat, top with the chocolate chips in an even layer and arrange the marshmallows standing up to cover all of the chocolate.
4. Close the lid and smoke for 5 to 7 minutes, or until the marshmallows are lightly toasted.
5. Remove from the heat and serve immediately with graham crackers and apple wedges for dipping.

Nutrition:

Calcium, Ca235 mg

Magnesium, Mg562 mg

Phosphorus, P759 mg

Iron, Fe15.75 mg

Potassium, K1761 mg

Sodium, Na533 mg

Zinc, Zn8.07 mg

261. Blackberry Pie

Preparation Time: 15 minutes

Cooking Time: 20 – 25 minutes

Servings: 4 - 6

Ingredients:

- Nonstick cooking spray or butter, for greasing
- 1 box (2 sheets) refrigerated piecrusts
- 8 tablespoons (1 stick) unsalted butter, melted, plus 8 tablespoons (1 stick) cut into pieces
- ½ cup all-purpose flour
- 2 cups sugar, divided
- 2 pints' blackberries
- ½ cup milk
- Vanilla ice cream, for serving

Directions:

1. Supply your smoker with wood pellets and follow the manufacturer's specific start-up procedure. Preheat, with the lid closed, to 375F (191C).

2. Coat a cast iron skillet with cooking spray.
3. Unroll 1 refrigerated piecrust and place in the bottom and up the side of the skillet. Using a fork, poke holes in the crust in several places.
4. Set the skillet on the grill grate, close the lid, and smoke for 5 minutes, or until lightly browned. Remove from the grill and set aside.
5. In a large bowl, combine the stick of melted butter with the flour and 1½ cups of sugar.
6. Add the blackberries to the flour-sugar mixture and toss until well coated.
7. Spread the berry mixture evenly in the skillet and sprinkle the milk on top. Scatter half of the cut pieces of butter randomly over the mixture.
8. Unroll the remaining piecrust and place it over the top of skillet or slice the dough into even strips and weave it into a lattice. Scatter the remaining pieces of butter along the top of the crust.
9. Sprinkle the remaining ½ cup of sugar on top of the crust and return the skillet to the smoker.
10. Close the lid and smoke for 15 to 20 minutes, or until bubbly and brown on top. It may be necessary to use some aluminum foil around the edges near the end of the cooking time to prevent the crust from burning.
11. Serve the pie hot with vanilla ice cream.

Nutrition:

Calcium, Ca224 mg

Magnesium, Mg39 mg

Phosphorus, P226 mg

Iron, Fe4.34 mg

Potassium, K340 mg

Sodium, Na200 mg

Zinc, Zn1.35 mg

262. Frosted Carrot Cake

Preparation Time: 20 minutes

Cooking Time: 1 hour

Servings: 4 - 6

Ingredients:

- 8 carrots, peeled and grated
- 4 eggs, at room temperature
- 1 cup vegetable oil
- ½ cup milk
- 1 teaspoon vanilla extract
- 2 cups sugar
- 2 cups self-rising or cake flour
- 2 teaspoons baking soda
- 1 teaspoon salt
- 1 cup finely chopped pecans
- Nonstick cooking spray or butter, for greasing
- 8 ounces (227 g) cream cheese
- 1 cup confectioners' sugar
- 8 tablespoons (1 stick) unsalted butter, at room temperature
- 1 teaspoon vanilla extract
- ½ teaspoon salt
- 2 tablespoons to ¼ cup milk

Directions:

1. Supply your smoker with wood pellets and follow the manufacturer's specific start-up procedure. Preheat, with the lid closed, to 350F (177C).
2. In a food processor or blender, combine the grated carrots, eggs, oil, milk, vanilla, and process until the carrots are finely minced.
3. In a large mixing bowl, combine the sugar, flour, baking soda, and salt.
4. Add the carrot mixture to the flour mixture and stir until well incorporated. Fold in the chopped pecans.
5. Coat a 9-by-13-inch baking pan with cooking spray.
6. Pour the batter into prepared pan and place on the grill grate. Close the lid and smoke for about 1 hour, or until a toothpick inserted in the center comes out clean.
7. Remove the cake from the grill and let cool completely.
8. For the Frosting
9. Using an electric mixer on low speed, beat the cream cheese, confectioners' sugar, butter, vanilla, and salt, adding two tablespoons to ¼ cup of milk to thin the frosting as needed.
10. Frost the cooled cake and slice to serve.

Nutrition:

Calcium, Ca2052 mg

Magnesium, Mg383 mg

Phosphorus, P3294 mg

Iron, Fe31.86 mg

Potassium, K4100 mg

Sodium, Na11039 mg

Zinc, Zn15.09 mg

263. Lemony Smokin' Bars

Preparation Time: 30 minutes

Cooking Time: 1 hour

Servings: 8 - 12

Ingredients:

- ¾ cup lemon juice
- 1½ cup sugar
- 2 eggs
- 3 egg yolk
- 1½ teaspoon cornstarch
- Pinch sea salt
- 4 tablespoons unsalted butter
- ¼ cup olive oil

- ½ tablespoon lemon zest
- 1¼ cup flour
- ¼ cup granulated sugar
- 3 tablespoon confectioner's sugar
- 1 teaspoon lemon zest
- ¼ teaspoon sea salt, fine
- 10 tablespoons unsalted butter, cut into cubes

Directions:

1. When ready to cook, set grill temperature to 180F (82C) and preheat, lid closed for 15 minutes.
2. In a small mixing bowl, whisk together lemon juice, sugar, eggs and yolks, cornstarch and fine sea salt. Pour into a sheet tray or cake pan and place on grill. Smoke for 30 minutes whisking mixture halfway through smoking. Remove from grill and set aside.
3. Pour mixture into a small saucepan. Place on stove top set to medium heat until boiling. Once boiling, boil for 60 seconds. Remove from heat and strain through a mesh strainer into a bowl. Whisk in cold butter, olive oil, and lemon zest.
4. To make a crust, pulse together the flour, granulated sugar, confectioners' sugar, lemon zest and salt in a food processor. Add butter and pulse until just mixed into a crumbly dough.
5. Press dough into a prepared 9" by 9" baking dish lined with parchment paper that is long enough to hang over 2 of the sides.
6. When ready to cook, set the Wood Pellet Grill to 350F (177C) and preheat, lid closed for 15 minutes.
7. Bake until crust is very lightly golden brown, about 30 to 35 minutes.
8. Remove from grill and pour the lemon filling over the crust. Return to grill and continue to bake until filling is just set about 15 to 20 minutes.
9. Allow to cool at room temperature, then refrigerate until chilled before slicing into bars.
10. Sprinkle with confectioners' sugar and flaky sea salt right before serving. Enjoy!

Nutrition:

Calcium, Ca287 mg
Magnesium, Mg82 mg
Phosphorus, P759 mg
Iron, Fe16.76 mg
Potassium, K879 mg
Sodium, Na891 mg
Zinc, Zn4.87 mg

264. Grilled Pound Cake with Fruit Dressing

Preparation Time: 20 min
Cooking Time: 50 min
Servings: 12
Ingredients:

- 1buttermilk pound cake, sliced into 3/4 inch slices
- 1/8 cup butter, melted
- 1.1/2 cup whipped cream
- 1/2 cup blueberries
- 1/2 cup raspberries
- 1/2 cup strawberries, sliced

Directions:

1. Preheat pellet grill to 400°F. Turn your smoke setting to high, if applicable.
2. Brush both sides of each pound cake slice with melted butter.
3. Place directly on the grill grate and cook for 5 minutes per side. Turn 90 halfway through cooking each side of the cake for checkered grill marks.
4. You can cook a couple of minutes longer if you prefer deeper grill marks and smoky flavor.
5. Remove pound cake slices from the grill and allow it to cool on a plate.
6. Top slices with whipped cream, blueberries, raspberries, and sliced strawberries as desired. Serve and enjoy!

Nutrition:

Calories: 222.1
Fat: 8.7 g
Cholesterol: 64.7 mg
Carbohydrate: 33.1 g
Fiber: 0.4 g
Sugar: 20.6 g
Protein: 3.4 g

265. Grilled Pineapple with Chocolate Sauce

Preparation Time: 10 min
Cooking Time: 25 min
Servings: 6 to 8
Ingredients:

- 1pineapple
- 8 oz. bittersweet chocolate chips
- 1/2 cup spiced rum
- 1/2 cup whipping cream
- 2tbsp light brown sugar

Directions:

7. Preheat pellet grill to 400°F.
8. De-skin the pineapple and slice pineapple into 1 in cubes.
9. In a saucepan, combine chocolate chips. When chips begin to melt, add rum to the saucepan. Continue to stir until combined, then add a splash of the pineapple's juice.
10. Add in whipping cream and continue to stir the mixture. Once the sauce is smooth and thickening, lower heat to simmer to keep warm.
11. Thread pineapple cubes onto skewers. Sprinkle skewers with brown sugar.

12. Place skewers on the grill grate. Grill for about 5 minutes per side, or until grill marks begin to develop.
2. Remove skewers from grill and allow to rest on a plate for about 5 minutes. Serve alongside warm chocolate sauce for dipping.

Nutrition:
Calories: 112.6
Fat: 0.5 g
Cholesterol: 0
Carbohydrate: 28.8 g
Fiber: 1.6 g
Sugar: 0.1 g
Protein: 0.4 g

266. Nectarine and Nutella Sundae

Preparation Time: 10 min
Cooking Time: 25 min
Servings: 4
Ingredients:

- 2nectarines, halved and pitted
- 2tsp honey
- 4tbsp Nutella
- 4scoops vanilla ice cream
- 1/4 cup pecans, chopped
- Whipped cream, to top
- 4cherries, to top

Directions:

1. Preheat pellet grill to 400°F.
2. Slice nectarines in half and remove the pits.
3. Brush the inside (cut side) of each nectarine half with honey.
4. Place nectarines directly on the grill grate, cut side down. Cook for 5-6 minutes, or until grill marks develop.
5. Flip nectarines and cook on the other side for about 2 minutes.
6. Remove nectarines from the grill and allow it to cool.

2. Fill the pit cavity on each nectarine half with 1 tbsp. Nutella.
3. Place 1 scoop of ice cream on top of Nutella. Top with whipped cream, cherries, and sprinkle chopped pecans. Serve and enjoy!

Nutrition:
Calories: 90
Fat: 3 g
Cholesterol: 0
Carbohydrate: 15g
Fiber: 0
Sugar: 13 g
Protein: 2 g

267. Cinnamon Sugar Donut Holes

Preparation Time: 10 min
Cooking Time: 35 min
Servings: 4
Ingredients:

- 1/2 cup flour
- 1 tbsp. cornstarch
- 1/2 tsp baking powder
- 1/8 tsp baking soda
- 1/8 tsp ground cinnamon
- 1/2 tsp kosher salt
- 1/4 cup buttermilk
- 1/4 cup sugar
- 1 1/2 tbsp. butter, melted
- 1 egg
- 1/2 tsp vanilla
- Topping
- 2 tbsp. sugar
- 1 tbsp. sugar
- 1 tsp ground cinnamon

Directions:

1. Preheat pellet grill to 350°F.
2. In a medium bowl, combine flour, cornstarch, baking powder, baking soda, ground cinnamon, and kosher salt. Whisk to combine.
3. In a separate bowl, combine buttermilk, sugar, melted butter, egg, and vanilla. Whisk until the egg is thoroughly combined.
4. Pour wet mixture into the flour mixture and stir. Stir just until combined, careful not to overwork the mixture.
5. Spray mini muffin tin with cooking spray.
6. Spoon 1 tbsp. of donut mixture into each mini muffin hole.

3. Place the tin on the pellet grill grate and bake for about 18 minutes, or until a toothpick can come out clean.
4. Remove muffin tin from the grill and let rest for about 5 minutes.
5. In a small bowl, combine 1 tbsp. sugar and 1 tsp ground cinnamon.
6. Melt 2 tbsp. of butter in a glass dish. Dip each donut hole in the melted butter, then mix and toss with cinnamon sugar. Place completed donut holes on a plate to serve.

Nutrition:
Calories: 190
Fat: 17 g
Cholesterol: 0
Carbohydrate: 21 g
Fiber: 1 g
Sugar: 8 g
Protein: 3 g

268. Pellet Grill Chocolate Chip Cookies

Preparation Time: 20 min
Cooking Time: 45 min
Servings: 12
Ingredients:

- 1cup salted butter, softened
- 1cup of sugar
- 1cup light brown sugar
- 2tsp vanilla extract
- 2large eggs

- 3cups all-purpose flour
- 1tsp baking soda
- 1/2 tsp baking powder
- 1tsp natural sea salt
- 2cups semi-sweet chocolate chips, or chunks

Directions:

1. Preheat pellet grill to 375°F.
2. Line a large baking sheet with parchment paper and set aside.
3. In a medium bowl, mix flour, baking soda, salt, and baking powder. Once combined, set aside.
4. In stand mixer bowl, combine butter, white sugar, and brown sugar until combined. Beat in eggs and vanilla. Beat until fluffy.
5. Mix in dry ingredients, continue to stir until combined.
6. Add chocolate chips and mix thoroughly.
7. Roll 3 tbsps. of dough at a time into balls and place them on your cookie sheet. Evenly space them apart, with about 2-3 inches in between each ball.
8. Place cookie sheet directly on the grill grate and bake for 20-25 minutes, until the outside of the cookies is slightly browned.
9. Remove from grill and allow to rest for 10 minutes. Serve and enjoy!

Nutrition:

Calories: 120
Fat: 4 Cholesterol: 7.8 mg
Carbohydrate: 22.8 g
Fiber: 0.3 g
Sugar: 14.4 g
Protein: 1.4 g

269. Delicious Donuts on a Grill

Preparation Time: 5 minutes
Cooking Time: 10 Minutes
Servings: 6
Ingredients:

- 1-1/2 cups sugar, powdered
- 1/3 cup whole milk
- 1/2 teaspoon vanilla extract
- 16 ounces of biscuit dough, prepared
- Oil spray, for greasing
- 1cup chocolate sprinkles, for sprinkling

Directions:

1. Take a medium bowl and mix sugar, milk, and vanilla extract.
2. Combine well to create a glaze.
3. Set the glaze aside for further use.
4. Place the dough onto the flat, clean surface.
5. Flat the dough with a rolling pin.
6. Use a ring mold, about an inch, and cut the hole in the center of each round dough.

10. Place the dough on a plate and refrigerate for 10 minutes.
11. Open the grill and install the grill grate inside it.
12. Close the hood.
13. Now, select the grill from the menu, and set the temperature to medium.
14. Set the time to 6 minutes.
15. Select start and begin preheating.
16. Remove the dough from the refrigerator and coat it with cooking spray from both sides.
17. When the unit beeps, the grill is preheated; place the adjustable amount of dough on the grill grate.
18. Close the hood, and cook for 3 minutes.
19. After 3 minutes, remove donuts and place the remaining dough inside.
20. Cook for 3 minutes.
21. Once all the donuts are ready, sprinkle chocolate sprinkles on top.
22. Enjoy.

Nutrition:

Calories: 400
Total Fat: 11g
Saturated Fat: 4.2g
Cholesterol: 1mg
Sodium: 787mg
Total Carbohydrate: 71.3g
Dietary Fiber 0.9g
Total Sugars: 45.3g
Protein: 5.7g

270. Smoked Pumpkin Pie

Preparation Time: 10 minutes
Cooking Time: 50 minutes
Servings: 8
Ingredients:

- 1tbsp cinnamon
- 1-1/2 tbsp. pumpkin pie spice
- 15oz can pumpkin
- 14oz can sweetened condensed milk
- 2beaten eggs
- 1unbaked pie shell
- Topping: whipped cream

Directions:

1. Preheat your smoker to 325oF.
2. Place a baking sheet, rimmed, on the smoker upside down, or use a cake pan.
3. Combine all your ingredients in a bowl, large, except the pie shell, then pour the mixture into a pie crust.
4. Place the pie on the baking sheet and smoke for about 50-60 minutes until a knife comes out clean when inserted. Make sure the center is set.
5. Remove and cool for about 2 hours or refrigerate overnight.

6. Serve with a whipped cream dollop and enjoy it!

Nutrition:
Calories: 292
Total Fat: 11g
Saturated Fat: 5g
Total Carbs: 42g
Net Carbs: 40g
Protein: 7g
Sugars: 29g
Fiber: 5g
Sodium: 168mg

271. Wood Pellet Smoked Nut Mix

Preparation Time: 15 minutes
Cooking Time: 20 minutes
Servings: 8-12
Ingredients:

- 3cups mixed nuts (pecans, peanuts, almonds, etc.)
- 1/2 tbsp. brown sugar
- 1tbsp thyme, dried
- 1/4 tbsp. mustard powder
- 1tbsp olive oil, extra-virgin

Directions:

1. Preheat your pellet grill to 250oF with the lid closed for about 15 minutes.
2. Combine all ingredients in a bowl, large, then transfer into a cookie sheet lined with parchment paper.
3. Place the cookie sheet on a grill and grill for about 20 minutes.
4. Remove the nuts from the grill and let cool.
5. Serve and enjoy.

Nutrition:
Calories: 249
Total Fat: 21.5g
Saturated Fat: 3.5g
Total Carbs: 12.3g
Net Carbs: 10.1g
Protein: 5.7g
Sugars: 5.6g
Fiber: 2.1g
Sodium: 111mg

272. Grilled Peaches and Cream

Preparation Time: 15 minutes
Cooking Time: 8 minutes
Servings: 8
Ingredients:

- 4halved and pitted peaches
- 1tbsp vegetable oil
- 2tbsp clover honey
- 1cup cream cheese, soft with honey and nuts

Directions:

1. Preheat your pellet grill to medium-high heat.
2. Coat the peaches lightly with oil and place on the grill pit side down.
3. Grill for about 5 minutes until nice grill marks on the surfaces.
4. Turn over the peaches then drizzle with honey.
5. Spread and cream cheese dollop where the pit was and grill for additional 2-3 minutes until the filling becomes warm.
6. Serve immediately.

Nutrition:
Calories: 139
Total Fat: 10.2g
Saturated Fat: 5g
Total Carbs: 11.6g
Net Carbs: 11.6g
Protein: 1.1g
Sugars: 12g
Fiber: 0g
Sodium: 135mg

273. Pellet Grill Apple Crisp

Preparation Time: 20 minutes
Cooking Time: 1 hour
Servings: 15
Ingredients:

- Apples
- 10 large apples
- 1/2 cup flour
- 1cup sugar, dark brown
- 1/2 tbsp. cinnamon
- 1/2 cup butter slices
- Crisp
- 3cups oatmeal, old-fashioned
- 1-1/2 cups softened butter, salted
- 1-1/2 tbsp. cinnamon
- 2cups brown sugar

Directions:

1. Preheat your grill to 350F.
2. Wash, peel, core, and dice the apples into cubes, medium-size
3. Mix flour, dark brown sugar, and cinnamon, then toss with your apple cubes.
4. Spray a baking pan, 10x13", with cooking spray then place apples inside. Top with butter slices.
5. Mix all crisp ingredients in a medium bowl until well combined. Place the mixture over the apples.
6. Place on the grill and cook for about 1-hour checking after every 15-20 minutes to ensure cooking is even. Do not place it on the hottest grill part.
7. Remove and let sit for about 20-25 minutes
8. It's very warm.

Nutrition:
Calories: 528
Total Fat: 26g

Saturated
Fat: 16g
Total Carbs: 75g
Net Carbs: 70g
Protein: 4g
Sugars: 51g
Fiber: 5g
Sodium: 209mg

274. Grilled Fruit with Cream

Preparation Time: 15 minutes

Cooking Time: 10min

Servings: 4 - 6

Ingredients:

- 2 halved Apricot
- 1 halved Nectarine
- 2 halved peaches
- ¼ cup of Blueberries
- ½ cup of Raspberries
- 2 tablespoon of Honey
- 1 orange, the peel
- 2 cups of Cream
- ½ cup of Balsamic Vinegar

Directions:

1. Preheat the grill to 400F with closed lid.
2. Grill the peaches, nectarines and apricots for 4 minutes on each side.
3. Place a pan over the stove and turn on medium heat. Add 2 tablespoon of honey, vinegar, and orange peel. Simmer until medium thick.
4. Add honey and cream in a bowl. Whip until it reaches a soft form.
5. Place the fruits on a serving plate. Sprinkle with berries. Drizzle with balsamic reduction.
6. Serve with cream.

Nutrition:

Calories: 230

Protein: 3g

Fiber: 0g

Carbohydrates: 35g

Fat: 3g

275. Apple Pie On the Grill

Preparation Time: 20 minutes

Cooking Time: 30 minutes

Servings: 4 - 6

Ingredients:

- ¼ cup of Sugar
- 4 Apples, sliced
- 1 tablespoon of Cornstarch
- 1 teaspoon Cinnamon, ground
- 1 Pie Crust, refrigerated, soften in according to the directions on the box
- ½ cup of Peach preserves

Directions:

1. Preheat the grill to 375F with closed lid.
2. In a bowl combine the cinnamon, cornstarch, sugar, and apples. Set aside.
3. Place the piecrust in a pie pan. Spread the preserves and then place the apples. Fold the crust slightly.
4. Place a pan on the grill (upside - down) so that you don't brill/bake the pie directly on the heat.
5. Cook 30 - 40 minutes. Once done, set aside to rest.
6. Serve and enjoy!

Nutrition:

Calories: 160

Protein: 0.5g

Fiber: 0g

Carbohydrates: 35g

Fat: 1g

276. Grilled Layered Cake

Preparation Time: 10 minutes

Cooking Time: 14 minutes

Servings: 6

Ingredients:

- 2 x pound cake
- 3 cups of whipped cream
- ¼ cup melted butter
- 1 cup of blueberries
- 1 cup of raspberries
- 1 cup sliced strawberries

Directions:

1. Preheat the grill to high with closed lid.
2. Slice the cake loaf (3/4 inch), about 10 per loaf. Brush both sides with butter.
3. Grill for 7 minutes on each side. Set aside.
4. Once cooled completely start layering your cake. Place cake, berries then cream.
5. Sprinkle with berries and serve.

Nutrition:

Calories: 160

Protein: 2.3g

Carbohydrates: 22g

Fiber: 0g

Fat: 6g

277. Cinnamon Sugar Pumpkin Seeds

Preparation Time: 30 minutes

Cooking Time: 30 minutes

Servings: 8-12

Ingredients:

- 2 tablespoon sugar
- Seeds from a pumpkin
- 1 teaspoon cinnamon
- 2 tablespoon melted butter

Directions:

1. Add wood pellets to your smoker and follow your cooker's startup procedure.
2. Preheat your smoker, with your lid closed, until it reaches 350.
3. Clean the seeds and toss them in the melted butter. Add them to the sugar and cinnamon.
4. Spread them out on a baking sheet, place on the grill, and smoke for 25 minutes.
5. Serve.

Nutrition:

Calories: 127

Protein: 5mg

Carbohydrates: 15g

Fiber: 0g

Fat: 21g

278. S'mores Dip

Preparation Time: 30 minutes

Cooking Time: 20 minutes

Servings: 6-8

Ingredients:

- 12 ounces' semisweet chocolate chips
- ¼ cup milk
- 2 tablespoon melted salted butter
- 16 ounces' marshmallows
- Apple wedges
- Graham crackers

Directions:

1. Add wood pellets to your smoker and follow your cooker's startup procedure. Preheat your smoker, with your lid closed, until it reaches 450.
2. Put a cast iron skillet on your grill and add in the milk and melted butter. Stir together for a minute.
3. Once it has heated up, top with the chocolate chips, making sure it makes a single layer. Place the marshmallows on top, standing them on their end and covering the chocolate.
4. Cover, and let it smoke for five to seven minutes. The marshmallows should be toasted lightly.
5. Take the skillet off the heat and serve with apple wedges and graham crackers.

Nutrition:

Calories: 216.7

Protein: 2.7g

Fiber: 0g

Carbohydrates: 41g

Fat: 4.7g

279. Ice Cream Bread

Preparation Time: 30 minutes

Cooking Time: 1 hour

Servings: 12-16

Ingredients:

- 1 ½ quart full-fat butter pecan ice cream, softened
- One teaspoon salt
- Two cups semisweet chocolate chips
- One cup sugar
- One stick melted butter
- Butter, for greasing
- 4 cups self-rising flour

Directions:

1. Add wood pellets to your smoker and follow your cooker's startup procedure. Preheat your smoker, with your lid closed, until it reaches 350.
2. Mix the salt, sugar, flour, and ice cream with an electric mixer set to medium for two minutes.
3. As the mixer is still running, add in the chocolate chips, beating until everything is blended.
4. Spray a Bundt pan or tube pan with cooking spray. If you choose to use a pan that is solid, the center will take too long to cook. That's why a tube or Bundt pan works best.
5. Add the batter to your prepared pan.

6. Set the cake on the grill, cover, and smoke for 50 minutes to an hour. A toothpick should come out clean.
7. Take the pan off of the grill. For 10 minutes., cool the bread. Remove carefully the bread from the pan and then drizzle it with some melted butter.

Nutrition:

Calories: 148.7

Protein: 3.5g

Fiber: 0g

Carbohydrates: 27g

Fat: 3g

280. Bacon Chocolate Chip Cookies

Preparation Time: 30 minutes

Cooking Time: 30 minutes

Servings: 12

- 8 slices cooked and crumbled bacon
- 2 ½ teaspoon apple cider vinegar
- One teaspoon vanilla
- Two cup semisweet chocolate chips
- Two room temp eggs
- 1 ½ teaspoon baking soda
- One cup granulated sugar
- ½ teaspoon salt
- 2 ¾ cup all-purpose flour
- One cup light brown sugar
- 1 ½ stick softened butter

Directions:

1. Mix together salt, baking soda and flour.
2. Cream the sugar and the butter together. Lower the speed. Add in the eggs, vinegar, and vanilla.
3. Still on low, slowly add in the flour mixture, bacon pieces, and chocolate chips.
4. Add wood pellets to your smoker and follow your cooker's startup procedure. Preheat your smoker, with your lid closed, until it reaches 375.
5. Place some parchment on a baking sheet and drop a teaspoonful of cookie batter on the baking sheet. Let them cook on the grill, covered, for approximately 12 minutes or until they are browned. Enjoy.

Nutrition:

Calories: 133

Protein: 2.6g

Fiber: 0g

Carbohydrates: 11.8g

Fat: 9.2g

281. Chocolate Chip Cookies

Preparation Time: 30 minutes

Cooking Time: 30 minutes

Servings: 12

Ingredients:

- 1 ½ cup chopped walnuts
- One teaspoon vanilla
- Two cup chocolate chips
- One teaspoon baking soda
- 2 ½ cups plain flour
- ½ teaspoon salt
- 1 ½ stick softened butter
- Two eggs
- One cup brown sugar
- ½ cup sugar

Directions:

1. Add wood pellets to your smoker and follow your cooker's startup procedure. Preheat your smoker, with your lid closed, until it reaches 350.
2. Mix together the baking soda, salt, and flour.
3. Cream the brown sugar, sugar, and butter. Mix in the vanilla and eggs until it comes together.
4. Slowly add in the flour while continuing to beat. Once all flour has been incorporated, add in the chocolate chips and walnuts. Using a spoon, fold into batter.
5. Place an aluminum foil onto grill. In an aluminum foil, drop spoonsful of dough and bake for 17 minutes.

Nutrition:

Calories: 66.5

Protein: 1.8g

Fiber: 0g

Carbohydrates: 5.9g

Fat: 4.6g

282. Apple Cobbler

Preparation Time: 30 minutes

Cooking Time: 1 hour and 50 minutes

Servings: 8

Ingredients:

- 8 Granny Smith apples
- One cup sugar

- One stick melted butter
- One teaspoon cinnamon
- Pinch salt
- ½ cup brown sugar
- Two eggs
- Two teaspoon baking powder
- Two c. plain flour
- 1 ½ cup sugar

Directions:

1. Peel and quarter apples, place into a bowl.
2. Add in the cinnamon and one c. sugar. Stir well to coat and let it set for one hour.
3. Add wood pellets to your smoker and follow your cooker's startup procedure. Preheat your smoker, with your lid closed, until it reaches 350.
4. In a large bowl add the salt, baking powder, eggs, brown sugar, sugar, and flour. Mix until it forms crumbles.
5. Place apples into a Dutch oven. Add the crumble mixture on top and drizzle with melted butter.
6. Place on the grill and cook for 50 minutes.

Nutrition:

Calories: 216.7

Protein: 2.7g

Fiber: 0g

Carbohydrates: 41g

Fat: 4.7g

283. Pineapple Cake

Preparation Time: 30 minutes

Cooking Time: 1 hour and 20 minutes

Servings: 8

Ingredients:

- One cup sugar
- One tablespoon baking powder
- One cup buttermilk
- ½ teaspoon salt
- One jar maraschino cherries
- One stick butter, divided
- ¾ cup brown sugar
- One can pineapple slices
- 1 ½ cup flour

Directions:

1. Add wood pellets to your smoker and follow your cooker's startup procedure. Preheat your smoker, with your lid closed, until it reaches 350.
2. Take a medium-sized cast iron skillet, melt one half stick butter. Be sure to coat the entire skillet. Sprinkle brown sugar into a cast iron skillet.
3. Lay the sliced pineapple on top of the brown sugar. Put a cherry into each individual pineapple ring.
4. Mix together the salt, baking powder, flour, and sugar. Add in the eggs, one-half stick melted butter, and buttermilk. Whisk to combine.
5. Put the cake on the grill and cook for an hour.
6. Take off from the grill and let it set for ten minutes. Flip onto serving platter.

Nutrition:

Calories: 120

Protein: 1g

Fiber: 0g

Carbohydrates: 18g

Fat: 5g

CHAPTER 21. RUBS, SAUCES, MARINADES, AND GLAZES

284. Smoked Tomato Cream Sauce

Preparation Time: 15 minutes

Cooking Time: 1 hour 20 minutes

Servings: 1

Ingredients:

- 1 lb. beefsteak tomatoes, fresh and quartered
- 1-1/2 tbsps. olive oil
- Black pepper, freshly ground
- Salt, kosher
- 1/2 cup yellow onions, chopped
- 1 tbsp. tomato paste
- 2 tbsps. minced garlic
- Pinch cayenne
- 1/2 cup chicken stock
- 1/2 cup heavy cream

Directions:

1. Prepare your smoker using directions from the manufacturer.
2. Toss tomatoes and 1 tbsp. oil in a bowl, mixing, then season with pepper and salt.
3. Smoke the tomatoes placed on a smoker rack for about 30 minutes. Remove and set aside reserving tomato juices.
4. Heat 1/2 tbsp. oil in a saucepan over high-medium heat.
5. Add onion and cook for about 3-4 minutes. Add tomato paste and garlic then cook for an additional 1 minute.
6. Add smoked tomatoes, cayenne, tomato juices, pepper, and salt then cook for about 3-4 minutes. Stir often.
7. Add chicken stock and boil for about 25-30 minutes under a gentle simmer. Stir often.
8. Place the mixture in a blender and puree until smooth. Now squeeze the mixture through a sieve, fine-mesh, to discard solids and release the juices,
9. Transfer the sauce in a saucepan, small, and add the cream.
10. Simmer for close to 6 minutes over low-medium heat until thickened slightly. Season with pepper and salt.
11. Serve warm with risotto cakes.

Nutrition:

Calories 50

Total fat 5g

Saturated fat 1g

Total carbs 2g

Net carbs 2g

Protein 0g, Sugar 0g

Fiber 0g

Sodium: 69mg

285. Smoked Mushroom Sauce

Preparation Time: 30 minutes

Cooking Time: 1 hour

Servings: 4

Ingredients:

- 1-quart chef mix mushrooms
- 2 tbsps. canola oil
- 1/4 cup julienned shallots
- 2 tbsps. chopped garlic
- Salt and pepper to taste
- 1/4 cup alfasi cabernet sauvignon
- 1 cup beef stock
- 2 tbsps. margarine

Directions:

1. Crumple four foil sheets into balls. Puncture multiple places in the foil pan then place mushrooms in the foil pan. Smoke in a pellet grill for about 30 minutes. Remove and cool.
2. Heat canola oil in a pan, sauté, add shallots and sauté until translucent.
3. Add mushrooms and cook until supple and rendered down.
4. Add garlic and season with pepper and salt. Cook until fragrant.
5. Add beef stock and wine then cook for about 6-8 minutes over low heat. Adjust seasoning.
6. Add margarine and stir until sauce is thickened and a nice sheen.
7. Serve and enjoy!

Nutrition:

Calories 300

Total fat 30g

Saturated fat 2g

Total carbs 10g

Net carbs 10g

Protein 4g

Sugar 0g

Fiber 0g

Sodium: 514mg

286. Smoked Cranberry Sauce

Preparation Time: 10 minutes

Cooking Time: 1 hour

Servings: 2

Ingredients:

- 12 oz. bag cranberries

- 2 chunks ginger, quartered
- 1 cup apple cider
- 1 tbsp. honey whiskey
    - oz. fruit juice
- 1/8 tbsp. ground cloves
- 1/8 tbsp. cinnamon
- 1/2 orange zest
- 1/2 orange
- 1 tbsp. maple syrup
- 1 apple, diced and peeled
- 1/2 cup sugar
- 1/2 brown sugar

Directions:

1. Preheat your pellet grill to 375oF.
2. Place cranberries in a pan then add all other ingredients.
3. Place the pan on the grill and cook for about 1 hour until cooked through.
4. Remove ginger pieces and squeeze juices from the orange into the sauce.
5. Serve and enjoy!

Nutrition:

Calories 48

Total fat 0.1g

Saturated fat 0g

Total carbs 12.3g

Net carbs 10g

Protein 0.4g

Sugar 7.5g

Fiber 2.3g

Sodium: 26mg

287. Smoked sriracha sauce

Preparation Time: 10 minutes

Cooking Time: 1 hour

Servings: 2

Ingredients:

- 1 lb. Fresno chiles, stems pulled off and seeds removed
- 1/2 cup rice vinegar
- 1/2 cup red wine vinegar
- 1 carrot, medium and cut into rounds, 1/4 inch
- 1-1/2 tbsp. sugar, dark-brown
- 4 garlic cloves, peeled
- 1 tbsp. olive oil
- 1 tbsp. kosher salt
- 1/2 cup water

Directions:

1. Smoke chiles in a smoker for about 15 minutes.
2. Bring to boil both vinegars then add carrots, sugar, and garlic. Simmer for about 15 minutes while covered. Cool for 30 minutes.
3. Place the chiles, olive oil, vinegar-vegetable mixture, salt, and 1/4 cup water into a blender.
4. Blend for about 1-2 minutes on high. Add remaining water and blend again. You can add another 1/4 cup water if you want your sauce thinner.
5. Pour the sauce into jars and place in a refrigerator.
6. Serve.

Nutrition:

Calories 147

Total fat 5.23g

Saturated fat 0.7g

Total carbs 21g

Net carbs 18g

Protein 3g

Sugar 13g

Fiber 3g

Sodium: 671mg

288. Smoked soy sauce

Preparation Time: 15 minutes

Cooking Time: 1 hour

Servings: 1

Ingredients:

- 100ml soy sauce
- Bradley flavor bisquettes cherry

Directions:

1. Put soy sauce in a heat-resistant bowl, large-mouth.
2. Smoke in a smoker at 158-176oF for about 1 hour. Stir a few times.
3. Remove and cool then put in a bottle. Let sit for one day.
4. Serve and enjoy!

Nutrition:

Calories 110

Total fat 0g

Saturated fat 0g

Total carbs 25g

Net carbs 25g

Protein 2g

Sugar 25g

Fiber 0g

Sodium: 270mg

289. Smoked Garlic Sauce

Preparation Time: 5 minutes

Cooking Time: 30 minutes

Servings: 2

Ingredients:

- 3 whole garlic heads
- 1/2 cup mayonnaise
- 1/4 cup sour cream
- 2 tbsps. lemon juice
- 2 tbsps. cider vinegar
- Salt to taste

Directions:

1. Cut the garlic heads off then place in a microwave-safe bowl, add 2 tbsps. water and cover. Microwave for about 5-6 minutes on medium.
2. Heat your grill on medium.
3. Place the garlic heads in a shallow 'boat' foil and smoke for about 20-25 minutes until soft.
4. Transfer the garlic heads into a blender. Process for a few minutes until smooth.
5. Add remaining ingredients and process until everything is combined.
6. Enjoy!

Nutrition:

Calories 20

Total fat 0g

Saturated fat 0g

Total carbs 10g

Net carbs 9g

Protein 0g

Sugar 0g

Fiber 1g

Sodium: 0mg

290. Smoked Cherry BBQ Sauce

Preparation Time: 20 minutes

Cooking Time: 1 hour

Servings: 2

Ingredients:

- 2 lb. dark sweet cherries, pitted
- 1 large chopped onion
- 1/2 tbsps. red pepper flakes, crushed
- 1 tbsps. kosher salt or to taste
- 1/2 tbsp. ginger, ground
- 1/2 tbsp. black pepper
- 1/2 tbsp. cumin
- 1/2 tbsp. cayenne pepper
- 1 tbsp. onion powder
- 1 tbsp. garlic powder
- 1 tbsp. smoked paprika
- 2 chopped garlic cloves
- 1/2 cup pinot noir
- 2 tbsps. yellow mustard
- 1-1/2 cups ketchup
- 2 tbsps. balsamic vinegar
- 1/3 cup apple cider vinegar
- 2 tbsps. dark soy sauce
- 1 tbsp. liquid smoke
- 1/4 cup Worcestershire sauce
- 1 tbsp. hatch Chile powder
- 3 tbsps. honey
- 1 cup brown sugar
- 3 tbsps. molasses

Directions:

1. Preheat your smoker to 250F.
2. Place cherries in a baking dish, medium, and smoke for about 2 hours.
3. Sauté onions and red pepper flakes in a pot, large, with 2 tbsps. oil for about 4 minutes until softened.
4. Add salt and cook for an additional 1 minute.
5. Add ginger, black pepper, cumin, onion powder, garlic powder, and paprika then drizzle with oil and cook for about 1 minute until fragrant and spices bloom.
6. Stir in garlic and cook for about 30 seconds.
7. Pour in pinot noir scraping up for 1 minute for any bits stuck to your pan bottom.
8. Add yellow mustard, ketchup, balsamic vinegar, apple cider vinegar, dark soy sauce, liquid smoke, and Worcestershire sauce. Stir to combine.
9. Add cherries and simmer for about 10 minutes.
10. Add honey, brown sugar, and molasses and stir until combined. Simmer for about 30-45 minutes over low heat until your own liking.
11. Place everything into a blender and process until a smooth sauce.
12. Enjoy with favorite veggies or protein. You can refrigerate in jars for up to a month.

Nutrition:

Calories 35

Total fat 0g

Saturated fat 0g

Total carbs 9g

Net carbs 9g

Protein 0g, Sugar 0g

Fiber 0g, Sodium: 0mg

291. Smoked Garlic White Sauce

Preparation Time: 15 minutes

Cooking Time: 1 hour

Servings: 2

Ingredients:

- 2 cups hickory wood chips, soaked in water for 30 minutes
- 3 whole garlic heads
- 1/2 cup mayonnaise
- 1/3 cup sour cream
- 1 juiced lemon
- 2 tbsps. apple cider vinegar
- Salt to taste

Directions:

1. Cut garlic heads to expose the inside and place in a container, microwave-safe,

with 2 tbsps. water. Microwave for about 5-6 minutes on medium.

2. Preheat your grill. Place garlic heads on a shallow foil "boat" and place it on the grill.
3. Close the grill and cook for about 20-25 minutes until soft completely. Remove and cool.
4. Transfer into a blender then add the remaining ingredients. Process until smooth.
5. Serve immediately or store in a refrigerator for up to 5 days.

Nutrition:

Calories 20

Total fat 0g

Saturated fat 0g

Total carbs 8g

Net carbs 8g

Protein 0g

Sugar 0g

Fiber 0g

Sodium: 45mg

292. Texas-Style Brisket Rub

Preparation Time: 5 minutes

Cooking Time: 15 minutes

Servings: 1

Ingredients:

- 2 tsp Sugar
- 2 Tbsps. Kosher salt
- 2 tsp Chili powder
- 2 Tbsps. Black pepper
- 1 tbsp. Cayenne pepper
- 1 tbsp. Powdered garlic
- 1 tsp Grounded cumin
- 2 Tbsps. Powdered onion
- 1/4 cup paprika, smoked

Directions:

1. Mix all the ingredients in a small bowl until it is well blended.
2. Transfer to an airtight jar or container. Store in a cool place.

Nutrition:

Calories: 18kcal

Carbs: 2g

Fat: 1g

Protein: 0.6g

293. Pork Dry Rub

Preparation Time: 5 minutes

Cooking Time: 10 minutes

Servings: 1

Ingredients:

- 1 tbsp. Kosher salt
- 2 tbsp. Powered onions
- 1 tbsp. Cayenne pepper
- 1tsp Dried mustard
- 1/4 cup brown sugar
- 1 tbsp. Powdered garlic
- 1 tbsp. Powdered chili pepper
- 1/4 cup smoked paprika
- 2 tbsps. Black pepper

Directions:

1. Combine all the ingredients in a small bowl.
2. Transfer to an airtight jar or container.
3. Keep stored in a cool, dry place.

Nutrition:

Calories: 16kcal

Carbs: 3g

Fat:0.9g

Protein: 0.8g

294. Texas Barbeque Rub

Preparation Time: 5 minutes

Cooking Time: 10 minutes

Servings: ½ cup

Ingredients:

- 1 tsp Sugar
- 1 tbsp. Seasoned salt
- 1 tbsp. Black pepper
- 1 tsp Chili powder
- 1 tbsp. Powdered onions
- 1 tbsp. Smoked paprika
- 1 tsp Sugar
- 1 tbsp. Powdered garlic

Directions:

1. Pour all the ingredients into a small bowl and mix thoroughly.
2. Keep stored in an airtight jar or container.

Nutrition:

Calories: 22kcal

Carbs: 2g

Fat: 0.2g

Protein: 0.6g

295. Barbeque Sauce

Preparation Time: 5 minutes

Cooking Time: 10 minutes

Servings: 2

Ingredients:

- 1/4 cup of water
- 1/4 cup red wine vinegar
- 1 tbsp. Worcestershire sauce
- 1 tsp Paprika
- 1 tsp Salt
- 1 tbsp. Dried mustard
- 1 tsp black pepper
- 1 cup ketchup
- 1 cup brown sugar

Directions:

1. Pour all the ingredients into a food processor, one after the other.
2. Process until they are evenly mixed.
3. Transfer sauce to a close lid jar. Store in the

refrigerator.

Nutrition:

Calories: 43kcal

Carbs: 10g

Fat: 0.3g,

Protein: 0.9g

296. Steak Sauce

Preparation Time: 15 minutes

Cooking Time: 10 minutes

Servings: ½ cup

Ingredients:

- 1 tbsp. Malt vinegar
- 1/2 tsp Salt
- 1/2 tsp black pepper
- 1 tbsp. Tomato sauce
- 2 tbsps. brown sugar
- 1 tsp hot pepper sauce
- 2 tbsps. Worcestershire sauce
- 2 tbsps. Raspberry jam.

Directions:

1. Preheat your grill for indirect cooking at 150°F
2. Place a saucepan over grates, add all your ingredients, and allow to boil.
3. Reduce the temperature to Smoke and allow the sauce to simmer for 10 minutes or until sauce is thick.

Nutrition:

Calories: 62.1kcal

Carbs: 15.9g

Fat: 0.3g

Protein:0.1g

297. Bourbon Whiskey Sauce

Preparation Time: 10 minutes

Cooking Time: 35 minutes

Servings: 3

Ingredients:

- 1 cups ketchup
- 1/4 cup Worcestershire sauce
- 3/4 cup bourbon whiskey
- 1/3 cup apple cider vinegar
- 1/2 onions, minced
- 1/4 cup of tomato paste
- cloves of garlic, minced
- 1/2 tsp Black pepper
- 1/2 cup brown sugar
- 1/2 tbsp. Salt
- Hot pepper sauce to taste
- 1 tbsp. Liquid smoke flavoring

Directions:

1. Preheat your grill for indirect cooking at 150°F

2. Place a saucepan over grates, then add the whiskey, garlic, and onions.
3. Simmer until the onion is translucent. Then add the other ingredients and adjust the temperature to Smoke. Simmer for 20 minutes. For a smooth sauce, sieve.

Nutrition:

Calories: 107kcal

Carbs:16.6g

Fat: 1.8g,

Protein:0.8g

298. Carne Asada Marinade

Preparation Time: 15 minutes

Cooking Time: 2 hours

Servings: 5

Ingredients:

- 1 cloves garlic, chopped
- 1 tsp Lemon juice
- 1/2 cup extra virgin olive oil
- 1/2 tsp Salt
- 1/2 tsp Pepper

Directions:

1. Mix all your ingredients in a bowl.
2. Pour the beef into the bowl and allow to marinate for 2-3hours before grilling.

Nutrition:

Calories: 465kcal

Carbs: 26g

Fat: 15g

Protein: 28g

299. Grapefruit Juice Marinade

Preparation Time: 10 minutes

Cooking Time: 1 hour

Servings: 3

Ingredients:

- 1/2 reduced-sodium soy sauce
- 1 cups grapefruit juice, unsweetened
- 1-1/2 lb. Chicken, bone and skin removed
- 1/4 brown sugar

Directions:

1. Thoroughly mix all your ingredients in a large bowl.
2. Add the chicken and allow it to marinate for 2-3 hours before grilling.

Nutrition:

Calories: 489kcal

Carbs: 21.3

Fat: 12g

Protein: 24g

300. Steak Marinade

Preparation Time: 5 minutes

Cooking Time: 10 minutes

Servings: 2

Ingredients:

- 1 tbsp. Worcestershire sauce
- 1 tbsp. Red wine vinegar
- 1/2 cup barbeque sauce
- 1 tbsp. soy sauce
- 1/4 cup steak sauce
- 1 clove garlic (minced)
- 1 tsp Mustard
- Pepper and salt to taste

Directions:

1. Pour all the ingredients in a bowl and mix thoroughly.
2. Use immediately or keep refrigerated.

Nutrition:

Calories: 303kcal

Carbs: 42g

Fat: 10g

Protein:2.4g

CHAPTER 22. CONCLUSION

In conclusion, there are many different models of smokers. You can always get the charcoal chimney or some simple charcoal lighter. These are not the best smokers for you. They do not give you a good flavor on the meat. With wood pellets, you can achieve a potent smoking flavor, but you will need to find a way to light it with a chimney. The best way to achieve the best flavor is to use a wood pellet grill and smoker box.

The best grills for smoking are the ones that provide easy ways to light the fire and also that give a good flavor to your meat. The types of grills that I prefer are wood pellet grills. With this type of grill, you can smoke your meat easily and also bake it. To give you the flavor that you have been looking for, you need to use wood chips. You should be able to smoke your meat with these grills and get a good flavor. They are the type of grills that you can depend on.

Another thing is that you should always use a thermometer to check if the meat is ready. You can use a simple indicator like the smoke, and we could be able to know if the meat is ready. It is a good idea to use a meat probe rather than an indicator. This is because it's in a better position to detect the meat temperature rather than watching the indicator. It's instant feedback that you are getting the right temperature. This will help you massively if you are smoking something rare or smoking in the wind. Again, it is very easy to detect the meat temperature with a thermometer.

As you can guess, a Wood Pellet Grill and Smoker provides you with better smoke flavor and because it's on the outside, it will cook more food instead of collecting the smoke flavor. This is very important. You will give a better flavor to your meat and get a more expensive taste without the smoke flavor. As the pellets are burned, there is a huge amount of extra heat. This means that you can get the grill more temperature for your meat and that you can grill using the pellets and also and grill something which is not smoked.

A great thing about these grills is a large capacity. The grills have a large space. This means that you can put a lot of food inside and you will still be able to smoke it. The large space means that you can cook a lot of food and that you can put a lot of meat on the grill. You will be able to enjoy the meat for a long time because you can keep cooking food and you can provide your guests with better types of food. The grills are very easy to manage and they come with all the necessary features.

A Wood Pellet Grill and Smoker is the best option that you have. It is a good option for you. The combination of the cooker and the smoker will make a very slow cooker. When food is cooked, there is a natural way of smoking. You will be able to sleep and your meat will be ready.

The Wood Pellet Grill and Smoker is a great addition to any home.

CPSIA information can be obtained
at www.ICGtesting.com
Printed in the USA
BVHW050103020321
601387BV00013B/1179